Discover Acadia National Park

Third Edition

AMC's Guide to the Best Hiking, Biking, and Paddling

JERRY AND MARCY MONKMAN

Appalachian Mountain Club Books
Boston, Massachusetts

The AMC is a nonprofit organization and sales of AMC books fund our mission of protecting the Northeast outdoors. If you appreciate our efforts and would like to make a donation to the AMC, contact us at Appalachian Mountain Club, 5 Joy Street, Boston, MA 02108.

www.outdoors.org/publications/books/

Distributed by National Book Network.

Front cover images: (top l-r) © 2006 Geir Olav Lyngfjell, BigStockPhoto.com; © Kenneth C. Zirkeli, iStock.com; © Ron Chapple Stock, iStock.com; (bottom) © Jerry and Marcy Monkman, EcoPhotography.com
Back cover images © Jerry and Marcy Monkman, EcoPhotography.com
All interior images © Jerry and Marcy Monkman, EcoPhotography.com
Book design by Eric Edstam
Cartography for pull-out map by Larry Garland, © Appalachian Mountain Club
Interior maps by Ken Dumas, © Appalachian Mountain Club

Library of Congress Cataloging-in-Publication Data
Monkman, Jerry.
Discover Acadia National Park : AMC's guide to the best hiking, biking, and paddling / Jerry & Marcy Monkman. — 3rd ed.
    p. cm.
Includes bibliographical references and index.
ISBN 978-1-934028-29-2 (alk. paper)
1. Hiking—Maine—Acadia National Park—Guidebooks. 2. Cycling—Maine—Acadia National Park—Guidebooks. 3. Canoes and canoeing—Maine—Acadia National Park—Guidebooks. 4. Acadia National Park (Me.)—Guidebooks. I. Monkman, Marcy. II. Appalachian Mountain Club. III. Title.
GV199.42.M22A326 2010
917.41'450444—dc22
                    2009046248

The paper used in this publication meets the minimum requirements of the American National Standard for Information Sciences-Permanence of Paper for Printed Library Materials, ANSI Z39.48-1984. ∞

Outdoor recreation activities by their very nature are potentially hazardous. This book is not a substitute for good personal judgment and training in outdoor skills. Due to changes in conditions, use of the information in this book is at the sole risk of the user. The author and the Appalachian Mountain Club assume no liability for accidents happening to, or injuries sustained by, readers who engage in the activities described in this book.

Interior pages contain 30% post-consumer recycled fiber.
Cover contains 10% post-consumer recycled fiber.
Printed in the United States of America,
using vegetable-based inks.

10 9 8 7 6 5 4 3   14 15 16 17 18

MIX
Paper from responsible sources
FSC
www.fsc.org FSC® C005010

*To all the photographers
who devote their lives to telling
conservation stories with pictures*

Locator Map

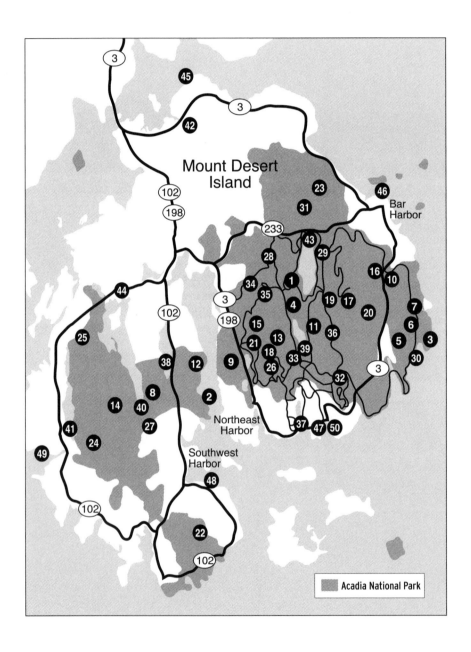

Contents

At-a-Glance Trip Planner

Trip	Page	Location	Rating	Distance and Elevation Gain
HIKES				
1 Conners Nubble	6	Eastern District	Easy	3.4 mi, 300 ft.
2 Flying Mountain	8	Western District	Moderate	1.2 mi, 275 ft
3 Great Head and Sand Beach	10	Eastern District	Moderate	1.8 mi, 200 ft
4 The Bubbles	13	Eastern District	Strenuous, but short	1.6 mi, 550 ft
5 Gorham Mountain and Ocean Path	18	Eastern District	Moderate, then easy	3.5 mi, 500 ft
6 The Beehive and the Bowl	21	Eastern District	Strenuous	1.3 mi, 450 ft
7 Bar Harbor to Sand Beach	24	Eastern District	Moderate	4.7 mi, 100 ft
8 Beech Mountain	27	Western District	Moderate	2.0 mi, 700 ft

Estimated Time	Public Transit	Good for kids	Dogs Allowed	X-C Skiing	Snow-shoeing	Trip highlights
2.0 hrs	🚌	🚶	🐕		🏷️🏷️	A flat, easy carriage road walk followed by a short hike up to great views.
45 min		🚶	🐕			A short hike to nice views of water.
1.0 hr	🚌	🚶				A beach walk followed by a wooded climb to the cliffs of Great Head.
1.5 hrs	🚌	🚶	🐕		🏷️🏷️	Great reward for a short hike.
2.0 hrs	🚌	🚶	🐕			A moderate hike to a walk along a dramatic coastline.
1.0 hr	🚌					A challenging climb to spectacular views and a mountain pond.
2.0 hrs		🚶	🐕			A walk from Bar Harbor that includes mountain and ocean views.
1.5 hrs		🚶	🐕			An enjoyable hike over rocky ledges to the summit of Beech Mountain.

Estimated Time	Public Transit	Good for kids	Dogs Allowed	X-C Skiing	Snow-shoeing	Trip highlights
2.5 hrs	🚌		🐕			A quick climb to views of Somes Sound.
2.5 hrs			🐕			A classic Acadia hike up steep pink granite to extraordinary mountain and ocean views.
2.5 hrs	🚌		🐕	🎿		A strenuous hike to some of Mt. Desert Island's most spectacular views.
3.0 hrs	🚌	🚶	🐕			A strenuous hike through a beautiful pitch pine forest to the best views of Somes Sound.
3.5 hrs	🚌					A strenuous hike with long periods of hiking on open ledges with magnificent views.
3.5 hrs			🐕	🎿		A peaceful, yet strenuous hike to the highest peaks on the western side of the island.
3.5 hrs	🚌		🐕		🥾🥾	A challenging hike over four peaks, including Sargent Mountain, Acadia's second highest peak.
4.0 hrs						A challenging hike to spectacular views and a narrow gorge.
4.0 hrs	🚌	🚶	🐕	🎿		A relatively long hike over open ledges with great views during most of this hike.
5.0 hrs	🚌		🐕	🎿		Wide open ridge hiking combined with scenic shoreline walks.
6.0 hrs	🚌					A strenuous hike starting with a walk from Bar Harbor to three of Acadia's four highest peaks.

Estimated Time	Public Transit	Good for kids	Dogs Allowed	X-C Skiing	Snow-shoeing	Trip highlights
6.5 hrs	🚌					A traverse of the eastern half of Mount Desert Island to some of Acadia's best known features.
1.25 hrs	🚌	✓	✓	✓	✓	A relatively easy ride to a 40 ft. waterfall and a visit to Upper Hadlock pond.
1.0 hr	🚌	✓	✓			An easy ride for the family on a dirt road in prime birdwatching habitat.
1.25 hrs		✓	✓		✓	An easy ride through beaver ponds and bogs to great view.
1.25 hrs		✓				An easy ride through a boreal forest that is frequented by moose.
2.0 hrs		✓				An easy ride on a dirty road to a secluded cove on Long Pond.
2.0 hrs	🚌	✓	✓		✓	A ride through an evergreen forest past streams lined with pink granite stones.
2.0 hrs	🚌					A ride through spruce woods from Echo Lake to Seal Cove Pond.
1.5 hrs	🚌	✓	✓		✓	A ride with views of Sargent Mtn. and Eagle Lake and the chance to see beavers.
2.0 hrs	🚌	✓	✓		✓	A great ride for families through rich woodlands, with good views from Eagle Lake.
2.0 hrs	🚌					A road bike ride from Bar Harbor to scenic Ocean Drive.
2.0 hrs	🚌					A scenic bike ride from Bar Harbor to Jordan Pond.

	Trip	Page	Location	Rating	Distance and Elevation Gain
32	Day Mountain	104	Eastern District, Carriage Roads	Moderate	8.0 mi, 500 ft.
33	Jordan Pond—Bubble Pond Loop	107	Eastern District, Carriage Roads	Moderate	9.0 mi, 500 ft
34	Giant Slide Loop	111	Eastern District, Carriage Roads	Difficult	8.5 mi, 600 ft.
35	Around the Mountain Loop	113	Eastern District, Carriage Roads	Difficult	12.0 mi, 1,000 ft
36	Around the Mountain II	117	Eastern District, Carriage Roads	Difficult	18.7 mi, 900 ft

QUIET WATER PADDLING

	Trip	Page	Location	Rating	Distance and Elevation Gain
37	Little Long Pond	125	Eastern District	Easy	1.25 mi
38	Echo Lake	128	Western District	Easy	1.5 mi
39	Jordan Pond	130	Eastern District	Easy	2.5 mi
40	Long Pond—South End	133	Western District	Easy	3.0 mi
41	Seal Cove Pond	138	Western District	Easy	4.5 mi
42	Northeast Creek	140	Eastern District	Moderate	5.0 mi
43	Eagle Lake	143	Eastern District	Moderate	4.0 mi
44	Long Pond—North End	147	Western District	Strenuous	7.5 mi

Estimated Time	Public Transit	Good for kids	Dogs Allowed	X-C Skiing	Snow-shoeing	Trip highlights
2.5 hrs	🚌	👪	🐕		✿✿	A ride up a mountain to great views of the ocean islands.
2.5 hrs	🚌	👪	🐕		✿✿	A moderate ride next to spectacular scenery.
2.5 hrs	🚌		🐕		✿✿	A ride over rushing mountain streams to fantastic ocean and mountain views.
4.0 hrs	🚌		🐕		✿✿	This ride has it all: waterfalls, mountain and ocean views and 7 major bridge crossings.
5.5 hrs	🚌		🐕		✿✿	A long ride through gorgeous forests and scenic ponds.
1.0 hr		👪	🐕			A short and easy paddle on a most picturesque pond.
1.0 hr		👪	🐕			A short paddle beneath towering cliffs and a chance to see Peregrine Falcons.
2.0 hrs		👪	🐕			A pleasant paddle on an incredibly scenic pond.
2.0 hrs		👪	🐕			A paddle beneath the steep cliffs of Beech and Mansell Mountains.
2.5 hrs		👪	🐕			A paddle on the westernmost pond, with good opportunities to see waterfowl and bald eagles.
2.5 hrs		👪	🐕			A quiet paddle on a narrow creek through extensive wetlands and prime wildlife habitat.
3.0 hrs		👪	🐕			A paddle on a beautiful lake with mountain views and wild shorelines.
4.0 hrs		👪	🐕			A long and popular paddle that explores wooded coves.

	Trip	Page	Location	Rating	Distance and Elevation Gain
SEA KAYAKING					
45	Mount Desert Narrows	156	Ocean	Difficulty depends on weather conditions	6.0 mi
46	Frenchman Bay and the Porcupine Islands	161	Ocean	Difficulty depends on weather conditions	6.5 mi
47	Sutton and Bear Islands	168	Ocean	Difficulty depends on weather conditions	6.0 mi
48	Somes Sound	171	Ocean	Difficulty depends on weather conditions	7.5 mi
49	Seal Cove to Pretty Marsh	175	Ocean	Difficulty depends on weather conditions	10.0 mi
50	Cranberry Isles	180	Ocean	Advanced	12.0 mi

Estimated Time	Public Transit	Good for kids	Dogs Allowed	X-C Skiing	Snow-shoeing	Trip highlights
3.0 hrs						A relatively sheltered paddle in shallow waters.
3.0 hrs						An exciting paddle around the beautiful and wild Porcupine Islands.
3.0 hrs						A paddle past a remote lighhouse and a sea arch with great views of mountains.
4.0 hrs						A paddle in the only fjord in the eastern US.
7.0 hrs						A paddle filled with wooded shoreline, beautiful islands, and bountiful wildlife.
7.0 hrs						An all-day paddle to historic islands with excellent views of mountains.

Preface

SWEEPING MOUNTAIN VIEWS, RUGGED OCEAN SCENERY, and abundant wildlife all contribute to the splendor that is Acadia National Park. Acadia's 46,000 acres stretch from Isle au Haut in the southwest to the Schoodic Peninsula in the northeast. However, the heart and soul of Acadia is Mount Desert Island, a place of scenic pink-granite mountains, deep glacial ponds, cobblestone beaches, and oceanside cliffs. Bald eagles, ospreys, and peregrine falcons patrol the skies while seals, porpoises, and seabirds fish the cold waters of Frenchman Bay and beyond. Mount Desert Island is the third-largest island in the continental United States and boasts such natural wonders as Somes Sound, the only fiord on the East Coast, and Cadillac Mountain, the highest point on the North Atlantic seaboard.

While it is the dramatic scenery that lures most visitors, it is the more intimate moments in Acadia that become a part of those who come here: listening to the steady sound of the surf in Monument Cove on a quiet morning in June, inhaling the delicious smell of pitch pine on a rocky trail on a warm September day, or watching in surprise as a harbor porpoise surfaces next to your kayak on a calm August afternoon. Although your experiences in Acadia most likely will be different from ours, our hope is that this book will help you discover your own special moments in Acadia.

For this revised (third) edition, we have added some new trips in the book's main chapters, taking advantage of new trails and adding new visits to important locations. We have also detailed much of the trail work in the park, which includes 25 trail name changes. This is the most complete and accurate version of *Discover Acadia* yet!

Acknowledgments

IT IS HARD FOR US TO BELIEVE THAT IT HAS BEEN TEN YEARS since we wrote the first edition of this guide to one of our favorite places on earth. Over the course of the intervening decade, we have had conversations with probably dozens of individuals whose stories and insights about Acadia have no doubt influenced our work on this guide and other projects. However, we do want to specifically thank a few people who helped us out with this third edition of *Discover Acadia*. As always, the personnel at the Park Service were invaluable to us, and we extend a big thank-you to Gary Stellpflug, Charlie Jacoby, Wanda Moran, and Karen Anderson. We also want to thank Marla Stellpflug O'Byrne at Friends of Acadia for her insights into new conservation efforts in the park, Glen Tucker at Coastal Kayaking for his help with the kayaking section, and Elizabeth Ehrenfeld for her suggestions in revising the safety section of the sea kayaking section. Jeff Aceto at the AMC's Maine Chapter was also helpful with his review of the manuscript.

Of course, we could not have made this revision without the expert guidance of AMC Books, specifically Kevin Breunig, Heather Stephenson, Athena Lakri, Amy Brais, and, last but not least, our editor, Dan Eisner, who was instrumental in determining the changes needed in this revision to make it a truly excellent update. As always, we want to thank both the Monkman and Wolin families for continuing to unconditionally support us in our careers as writers and "ecophotographers." Lastly, we would like to dedicate this book to our children, Quinn and Acadia, whose enthusiasm for the outdoors constantly reminds us of the wonders of Acadia National Park.

Stewardship and Conservation

ACADIA NATIONAL PARK CONSISTENTLY RANKS AS ONE of the ten most visited national parks in the United States. With 2 million visitors entering the park every year, it sees the same amount of use as much bigger parks, such as Yellowstone and Yosemite. With that many peo-  ple enjoying Acadia's limited and fragile resources, everyone must remember to help protect the resource. It is imperative that everyone learn and adhere to Leave No Trace principles. In Acadia, follow these principles:

Plan Ahead and Prepare
When going into Acadia's backcountry, plan an outing that you know everyone in your group can finish. Be prepared for unexpected events by having extra food, water, and clothing. A well-planned day will prevent the need for an unnecessary night out in the woods, where you may be forced to build fires and trample delicate vegetation. Keep your group size to ten or fewer, splitting into smaller groups if necessary. Try to avoid travel in wet and muddy conditions, and use extra care when in Acadia's delicate subalpine zone.

Travel and Camp on Durable Surfaces
Camping in Acadia's backcountry is prohibited. When hiking, try to stay on trails and rocks. When you are on a trail, look up for blazes and cairns, and stay in the center of the trail, even when it is wet and muddy. Use your boots!

Trails are hardened sites where use should be concentrated. Avoid contributing to the widening and braiding of trails. Hiking off-trail into pristine areas is allowed, but it requires great understanding and diligence. First consider if hiking off-trail is necessary. If you decide to hike off-trail, do it only on durable surfaces such as rock, gravel, or grasses. Spread your group out, take different routes, and avoid places where unofficial "social" trails are just beginning to show.

Dispose of Waste Properly
Pack out all that you bring in. This includes any and all food you may drop while eating. Urinate at least 200 yards from any water source and pack out your used toilet paper. To dispose of solid human waste in the backcountry, dig an individual "cat hole" at least 200 yards from a trail or water source. Organic topsoil is preferable to sandy mineral soil. Dig a hole 4 to 8 inches deep and about 6 inches in diameter. After use, mix some soil into the cat hole with a stick and cover it with the remainder of the soil. Disguise the hole by covering it with leaves or other brush. Pack out your toilet paper in an odor-proof bag. It is especially important in Acadia not to pollute near watercourses, which probably lead to a town water source.

Leave What You Find
Leave all natural and historical items as you find them. Of particular concern to naturalists in the park is the moving of rocks, large and small, in order to build rock cairns or sculptures. This detracts from the natural and scenic qualities of the landscape. It wreaks havoc on the environment, causing soil erosion and removing vital habitats for small plants and animals. Building unauthorized cairns is also a safety concern, as an improperly located cairn can cause hikers to get lost. There is much human history in and around Acadia in the form of American Indian shell heaps and arrowheads, as well as stone walls and old cellar holes from early European settlements. It is illegal to disturb any such cultural artifacts in the national park. It is also illegal to move or take home natural features of the park, whether they are wildflowers, rocks, beach cobbles, or animal parts such as feathers or antlers. The only exception to this in Acadia is that you are allowed to pick fruit, nuts, and berries for personal consumption. However, the taking of pine or spruce cones, mushrooms, fungi, and fiddlehead ferns is prohibited.

Minimize Campfire Impacts
Campfires are allowed only in designated fire pits in campgrounds and picnic areas.

Respect Wildlife
Remain quiet while in the backcountry, and give animals enough space so that they feel secure. If you notice wildlife changing their behavior, it is most likely because you are too close. In that case, back off and give the animals space. Avoid nesting or calving sites, and never attempt to feed any wildlife, not even sea gulls or those cute little red squirrels. While kayaking around the island, do not land on any island that has an active seabird colony or nesting bald eagles. To verify the location of any such islands, check with the Park Service before your paddle. Also, remember that residents of the intertidal zone are wildlife too. Do not remove starfish, sea urchins, or other creatures from their natural habitat. For low-impact wildlife-watching tips, visit Watchable Wildlife's website, www.watchablewildlife.org.

Be Considerate of Other Visitors
Stay quiet. Refrain from using cell phones and radios. When hiking, take rests on the side of the trail (on a durable surface) so that other hikers do not have to walk around you. When on the water, remember that sound carries a long, long way. Also, it is required that you keep your dog on a leash while in the park. Dogs are not allowed on Sand Beach, Echo Lake Beach, or ladder trails.

You can learn more about the Leave No Trace Center for Outdoor Ethics by visiting the Leave No Trace website (www.lnt.org) or by writing LNT Inc., PO Box 997, Boulder, CO 80306.

Trail Maintenance
It takes a huge amount of work to keep hiking trails and carriage roads in good condition. Volunteering to help with trail maintenance is a great way to give back to the park. The AMC offers several one-week Volunteer Vacations in Acadia National Park in the summer. See www.outdoors.org/volunteer for details. Friends of Acadia runs a volunteer trail-maintenance program in conjunction with the national park. Currently, maintenance is scheduled for Tuesdays, Thursdays, and Saturdays. For more information, call Friends of

Acadia at 207-288-3934 or the Park Service at 207-288-3338. The AMC's Echo Lake Camp (207-244-3747) also leads trail-maintenance trips twice a week in season.

More Conservation Opportunities

Get involved in trails and river stewardship, land protection, or conservation advocacy on a regional landscape level by joining a conservation or recreation organization. Contributions to such organizations are key to the success of their missions. You can also get involved on the ground. The Appalachian Mountain Club (AMC) is a conservation *and* recreation organization, with opportunities to:

- Maintain trails near you as part of a volunteer trail crew or as a Trail Adopter.
- Participate in hands-on air- and water-quality research through the Mountain Watch program at AMC backcountry destinations.
- Patrol White Mountain ridges in the summer as an Alpine Steward and help raise the public's awareness of its impacts on the rare and fragile alpine environment.
- Support the Maine Woods Initiative, AMC's effort to promote conservation, recreation, sustainable forestry, and community partnerships in Maine's 100-Mile Wilderness.

You can also join the AMC's Conservation Action Network (CAN) and help increase public influence on critical conservation issues at www.outdoors .org/conservation/can.

Introduction to Acadia National Park

IT IS HARD TO SAY EXACTLY WHAT DRAWS SO MANY PEOPLE TO ACADIA, although the juxtaposition of granite-clad mountain peaks overlooking the deep blue waters of the Atlantic Ocean probably lures most visitors. With mountains next to the ocean, Acadia gives visitors the chance to participate in almost any outdoor activity they can dream up, all with spectacular scenic rewards. Of course, the mountains of Acadia are modest, even by New England standards, with the tallest peak, Cadillac Mountain, reaching a height of only 1,528 feet. Nonetheless, hiking is probably the most popular park activity, as most of the summits are treeless and provide spectacular views of the surrounding bays and islands. Trails vary from easy ocean-side walks to steep cliff-side climbs up iron ladders. Biking is also a popular activity in the park, particularly on the scenic system of gravel carriage roads built by John Rockefeller Jr. in the 1920s and 1930s. Just a few thousand years ago, glaciers left behind numerous deep lakes and ponds that now give visitors the opportunity to canoe or kayak below the rocky scenery of the mountains. Over the last ten years, sea kayaking has become one of the premier activities of the more adventurous visitors to Acadia National Park. Chapters 2 through 5 give detailed descriptions of hiking, biking, and paddling trips, from one-hour excursions to all-day adventures.

Other activities such as rock climbing, birding, and whale watching give the outdoor enthusiast plenty of alternative ways to experience Acadia. See the appendixes for information about participating in these other vacation adventures. The rest of this introductory chapter provides some basic information you can use to get started on your visit to Acadia National Park and Mount Desert Island.

Climate

Acadia has a typical New England coastal climate. Cold, wet conditions are common, but so are sunny and warm days. In general, Acadia's climate is no problem for the outdoor adventurer who comes prepared for unexpected weather. Spring is often foggy, with temperatures ranging between 30 and 70 degrees Fahrenheit. Summer is mild, with daytime temperatures usually in the 70s and 80s. Evenings are cool, especially when there is a sea breeze, and, with ocean temperatures in the 50s, any activity on the ocean requires an extra layer of clothing. Fall in Acadia varies from subfreezing temperatures at night to warm days in the 70s. Rain and fog are common, but so are perfect, clear leaf-peeping days. Winter is cold, with daytime temperatures usually in the 30s and lows ranging to below zero. Acadia averages 61 inches of snow per year.

Getting There

Bar Harbor and Acadia National Park are located 45 miles southeast of Bangor, Maine. From Bangor, drive east on Alternate Route 1 to Route 3 in Ellsworth. Following Route 3 south will take you to Mount Desert Island. The entrance to Acadia National Park is located off Route 3 in Hulls Cove, just north of Bar Harbor. During the summer months, Greyhound (800-231-2222) provides bus service to Bar Harbor. Once you are on the island, you can take advantage of the park's free bus system, Island Explorer, from late June through early October.

Island Explorer Bus System

One of the best things to happen in Acadia since we first wrote this guidebook in 1999 is the introduction of the Island Explorer Bus system. Using the Island Explorer opens up a whole new array of hiking and biking opportunities that let you explore the park without having to spot a car (or use a car at all), and it is a great way to help leave no trace. This system of propane-powered buses can help you to avoid spending your vacation driving and hunting for parking spots at crowded trailheads. Seven of the routes can be boarded at the village green in Bar Harbor. These routes go to Blackwoods and Seawall Campgrounds, Sand Beach and Otter Cliffs, Jordan Pond, Eagle

Lake, Northeast Harbor, Southwest Harbor, Bass Harbor, Tremont, private campgrounds, and many places in between. There is also a bus around the Schoodic Peninsula. Best of all, the buses are free! The system runs only during the busy summer months and into early fall, and the schedule changes from year to year based on current funding levels, so check with the Park Service or Downeast Transportation before planning your trip. For a schedule, contact Downeast Transportation at 207-667-5796 or visit their website at www.exploreacadia.com.

Lodging

There are two campgrounds in the national park: Blackwoods and Seawall. Blackwoods is open year-round, while Seawall is open from the Wednesday before Memorial Day through September 30. Bar Harbor, Northeast Harbor, and Southwest Harbor are full of inns, hotels, and bed-and-breakfasts. A complete listing of these can be attained by calling the local areas' chambers of commerce. AMC's Echo Lake Camp offers tent-based lodging, group meals, and daily activities led by volunteers. A week-long stay is usually required. Visit www.amcecholakecamp.org, or turn to page 129 for details.

Food

Restaurants are located throughout the island, with the biggest selection in Bar Harbor. The Hannaford on Cottage Street in Bar Harbor is the island's largest grocery store. The Alternative Market (located across from the Bar Harbor town green) and A and B Naturals (on Cottage Street in Bar Harbor) both have a good selection of health foods. In Southwest Harbor, you can buy groceries at the Southwest Harbor Food Mart.

National Park Service Information

First-time visitors to Acadia National Park should begin their visit by stopping in at the Hulls Cove Visitor Center on Route 3. Here you can pick up a schedule of ranger-led events, talk to a ranger about your park visit, and pick up fliers and books about Acadia. The Hulls Cove Visitor Center is open from April 15 through October 31. During the winter months, visitors should check in at the park headquarters on Route 233, west of Bar Harbor. The Park Service maintains a website at www.nps.gov/acad. You can also request information about the park before your visit by writing to the Park Service at Acadia National Park, PO Box 177, Bar Harbor, ME 04609, or by calling 207-288-3338.

Fees

There are fees for using the Park Loop Road and the park campgrounds. In 2009, a one-week pass for entrance to the park was $20 from June 23 to Columbus Day (when the bus system is running) and $10 from May 1 to June 22 and after Columbus Day (when the bus is not in operation). An Acadia annual pass is $40. A campsite at Blackwoods or Seawall costs $20 per night.

Handicapped Access

Most park facilities, including the visitor center and Blackwoods and Seawall Campgrounds, are accessible to handicapped persons. The exceptions are the Nature Center at Sieur de Monts, the Frazer and Pretty Marsh Picnic Areas, Sand Beach, and the Thunder Hole Gift Shop. To see the backcountry, the park's carriage roads are the best option since they tend to have level, firm surfaces. The two easiest sections of the carriage roads can be reached from Eagle Lake and Bubble Pond. Wildwood Stables near Jordan Pond also has carriage rides that are accessible to the handicapped. For more information, contact the Park Service and ask for their excellent eight-page access guide. Call 207-288-3338 and have them send you the guide, or pick one up at the visitor center. The TYY phone number for the hearing impaired is 207-288-8880. The official Park Service Web address is www.nps.gov/acad.

Emergencies

All injuries that happen in the park should be reported to a ranger. In the event of an emergency, you should dial 911. Other important phone numbers include the following:

- Bar Harbor Police (nonemergency calls): 207-288-3391
- Mount Desert Police (nonemergency calls): 207-276-5111
- Southwest Harbor (nonemergency calls): 207-244-7911
- State Police, Orono Barracks: 800-432-7381
- Acadia National Park (nonemergency calls): 207-288-3338
- U.S. Coast Guard Emergency: 207-244-5121

Choosing Your Trip

The dozens of hiking, biking, and paddling trips in this book provide a variety of outdoor experiences. Before heading out on the trail or on the water, you should decide what the focus of your trip is (beachcombing, mountain views, wildlife watching, etc.). You should also decide how strenuous a trip you and your group are willing and able to complete. The At-a-Glance Trip Planner that follows the table of contents has an easy-to-follow listing of all the trips, including their difficulty, length, and highlights. Once you have narrowed down your choices, read the detailed trip descriptions in the individual chapters to get a better idea of what the trip entails and what you might encounter. Hikers interested in trails other than those listed in the hiking chapter can read through a complete listing of hiking trails in Appendix A.

1

Hiking in Acadia National Park

HIKING THROUGH ACADIA'S FORESTS TO ITS STORIED ROCKY COAST OR its bare mountain summits has been a popular activity since the mid-1800s. With more than 100 miles of maintained trails providing access to almost every corner of the park, it is possible to explore ocean cliffs, rocky gorges, quiet mountain ponds, and wide-open granite mountaintops with spectacular views of forest and ocean. During a hike in Acadia, you may spot bald eagles and peregrine falcons flying overhead, deer and beaver feeding in and around ponds, or loons and harbor seals swimming in the Atlantic. While most of Acadia's trails are short, creative trip planning can make for some enjoyable extended hiking. This chapter suggests twenty hikes that are, in our opinion, some of the most scenic in the park. For some trips, we have combined several trails into one hike. For others, we have included walks on the park's carriage roads and dirt fire roads, as well as the park loop road. A complete listing of trails can be found in Appendix A.

Hiking Times and Trail Ratings

Our hiking times are estimates based on our experience as average 30-something hikers carrying 15 to 30 pounds of gear and no children. Obviously, these times can vary according to the weather, the physical-fitness level of your group, and how much gear you stuff into your pack. While we think these times are useful for planning a trip, your hiking times will undoubtedly differ from ours. Distances listed are the round-trip mileage, and elevation gains are calculated using the data from the AMC's Acadia National Park Discovery Map, which can be found in the pocket on the inside of the back cover of this guide. We have used the National Park Service's system for Rating trails, using a scale of easy, moderate, strenuous, and ladder. Easy trails are suitable for families with kids of any age. Moderate and strenuous trails can be fun for older children who have experience hiking steep and rocky trails. Expect a strenuous trail in Acadia to be like climbing a very steep staircase with large and uneven steps. Trails with ladders have at least one section of climbing iron rungs that are driven into granite cliffs. It is exactly like climbing a ladder on the side of a mountain. These can be challenging and fun trails, but they are also frightening for small children or people with a fear of heights. It is also illegal to bring a dog on a ladder trail, and you should consider your dog's fitness level before bringing him or her along on any hike.

Safety and Etiquette

Its mild summer climate makes Acadia an enjoyable and relatively safe hiking destination. Of course, bad weather or poor planning can spoil any hiking adventure. Before heading into Acadia's backcountry, consider the following tips:

- Leave behind your plans with a friend or, if you are on vacation, with a staff person at the lodge or campground where you are staying.
- Select a trip that is appropriate for everyone in the group. Match the hike to the abilities of the least capable person in the group.
- Plan to be back at the trailhead before dark. Determine a turn-around time and stick to it—even if you have not reached your goal for the day.
- Check the weather. Wet weather can make Acadia's granite very slick, and high winds and pelting rain can make the summits an uncomfortable place to be. Avoid trails with iron rungs and ladders in the rain, as they become very slippery and dangerous when wet. You can get current weather forecast from local radio station WDEA's weather phone: 207-667-8910.
- Bring a pack with the following items:
  - ✓ Water: Two quarts per person is adequate depending on the weather and length of the trip. (Be sure to bring water purification items for longer trips.)
  - ✓ Food: Even for a short hike, it is a good idea to bring some high-energy snacks like nuts, dried fruit, or snack bars. Bring a lunch for longer trips.

- ✓ Map and compass: Be sure you know how to use them!
- ✓ Headlamp or flashlight, with spare batteries and lightbulb.
- ✓ Extra clothing: Bring rain gear, a wool or fleece sweater, a hat, and mittens.
- ✓ First-aid kit: It should include adhesive bandages, gauze, and nonprescription painkiller.
- ✓ Sunscreen.
- ✓ Pocketknife.
- ✓ Waterproof matches and a lighter.
- ✓ Insect repellent: Mosquitoes are always present during the warm weather months in Acadia. Be aware that black flies can be a significant nuisance in July and August.
- ✓ A trash bag.
- ✓ Toilet paper.
- ✓ Binoculars for wildlife viewing.
- Wear appropriate footwear and clothing. Hiking shoes should be waterproof and provide good ankle support. Wear wool hiking socks and comfortable, sturdy hiking boots that give you good traction and support. Bring rain gear even in sunny weather, since unexpected rain, fog, or wind is possible at any time in Acadia National Park. Avoid wearing cotton clothing, which absorbs sweat and rain, making for cold, damp hiking. Polypropylene, fleece, silk, and wool are all good materials for keeping moisture away from your body and keeping you warm in wet or cold conditions.

In addition to practicing the no-impact techniques described in this book's introduction, it is also a good idea to keep the following things in mind while hiking:

- Try not to disturb other hikers. While you may often feel alone in the wilderness, wild yelling or cell-phone usage will undoubtedly upset another person's quiet backcountry experience.
- When you are in front of the rest of your hiking group, wait at all trail junctions. This avoids confusion and keeps people in your group from getting lost or separated.
- If you see downed wood that appears to be purposely covering a trail, it probably means the trail is closed due to overuse or hazardous conditions.

- If a trail is muddy, walk through the mud or on rocks, never on tree roots or plants. Wearing waterproof boots will keep your feet comfortable, and by staying in the center of the trail you will keep the trail from eroding into a wide "hiking highway."

For the most part, Acadia is not a frightening place to be. Cool, quiet forests and tranquil ocean views are the norm. When hiking, expect an enjoyable time and keep your senses tuned to your surroundings. Every one of the trips in this chapter passes through two or more different natural habitats, adding variety to every outing. Don't expect to see eagles and bears and moose on every hike. However, by paying attention to details such as a rare alpine flower on Saint Sauveur, the jack pines on Cadillac, or the salamanders in a forested wetland, you can finish a hike with a satisfying sense of wonder.

The following hikes will take you from the shores of Sand Beach to the summit of Cadillac Mountain. You will encounter forests shaped by fire and people and nature. You will hike through valleys and over hills created deep within the Earth before being pushed up by earthquakes and scoured by glaciers. Eagles, falcons, and hawks will soar over head, and warblers will fill the forest with bird song. If you have visited Acadia before, you may find some new and interesting hikes that you have yet to try. If you are new to the park, you should find the trips described in this book to be a great way to explore this special place.

Flat and Easy Walks
While many of Acadia's trails consist of steep hikes with rough footing, a few trails are flat, easy, yet worthwhile destinations. In midsummer, these trails do attract the crowds; however, early mornings and evenings tend to be less crowded than the middle of the day.

Shore Path
This 1.5-mile path conveniently starts in downtown Bar Harbor. It begins on the shoreline at the pier of the Bar Harbor Inn, next to the parking lot at the municipal pier. From the path, you can look out over the harbor at Bar Island and the Porcupine Islands as well as the Schoodic Peninsula. You will also get a good view of the most impressive homes in Bar Harbor. The path ends at Hancock Street, which will lead you back to Main Street.

Ocean Path

This trail (which is also part of the Gorham Mountain hike, Trip 5 in this chapter), is an easy walk from Sand Beach to Otter Point. It provides an up-close experience with the shoreline of Acadia over the course of about 2.0 miles. There are cobble beaches and tide pools to explore, as well as Thunder Hole and Otter Cliffs. The soothing sounds, smells, and sights of the Atlantic Ocean are so captivating that you hardly notice the nearby Park Loop Road.

Jordan Pond Path

The 1.5 miles of this trail on the east side of Jordan Pond are flat and have relatively good footing. Look for mergansers and loons on the pond as well as peregrine falcons on the cliffs of Penobscot Mountain. This is an especially good destination for children. Please note that the portion of this trail on the west side of Jordan Pond has extremely difficult footing and is rated as a moderate hike.

Jesup Path

Close to Bar Harbor, this trail is almost a mile long. A hike on the Jesup Path is an easy walk past the beaver ponds of the Great Meadow and through hemlock and mixed hardwood forests. It also passes by Sieur de Monts Spring, home of the Abbe Museum, specializing in American Indian history; the Wild Gardens of Acadia; and the Acadia National Park Nature Center.

Wonderland

Located between Seawall Campground and the Ship Harbor Nature Trail on Route 102A, the Wonderland area can be explored via a gravel fire road that takes you to a cobble beach in about 0.5 mile. From the beach, you can see the Duck Islands to the southeast and Great Cranberry Island to the northeast. This is a good place to bring kids for beach and tide-pool exploration.

Ship Harbor Nature Trail

This trail leaves Seawall Road 1.5 miles from Seawall Campground and gives hikers the opportunity to enjoy ocean views from the western side of Mount Desert Island and to see tidal currents at work as Ship Harbor empties into the Atlantic, only to be filled back in a few hours later. It is flat, only 1.3 miles long, and the first 0.3 mile is wheelchair accessible.

TRIP 1
CONNERS NUBBLE

NPS Rating: Easy
Distance: 3.4 miles
Elevation Gain: 300 feet
Estimated Time: 2.0 hours
Map: AMC's Acadia National Park Discovery Map: D7

This flat, easy carriage-road walk is followed by a short hike up to 360-degree views of Eagle Lake and Cadillac Mountain.

Directions
From the intersection of Route 3 and Route 233 in Bar Harbor, take Route 233 west toward Cadillac Mountain. After 2.1 miles, you will see two parking areas for the carriage road, one on the right and one on the left. The parking area is stop B on the Island Explorer Brown Mountain route (route 6). *GPS coordinates*: 44° 22.648' N, 68° 15.141' W.

Trip Description
Conners Nubble provides excellent views for little effort, with much of the hike following a carriage road next to Eagle Lake. The summit is typical Acadia—a pink granite dome, devoid of trees and providing views in all directions. The carriage road walk is followed by a short ascent in the woods that is relatively easy but makes for great adventure for young children.

If you parked on the north side of Route 233, turn left on the carriage road, which soon passes under Route 233. Go straight at post 6. If you parked on the south side of Route 223, go right on the carriage road and turn left at post 6. About 100 yards past post 6, stay to the left at post 9. The carriage road rises gradually through tall spruce trees on its way to views of Eagle Lake and Cadillac Mountain about 0.5 mile from the parking area. Soon afterward, the forest transitions to a mosaic forest. At 1.3 miles from the parking area, you will see the Eagle Lake Trail on the left. Turn here and follow the trail for about 100 yards and turn right on the Bubbles Trail.

The Bubbles Trail makes for a moderate 0.4-mile hike up to the summit of Conners Nubble, which rises above a stand of short, shrub-sized paper

Eagle Lake, which can be seen from Conners Nubble, is the largest freshwater lake in Acadia National Park.

birch trees to reveal a dome of pink, lichen-encrusted Cadillac granite. Low-bush blueberries grow wherever enough soil has collected in the cracks in the granite. There are excellent views of nearby Cadillac and Pemetic mountains, as well as the waters of Frenchman Bay and Mount Desert Narrows to the east and north. To the west looms Sargent Mountain, and of course, directly below the summit are the sparkling blue waters of 3-mile-long Eagle Lake.

Eagle Lake was the site of some of the first efforts to conserve land on Mount Desert Island in the early twentieth century. The deep, clean waters of the lake are used as a public water supply for the town of Bar Harbor. When a wealthy summer resident began plans for building a home on the lake, island residents became concerned that the development could compromise this water supply. By 1913, most of the land around Eagle Lake and nearby Jordan Pond had been acquired by George Dorr for the Hancock County Trustees of Public Reservations in order to protect the water supply.

Since this is an out-and-back trip, you should just retrace your steps to the parking area after enjoying the views from the summit. If you like what you see so far and want to make a long day out of it, consider making the strenuous Northeast Harbor to Eagle Lake hike described in Trip 18.

TRIP 2
FLYING MOUNTAIN

NPS Rating: Moderate
Distance: 1.2 miles
Elevation Gain: 275 feet
Estimated Time: 45 minutes
Map: AMC's Acadia National Park Discovery Map: F5

This short hike leads to good views of the waters surrounding the entrance of Somes Sound.

Directions

From the intersection of Routes 102 and 198 in Somesville, follow Route 102 south for 5.4 miles to Fernald Point Road. Turn left (west) onto Fernald Point Road. The Fernald Cove parking area is on the left, 0.9 mile from Route 102. There is no direct access to this trailhead via the Island Explorer. The closest stop (about two miles from the trailhead) is Smugglers Den (stop F) on the Southwest Harbor route (route 7). *GPS coordinates*: 44° 17.936′ N, 68° 18.871′ W.

Trip Description

Flying Mountain stands as a sentinel at the southern end of Somes Sound, jutting out into the water at a point that almost closes off the entrance to the sound. At 284 feet tall, Flying Mountain is more a hill than a mountain, but it provides good views for a small amount of effort. This hike loops over the mountain and over to Valley Cove, a protected tongue of water that laps up against 500 vertical feet of rock known as Eagle Cliff. For only 45 minutes of work, this hike has a lot to offer.

Start this hike on the Flying Mountain Trail, which begins on the west side of the Fernald Cove parking area. The trail, marked with blue blazes, climbs moderately through a pure spruce forest. The soil here is thin, and erosion has made the trail difficult to follow at first. Please do your part to prevent further erosion by seeking out the blazes and keeping to the intended footpath. You will reach the summit fairly quickly, 0.3 mile from the parking lot. There are views of the south end of Somes Sound and out to

Although its peak is one of the lowest in the park, Flying Mountain offers excellent views of Somes Sound.

Greening, Sutton, and Bear Islands as well as the Cranberries. Cadillac and Norumbega mountains are also visible across the sound.

Past the summit, a side path leads to the right to an overlook with more views of the sound and the large houses of Northeast Harbor. The Flying Mountain Trail leads to the left and then descends steeply to Valley Cove. Valley Cove is a place where you can explore tide pools and gaze up at the steep walls of Eagle Cliff. This cove is one of the safest places on Mount Desert Island for boats to drop anchor in big storms, as Flying Mountain extends into Somes Sound far enough to prevent large storm swells from making their way into the cove.

As you follow the shoreline, look for a path on the left just after climbing a set of wood-and-gravel steps. Turn left on this path and then left again when it reaches a gravel fire road in a few yards. Follow the fire road through a mature forest of spruce and cedar. The parking area is 0.6 mile from Valley Cove.

TRIP 3
GREAT HEAD AND SAND BEACH

NPS Rating: Moderate
Distance: 1.8 miles
Elevation Gain: 200 feet
Estimated Time: 1.0 hour
Map: AMC's Acadia National Park Discovery Map: E9

This is a beach walk followed by a wooded climb to the 145-foot cliffs of Great Head, which overlook the Atlantic Ocean.

Directions

From downtown Bar Harbor, drive south on Route 3 for 2.1 miles and turn right at the Sieur de Monts entrance to the Park Loop Road. Follow the signs for Sand Beach. The Sand Beach parking area is on the left, 3.25 miles south of the Sieur de Monts entrance. The parking area is stop C on the Island Explorer Sand Beach route (route 3) and stop D on the Loop Road route (route 4). *GPS coordinates*: 44° 19.783′ N, 68° 11.058′ W.

Trail Description

This hike starts at Sand Beach and climbs to the outlooks along the cliffs of Great Head. Great Head is a peninsula of granite, basalt, and sedimentary rock that juts out into the ocean just to the east of Sand Beach. The cliffs are as high as 145 feet and are a dramatic spot for looking at the wildlife plying the waters below. This loop hike returns to Sand Beach, which is composed of small grains of quartz and pieces of clamshells, blue mussel shells, and green sea urchins.

From the Sand Beach parking area, walk down the stairway that leads to Sand Beach. Walk east across the beach, which is about 300 yards long, to the beginning of the Great Head Trail. A stream cuts through the beach just before the trail. Depending on the tide and the season, the stream can be completely dry or a couple of feet deep. Be prepared to ford the stream, as there is no bridge. The current is not strong, so the crossing is easy, but you will want to wear waterproof boots or sport sandals because the bottom is rocky. The stream can be an interesting place to study the rocks that exist beneath

The cliffs along Great Head Trail provide an excellent spot for wildlife watching.

the beach, as the water tends to carry the sand here to the ocean. Pink granite, dark basalt, and brownish sedimentary rocks give the stream a multicolored presence.

The Great Head Trail begins by climbing a short stretch of granite steps, at the top of which is an old millstone. Turn right here and start a moderate climb over granite slabs. Keep an eye open for blue trail blazes painted on the rocks, as the footpath is not always obvious. The hike reaches what seems like the high point of the trip before descending to the right into the woods to an overlook with views of Sand Beach, Gorham Mountain, and the Beehive.

From this overlook, the trail follows the coast to the left and gradually climbs over rocky cliffs before reaching the high point of Great Head, marked by the stone foundation of an old teahouse. The house was part of the estate of Louisa Satterlee, who received Great Head and Sand Beach as a present from her father, the financier J. P. Morgan. The teahouse was destroyed in the fire of 1947, and the Morgan property was donated to the park two years later. Great Head is the highest point on the coast of Mount Desert Island. The entire walk over these cliffs is out in the open, with the sights and sounds of the ocean on the right. Open ocean is due south, while the mouth of Frenchman Bay and the Schoodic Peninsula are to the east. To the west are Otter Cliffs, probably named for otter-like sea minks that could be seen here until they went extinct in the mid-nineteenth century. The rocky shoal between Great Head and Otter Cliffs is called Old Soaker and is a favorite hangout for seabirds. The cliffs are a good place to sit and watch for porpoises, seals, gulls, terns, guillemots, and common eider ducks. In the fall and winter, common loons can be seen here as well.

From the top of Great Head, follow the trail north, then northwest, as it descends back into a forest of spruce. At the next trail junction, continue straight as the forest changes into a mix of white birch, aspen, and balsam fir. About 0.5 mile from Great Head, the trail reaches a junction with a narrow dirt service road. Turn left onto the service road, which seems much more like a woodland path than a road. In 0.3 mile, the road completes the Great Head loop at the millstone seen at the beginning of the hike. To finish your hike, go down the stairs to Sand Beach and walk back to the west end of the beach.

TRIP 4
THE BUBBLES

NPS Rating: Strenuous, but short
Distance: 1.6 miles
Elevation Gain: 550 feet
Estimated Time: 1.5 hours
Map: AMC's Acadia National Park Discovery Map: E7

**This short but irresistible climb goes to the summits of
Jordan Pond's distinctive mountains.**

Directions

From the Acadia National Park Visitor Center, drive south on the Park Loop
Road for 6.3 miles. Be sure to continue straight at the intersections marked
Sand Beach and Cadillac Mountain. The Bubble Rock parking area will be on
your right. The parking area is stop B on the Island Explorer Jordan Pond
route (route 5). *GPS coordinates*: 44° 20.461′ N, 68° 15.023′ W.

Trip Description

The Bubbles are two well-rounded granite hills that stand at the northern
end of Jordan Pond, home to loons and mergansers. Their shape and location are so distinctive, it is hard to imagine Jordan Pond without them. At
766 feet and 872 feet, they are far from being the tallest mountains in the
park, but they do provide good views of Jordan Pond and the taller surrounding peaks. South Bubble is also home to perhaps the most well-known
rock in the state of Maine: Bubble Rock.

This hike starts at the Bubble Rock parking lot, which is about 1.1 miles
south of Bubble Pond on the Park Loop Road. From the parking lot, follow
the Bubbles Divide Trail west for a short distance where it passes the Jordan
Pond Carry—continue straight. The footpath is wide and level as it passes
through one of the few true northern hardwood forests on the island. Birch
and American beech dominate. Search the forest floor for beechnuts, a
favorite food of bear, turkey, and other animals. With the demise of the
American chestnut, which was decimated by a fungus early in the twentieth
century, beechnuts became an even more important food source for the

Glacially scored granite can be found on South Bubble's summit.

animals of eastern North America. Now the American beech is being attacked by the combination of a fungus and a scale introduced by the importation of European beech trees. Without the natural defenses necessary to fight off this threat, it is possible that the American beech could go the way of the American chestnut.

The trail turns left and climbs up a set of stairs to another junction with the Bubbles Trail, where you should turn right, making a steep climb over granite ledges toward the North Bubble. Scree walls (small rock walls) built by the park's trail crew line the trail in an attempt to keep hikers on the footpath. Like most trails in Acadia, this one is heavily used. It is very important to stay on the trail in order to ensure that the surrounding vegetation remains healthy.

Views begin to open up as thick forest gives way to pitch pines and blue-berry bushes. The summit is reached 0.6 mile from the parking lot. The view takes in Jordan Pond and the surrounding group of Mount Desert's highest peaks—Cadillac, Pemetic, Penobscot, and Sargent.

To go to South Bubble, head back down the Bubbles Trail toward the parking lot. At the junction with the Bubbles Divide Trail, turn right. The trail is fairly level for 0.1 mile, until a trail junction where going straight will bring you down to the northern end of Jordan Pond. Turn left for a moderate 0.2-mile ascent to the summit of South Bubble. Although lower than North Bubble, this summit has better views of Jordan Pond.

Bubble Rock, which lies just to the east of South Bubble's summit, is the most conspicuous example of a glacial erratic on Mount Desert Island. Glacial erratics are rocks carried by glaciers and dropped far from their place of origin. They are easily identifiable by the fact that they are made of a different type of rock than their general surroundings. Bubble Rock is made of a coarse-grained white granite that contrasts markedly with the pink granite of the Bubbles and the other peaks on Mount Desert Island. Bubble Rock most likely came from Lucerne, 40 miles to the northwest. Another erratic from Lucerne, Balance Rock, can be seen from the Shore Path in Bar Harbor. Estimated to weigh between 8 and 12 tons, Bubble Rock is often described as being about the size of a living room.

To return to the car, retrace your steps to the Bubbles Divide Trail and the parking area.

Family Adventures in Acadia National Park

One big change for us since we first wrote this guide ten years ago is that we now have two young children to share the Acadia experience with us. It is rewarding and refreshing to see the park through their eyes, and many of the adventure opportunities in the park are well-suited to kids. It is no surprise that Acadia is a popular family destination, and there are numerous activities in and around the park that are geared toward families with kids of all ages.

Kids can easily be introduced to hiking on the park's trails. Except on the ladder trails, ambitious parents can carry babies and toddlers in a child carrier backpack without too much trouble, and we found that our kids loved napping while

Acadia contains a multitude of trails that kids will love.

being carried on the trail and were wide-eyed when awake. Once kids are scrambling around on their own, good first "mountain climbs" include Conners Nubble (Trip 1), Great Head (Trip 3), the Bubbles (Trip 4), and Gorham Mountain (Trip 5). A key for parents hiking with young kids is to be patient. Your pace will be slow, as everything in nature is interesting to young kids and they will want to stop and explore often. You will also need to have snack and water breaks more often and play games to keep them moving at times—hide and seek works well. By the time kids are 8 or 9 years old, they will be capable of all but the longest trips in this book, and they can usually handle 4 or 5 miles with elevation gain. Also, hiking with kids often goes smoother if you can bring a young friend or two along, as they are engaged in their own conversations and are less likely to complain about fatigue with their peers alongside them.

All of the canoe trips in this book are appropriate for families, and the carriage roads offer bike opportunities for any level of biking ability. Appendix D has suggestions for places that rent canoes and bikes, and all the kid gear that goes with them. Sea kayaking is another great activity for families with older kids, but it has inherent dangers that must be taken into consideration. All of the trips in this guide are *not* suggested for inexperienced paddlers, let alone kids without significant kayaking experience. For experienced sea kayaking families, the Mount Desert Narrows paddle (Trip 45) is a good first choice in good weather and calm seas, as it is more sheltered than other trips in this guide. For inexperienced paddlers who want to get their kids into the sport, we suggest taking a trip with one of the sea kayaking outfitters listed in Appendix D. Some have trips appropriate for kids as young as 8; on these trips, the kids are always in a tandem kayak with a parent or other adult.

Friends of Acadia and park officials are working to provide more opportunities for families. In addition to the usual campground and ranger-led programs, they have recently instituted Family Fun Day (a Sunday in July), which includes ranger programs geared toward kids, a climbing wall, and horse rides. They have also created Acadia Quest, a competition in which teams complete a series of six events and activities in Acadia National Park between April and November. To qualify, all a team needs is one member over 18 and one under 18. The teams that meet all of the Acadia Quest requirements are entered into the grand prize drawing at Take Pride in Acadia Day in November.

TRIP 5
GORHAM MOUNTAIN AND OCEAN PATH

NPS Rating: Moderate, then easy
Distance: 3.5 miles round-trip
Elevation Gain: 500 feet
Estimated Time: 2.0 hours
Map: AMC's Acadia National Park Discovery Map: E9

A moderate hike up to wide-open views of the ocean is followed by a walk along the dramatic coastline between Sand Beach and Otter Cliffs.

Directions
From downtown Bar Harbor, drive south on Route 3 for 2.1 miles and turn right at the Sieur de Monts entrance to the Park Loop Road. Follow the signs for Sand Beach. The Gorham Mountain parking area is on the right, 4.4 miles south of the Sieur de Monts entrance. The parking area is an unscheduled stop between Thunder Hole (stop D) and the Fabbri Picnic Area (stop E) on the Island Explorer Sand Beach route (route 3). *GPS coordinates*: 44° 19.024′ N, 68° 11.471′ W.

Trip Description
This hike makes the climb up Gorham Mountain from the Park Loop Road at a parking area opposite Monument Cove. A short detour explores the caves on the Cadillac Cliffs before reaching the summit and its views out over the Ocean Drive section of the Park Loop Road. After descending the north ridge of Gorham Mountain, the hike follows an easy footpath along Ocean Drive and passes Thunder Hole. This hike's moderate grades and relatively accessible views make it a good trip for families with young children.

From the parking area, the Gorham Mountain Trail enters a forest of paper birch and red spruce, but quickly reaches a forest of pitch pine spread out among the ledges of pink Cadillac granite. At 0.3 mile, a side trail goes to the right. If you are not up for some rough footing or a short but steep ascent, continue straight on the Gorham Mountain Trail. Otherwise, turn right and follow the 0.5-mile side trail along Cadillac Cliffs.

Numerous passages can be explored near the pink granite ledges that are adjacent to Ocean Path.

The trail meanders around and under modest, fern-covered cliffs and caves that were once at sea level. Huge boulders have broken off the cliffs and created a jumbled trail of tunnels and "lemon squeezers," places where the trail squeezes between large pieces of granite. In addition to challenging hiking, the cliffs also create a cool, moist microclimate where ferns and mosses grow thick.

After the last big set of boulders, the trail turns left and climbs quickly to rejoin the Gorham Mountain Trail. Turn right to hike over open ledges to the summit of Gorham Mountain in 0.4 mile. While only 522 feet above sea level, Gorham Mountain is less than half a mile from the waters of the Atlantic Ocean. The views of Ocean Drive, Otter Cliffs, and Sand Beach are excellent, as are the views of Champlain, Dorr, and Cadillac mountains.

To resume this trip, continue north on the Gorham Mountain Trail as it descends gently into a forest of mixed hardwoods. The hardwoods here grew up out of the ashes of the great fire of 1947. It is now difficult to imagine this area as the charred, treeless plain it was 50 years ago, but the fire here burned so hot that the ground was actually sterilized in some places, and it was many years before trees recolonized the area. As the trail descends, an unofficial and unmaintained trail leaves the Gorham Mountain Trail on the right. Continue straight on the Gorham Mountain Trail and avoid the unmaintained trail, which the Park Service is trying to let fade back into the forest.

The trail reaches a junction with the Bowl Trail 0.7 mile from the summit. Turn right here and follow the Bowl Trail 0.5 mile to the Park Loop Road. Cross the Park Loop Road and turn right onto the Ocean Path.

The Ocean Path follows the Ocean Drive section of the Park Loop Road for the entire mile from here to the Monument Cove parking area. The Ocean Path provides the park's best access to Mount Desert Island's famed pink-granite coastline. During this walk, you can scramble over smooth granite ledges and explore the cobble beaches of Newport and Monument Coves, all while watching and listening to the surf making landfall in typical Maine fashion. Herring and great black-back gulls are common. Unfortunately, they are often fed by tourists, even though the practice is prohibited in Acadia and is never a good idea, as it endangers the health of the animals and people. Eider ducks and double-crested cormorants cruise the waters, feeding on fish, crustaceans, and mollusks.

The biggest attraction along the Ocean Path is Thunder Hole, a narrow cleft in the granite shoreline. When the waters of the rising tide hit this hole in the rock just right, a giant splash of water hurtles skyward, emitting a thunderous crash and soaking any visitor who happens to be standing in the wrong spot. While it is rather tame most of the time, chances are good that Thunder Hole will be booming if you visit near high tide on a windy day. Be sure to not go beyond the barriers. Tides are usually listed in local papers such as the *Bar Harbor Times*, *Acadia Weekly*, and the National Park Service's *Beaver Log* (available at www.nps.gov/acad/parknews/newspaper.htm.) You can also buy official tide charts at local bookstores.

Just beyond where the Ocean Path reaches the parking area is Monument Cove. Take a few minutes to hike down to this cove filled with melon-sized cobbles of granite. These fascinating globe- and egg-shaped rocks have been smoothed and shaped over time by constantly rolling and grinding against one another as the waves wash over them. As time goes on, these cobbles will become smaller and smaller, eventually becoming a pebble beach. For more than 300 years, cobbles from Maine's beaches were harvested and used for ships' ballast, building materials, and cobblestone streets. Cobbles are now understood to be an important part of the environment, however, and should be left on the beach. The Gorham Mountain parking area is directly across the Park Loop Road from Monument Cove.

TRIP 6
THE BEEHIVE AND THE BOWL

NPS Rating: Strenuous, with ladders
Distance: 1.3 miles
Elevation Gain: 450 feet
Estimated Time: 1.0 hour
Map: AMC's Acadia National Park Discovery Map: E9

**Take a challenging climb up iron rungs to spectacular views
and a visit to a quiet and beautiful mountain pond.**

Directions
From downtown Bar Harbor, drive south on Route 3 for 2.1 miles and turn
right at the Sieur de Monts entrance to the Park Loop Road. Follow the signs
for Sand Beach. The Sand Beach parking area is on the left, 3.25 miles south
of the Sieur de Monts entrance. The Bowl Trail is across the road from the
parking area. The parking area is stop C on the Island Explorer Sand Beach
route (route 3), and stop D on the Loop Road route (route 4). *GPS coordinates*: 44° 19.783′ N, 68° 11.058′ W.

Trip Description
The challenging nature of this hike up the Beehive makes this one of the
more popular hikes in the park. The fact that it is just across the road from
Sand Beach and has good views probably adds a bit to its popularity as well.
The Bowl is a beautiful pond nestled between the Beehive and Champlain
Mountain and is one of two ponds in the park that are accessible only by
foot. (Sargent Pond is the other.)

Caution: This hike is very steep and traverses the cliffs of the Beehive using iron rungs and ladders. This hike is very dangerous in wet weather. People who have a fear of heights should consider climbing the Beehive from the
Bowl instead of up the Beehive Trail. It is not a recommended hike for people
with small children, and those with older children should consider hiking it
without kids first to determine if it is an appropriate hike for the family.

Begin this hike on the Bowl Trail, which is across the Park Loop Road
from the Sand Beach parking area. The Beehive Trail is the first trail junction,

The wooden walkway next to the Bowl provides a welcome respite after ascending the iron rungs and granite ledges of the Beehive Trail.

0.2 mile from the road. Turn right to follow the Beehive Trail toward the 350-foot cliffs of the Beehive. Like most of the mountains on Mount Desert Island (as well as many of the islands surrounding it), the Beehive has a gradual-sloping north face and steep cliffs on the south face. Glaciers during the last ice age created this landscape feature. The pressure of the ice caused water to fill the cracks on the south face of the peaks. The rock weakened as the water went through repeated cycles of freezing and thawing. As the glacier moved forward, it sheared off these weakened pieces of granite, creating the cliffs.

Designed and built by Rudolph Brunnow, the man who built the Precipice Trail on Champlain Mountain, the Beehive Trail quickly rises to meet the cliff wall and begins to climb almost straight up. The iron rungs and ladders alternate with stretches of granite ledges. Views of the Atlantic Ocean, Sand Beach, and Champlain Mountain get better and better as you climb, but be sure of your footing before you look back over your shoulder! While strenuous, the climb up the Beehive is relatively short, and most hikers can finish the 0.5-mile hike to the summit in about 30 minutes. The views of the ocean are good, but the view toward the interior of the island is one of the prettiest mountain views in the park. While looking over the Bowl toward Dorr and Cadillac mountains, you see no sign of man—no Park Loop Road, no carriage roads, no power lines.

To hike down to the Bowl, a small 9.5-acre pond, follow the Beehive Trail northwest, away from the cliffs. A side trail leads left back to the Bowl Trail but bypasses the Bowl. Continue straight on the Beehive Trail to reach the Bowl, a good example of a glacial tarn, which is a deep, typically circular lake that forms when an alpine glacier melts. The Bowl is a quiet place with a unique, southern view of Champlain Mountain. To finish the hike, follow the trail to the left, along the southern end of the pond. In the middle of a set of wooden puncheons built to protect the boggy shoreline, the Bowl Trail comes in from the left. Turn left on the Bowl Trail and follow it 0.6 mile back to the Park Loop Road.

TRIP 7
BAR HARBOR TO SAND BEACH

NPS Rating: Moderate
Distance: 4.7 miles
Elevation Gain: 100 feet
Estimated Time: 2.0 hours
Map: AMC's Acadia National Park Discovery Map: C9, D9, E9

Walk to the beach from downtown Bar Harbor and enjoy both mountain and ocean views.

Directions

Park anywhere in Bar Harbor. There are public lots on Rodick Street and at the municipal pier at the end of Main Street. The hike will start at the corner of Main Street and Mount Desert Street at the town green (see Bar Harbor map at the back of this book).

Trip Description

For more than a decade, Friends of Acadia has been working with the Park Service to create several village connector trails that allow residents and visitors to Mount Desert Island to walk into the park while leaving their cars behind at home or at a hotel. In 2009, trail crews completed work restoring the Schooner Head Path, a historic (but abandoned) trail that once connected Bar Harbor to Schooner Head and nearby Sand Beach in the park. This trip describes the route from Bar Harbor to Sand Beach using this trail, sidewalks, a short stretch of park road, and a section of the Great Head Trail. The hike is next to the road for most of its length, but there is something special about being able to walk from your home or hotel to enjoy the beauty of Sand Beach and views of Champlain Mountain and the Beehive. It is a flat 4.7 miles one way, and you can either walk back to town, or pick up the free Island Explorer shuttle bus at Sand Beach for your return trip.

This trip starts at the Bar Harbor Town Green on the corner of Main and Mount Desert streets. Follow Main Street south (away from the water and toward the mountains), taking the sidewalks past restaurants and motels. After about 1.0 mile, you will pass a National Park Service parking area on the left, where there are trails that lead 0.5 mile through the woods to the water at Dorr Point (worth a look if you have the time). Continue following Main Street until you reach Schooner Head Road, in another 0.2 mile. Turn left on Schooner Head Road and you will soon see the Schooner Head Path entering the woods on the left side of the ride.

The path is basically a gravel sidewalk in the woods. It crosses the road a few times and is never far from the pavement, but the road is quiet and there are few interruptions, especially after the Jackson Laboratory near the beginning of the path. About 1.4 miles from Main Street, you will pass the Orange and Black Trail on the right, which leads to the trails at the north end of Champlain Mountain. In another 0.5 mile, you pass another trail on the right, Murphy Lane, which leads to the Precipice Trail. Continuing on the Schooner Head Path, you soon pass through a beautiful forest of paper birch trees and get great views of Champlain Mountain over a large beaver pond.

After crossing the outlet of the pond, the trail crosses the road one last time and leads 0.1 mile through the woods to the Schooner Head Parking area. There are great ocean views here as well as a 0.25 mile side trail that leads down to the cliffs overlooking Schooner Head. At low tide, you can crawl into Anemone Cave, a popular destination since the heyday of Bar Harbor tourism in the nineteenth century. If you do wish to explore the cave, be aware that the trail to the cave is poorly marked, steep and follows the ledges at the water's edge. To continue to Sand Beach, follow the road from the parking area back toward Schooner Head Road, which is in 0.1 mile. Turn left here, and follow the road for 0.4 mile through the woods to the parking area for the Great Head Trail.

The Great Head Trail is a figure eight that leads to both Great Head and Sand Beach. From the parking area, follow the trail into the woods and follow the right fork for a 0.4-mile walk through the woods down to the beach, taking a second right fork in about 0.3 mile. As you reach the beach, you will break out into the open on a dune above a tidal creek with views of the Beehive to the right and the open ocean to the left. Cross the creek and you are on a beautiful sandy beach, which is surrounded by high cliffs on either end. Feeling brave? Take a dip in the Gulf of Maine waters, whose temperature rarely rises above the mid-50s even in the hottest days of summer.

If you are making this hike between late June and Columbus Day, you can grab a shuttle bus back to Bar Harbor. To do so, walk up the stairs at the far end of the beach to the Sand Beach parking area and wait for Island Explorer Bus 3.

The Great Fire of 1947

In 1947, an event occurred that still has an effect on Acadia today. That summer Maine received only 50 percent of its normal rainfall, and by October Mount Desert Island was as dry as it has ever been. On October 17 the fire department received a call that smoke was rising from a cranberry bog near a dump on Crooked Road, west of Hulls Cove. At the time it was a modest blaze, and it burned only 167 acres during the next three days. But on October 21 strong winds took control, and soon another 2,000 acres were burning. The fire continued to intensify as firefighters proved no match for the gale-force winds, which blew the fire south and east. At one point, the fire moved 6 miles in less than 3 hours and burned 67 summer cottages in the section of Bar Harbor known as Millionaires' Row. Downtown Bar Harbor itself was spared, although the fire came close enough that 400 people fled by sea to Winter Harbor across Frenchman Bay.

After burning more than 17,000 acres, 10,000 of them in Acadia, the fire burned itself out in a massive fireball over the Atlantic Ocean at Ocean Drive. For such an intense fire, casualties were low: one person died while trying to rescue a cat from his burning home, and two people died in a car accident while fleeing the island. Park rangers believed that most animals were able to outrun the fire and take refuge in lakes and ponds. However, the nature in the park was altered dramatically. Before the fire, spruce and fir dominated the landscape, but with the spruce-fir canopy gone, sun-loving species such as birch and aspen were able to grow. Today, a mosaic forest has reclaimed the burned areas of the park. This forest—a mix of spruce, fir, white pine, hemlock, beech, maple, birch, and aspen—supports a variety of wildlife, including beaver, white-tailed deer, and ruffed grouse. On the exposed, rocky ledges of the mountains that burned, fire-resistant pitch pine flourishes. All in all, the park now contains a more diverse mix of flora and fauna than it did before the fire.

The fire of 1947 brought about the end of the era of huge summer cottages (most bunred,) although the lavish lifestyle surrounding these coastal vacation mansionshad already been in decline due to such factors as the introduction of the income tax, the Great Depression, and World War II. However, tourism remains the largest part of the economy for Mount Desert Island, and more than 2 million people a year visit Acadia to walk its wooded paths, breathe in the salty scent of the Atlantic, and watch the wildlife of Maine's wild coast. Acadia National Park has healed its fire scars and is now a vibrant and healthy ecosystem.

TRIP 8
BEECH MOUNTAIN

NPS Rating: Moderate
Distance: 2.0 miles round-trip
Elevation Gain: 700 feet
Estimated Time: 1.5 hours
Map: AMC's Acadia National Park Discovery Map: F4

This enjoyable hike over rocky ledges leads to the summit of Beech Mountain and excellent views.

Directions

From the center of Southwest Harbor, go west on Seal Cove Road. Take the first paved road on the right, Long Pond Road. Follow Long Pond Road through a residential area until it ends at the south end of Long Pond. There is a small parking area to the right of the water-pumping station. There is no Island Explorer stop at this parking area. The closest stop (2 miles away) is Echo Lake (stop E) on the Southwest Harbor Route (route 7). *GPS coordinates:* 44° 18.898′ N, 68° 21.210′ W.

Trip Description

This hike begins at the southern end of Long Pond and makes its way up 700 feet of granite ledges to the fire tower atop Beech Mountain. Due to its relatively easy access and its good views, this is the most popular summit on the western side of Mount Desert Island. A longer walk down the open south ridge of Beech Mountain makes for a less steep return trip filled with good views.

From the parking area, follow the Beech West Ridge Trail along the eastern shore of Long Pond. The trail stays near the shore of the pond for 0.3 mile and passes two private residences along the way. Please respect these residents' privacy. After passing the second house, the trail turns right and begins climbing the relatively steep west ridge of Beech Mountain. The trail quickly reaches open granite ledges populated by white pines and scrub oak. Views begin to open up across Long Pond to Mansell Mountain.

The trail reaches the Beech Mountain Trail 0.9 mile from the parking area. Turn right on this trail for a 0.1-mile hike to the summit. The summit of

Beech West Ridge Trail leads to the summit of Beech Mountain and a fire tower, which is rarely open to the public.

Beech Mountain is only 841 feet above sea level, but, like most peaks on Mount Desert Island, it is treeless, making for excellent views in all directions. The fire tower is not currently staffed, as small planes are now used to patrol for fires. While you can't currently climb the tower, the summit still has excellent views of Somes Sound, Cadillac Mountain, Sutton and Greening islands, the Cranberry Isles, Isle au Haut, and all of the western mountains.

To return to your car, look for a trail that heads south. This is the Beech South Ridge Trail. This trail descends moderately through a forest of spruce that opens up regularly to provide more good views past Southwest Harbor and out to the Atlantic Ocean. The views finally end as the trail enters a thick forest of tall spruce. The trail descends steeply here, using switchbacks and stone steps to ease the hiking. You will reach a trail junction 0.6 mile from the summit, marking the end of the Beech South Ridge Trail. Turn right on the Valley Trail for a 0.4-mile forested walk back to the parking area at Long Pond.

TRIP 9
NORUMBEGA MOUNTAIN

NPS Rating: Strenuous
Distance: 3.5 miles round-trip
Elevation Gain: 700 feet
Estimated Time: 2.5 hours
Map: AMC's Acadia National Park Discovery Map: E6

Take a quick climb to good views of Somes Sound, followed by a visit to the quiet waters of scenic Lower Hadlock Pond.

Directions
Follow Routes 198/3 for 1.4 miles north from Northeast Harbor. The Norumbega Parking Area will be on the left (west) side of the road. The parking area is an unscheduled stop between Gate House (stop D) and MDI High School (stop C) on the Island Explorer Brown Mountain route (route 6). *GPS coordinates*: 44° 19.558′ N, 68° 17.489′ W.

Trip Description
At 850 feet tall, Norumbega Mountain is not one of the largest peaks in the park, but it is an important peak geologically because it forms the eastern wall of Maine's only fjord, Somes Sound. This loop hike has the typical Acadia features: great views, tranquil forests, and welcome moments of solitude. It makes a quick ascent to the summit before making a leisurely return trip along the shores of Lower Hadlock Pond, which is home to tall spruce trees and calling loons.

From the Norumbega parking lot on Route 198, hike up the Goat Trail, which seems to follow the steepest route possible to the summit. Besides being steep, the trail is rough; it is filled with roots and boulders as it gains 600 feet in the first 0.3 mile. A heavy pack will definitely work against you here, but once you complete that first 0.3 mile, you will be faced with easy walking up a ridge sparsely populated by short pitch pines and lowbush blueberries. Views open up in all directions as you near the summit, only 0.6 mile from the parking area. Scattered pine trees obscure the view from the top, but there are excellent views from a ledge 150 yards beyond the summit.

Follow the trail, now called the Norumbega Mountain Trail, beyond the summit, as it continues along semi-open granite ridge top, providing occasional views of the mountains to the east and west, Southwest Harbor, and the Cranberry Isles. At 1.3 miles, the trail reenters the forest and reaches a junction with the Golf Course Trail, where you should turn left, heading toward Lower Hadlock Pond. The descent along the south ridge of Norumbega is much gentler than the ascent you made earlier; here you can allow your mind to drift away from a concentration on the trail and take in the beautiful spruce forest that surrounds you.

At 1.8 mile, you'll reach the southern end of Lower Hadlock Pond, a small, quiet pond ringed with spruce trees; the mile or so of shoreline appears to be an impenetrable wall of green. When you reach the pond, turn left on the Hadlock Ponds Trail and follow the western shore for about 0.5 mile to the northern end. Here you will find a series of small cascades where Hadlock Brook tumbles into the pond. The trail follows the west side of the brook away from the pond, passing two other paths within about 200 yards. Stay left at both intersections, following a sign at the second intersection that reads "To Goat Trail." This is the Norumbega Connector Trail.

After leaving the brook, the trail rolls over uneven terrain through more spruce woods, paralleling Route 198 for 1.3 miles on its way to the Norumbega parking area, completing the loop.

TRIP 10
HUGUENOT HEAD AND CHAMPLAIN MOUNTAIN

NPS Rating: Moderate, with one short strenuous section
Distance: 3.3 miles
Elevation Gain: 1,100 feet
Estimated Time: 2.5 hours
Map: AMC's Acadia National Park Discovery Map: D9

This classic Acadia hike goes up steep pink granite to spectacular mountain and ocean views.

Directions
This hike begins at the Tarn parking area, 2.2 miles south of Bar Harbor on Route 3. Across Route 3 from the parking area, look for a granite staircase marking the beginning of the Beachcroft Trail. The closest Island Explorer stop is at Sieur de Monts (stop B, about 0.25 mile from the Tarn) on Sand Beach route (route 3). *GPS coordinates*: 44° 21.508′ N, 68° 12.344′ W.

Trip Description
Champlain Mountain is a popular wildlife-viewing spot due to its pair of nesting peregrine falcons. This is also one of the best places to view Frenchman Bay while visiting Mount Desert Island. The Beachcroft Trail makes a moderate ascent from the west and offers distinctive views of the Tarn and Dorr Mountain from Huguenot Head. This trail is a good alternative to the east face's Precipice Trail, a steep climb up iron rungs. The Precipice Trail is usually closed for much of the summer so that hikers do not disturb the nesting falcons. By combining the Beachcroft Trail with the Champlain North Ridge Trail and the Park Loop Road, it is possible to have a varied hike above treeline, watch for eagles and falcons, and visit an active beaver pond.

This hike starts on the east side of Route 3, across the road from the north end of the Tarn, a glacial pond nestled below the cliffs of Dorr Mountain. Look for a set of granite stairs and a wooden sign marking the Beachcroft Trail. George Dorr had the Beachcroft Trail built in 1915, using stones from the base of the mountain as the material for the 1,482 steps that ease

One way to get to the summit of Champlain Mountain is the Precipice Trail.

the climb. The first few hundred yards of the trail follow a sidewalk-like stretch of skillfully laid granite through a deciduous forest. The trail then rises quickly above the trees on switchbacks built into the steep face of Huguenot Head. At 0.4 mile, the trail reaches the southwestern shoulder of Huguenot Head, passing within 150 yards of the summit. This open granite ledge provides views of Dorr Mountain, the Tarn, and the Atlantic Ocean.

The trail drops back below the trees for 0.1 mile before beginning the climb to the summit of Champlain Mountain. The next section of the hike is the most difficult. A short, steep climb over rocks and through the trees brings you to a prime example of a pitch-pine forest. Due to its open nature, a pitch-pine forest looks like few others in New England. The widely spaced trees grow on exposed granite ledges, accompanied only occasionally by prostrate shrubs like lowbush blueberry and mountain cranberry. The trees themselves seldom grow to more than 20 feet in height and are gnarled and twisted by constant exposure to high winds. The open aspect of the forest makes it possible to see the summit of Cadillac Mountain, now visible directly behind Dorr Mountain.

The climb through the pines to the summit of Champlain is over smooth but steep granite. This part of the hike can be very slippery when wet, so

Impressive Speed: The Peregrine Falcon

The peregrine falcon is about the size of a crow, but it has the speed of a Corvette. A peregrine regularly attains speeds in excess of 100 miles per hour while diving to catch and kill its prey in flight. Even in regular flight, this awesome predator reaches speeds of 60 miles per hour. While flying, a peregrine looks like a typical falcon, with long, pointed wings and a long tail. The bird has a white or buff-colored breast, a slate-gray back, a small head made distinctive by long gray "sideburns," and yellow legs.

By the mid-1960s, the falcon was considered extinct in the eastern United States. Hunting caused much of its downfall, but the ingestion of chemical pesticides accelerated its extinction by making it nearly impossible to reproduce successfully. The peregrine was declared an endangered species in 1973. Acadia National Park began participating in a peregrine-reintroduction program in 1984. The park released 22 hand-raised chicks into the park between 1984 and 1986. In 1987 adult peregrines began returning to the park, and in 1991 peregrines successfully fledged chicks in Acadia for the first time since 1956.

The program has been such a success that, depending on the year, two or three pairs of peregrines now nest in the park, where they seek out small ledges on high cliffs. The nest sites are consistently on Champlain Mountain, Flying Mountain, Beech Mountain, and Jordan Cliffs on Penobscot Mountain. The park usually closes any hiking trails in nest areas if the nests are active.

The best opportunity to observe peregrines is on Champlain Mountain during the spring and summer. From the parking area for the Precipice Trail, it is possible to view the birds on the cliffs above with a spotting scope or a good pair of binoculars. (The Precipice Trail is closed while the birds are nesting.) The National Park Service often stations a volunteer in the parking area to answer questions and to help visitors locate the birds. It is also possible to see the birds soaring above the cliffs from the summit of Champlain Mountain.

To protect the peregrine falcon, Acadia National Park asks visitors to:

- Learn the characteristic field marks and behaviors of peregrines so that you can make a positive identification when you see one in the park.
- Report any peregrine sightings to a park information station.
- Keep away from areas where peregrines are nesting. Avoid observing the birds from a location higher than the nest. Adult peregrines generally won't tolerate people above them and may dive at intruders.

exercise caution in rainy and foggy conditions. The Beachcroft Trail ends at the summit, 0.8 mile from Route 3. Champlain's open, rocky peak is a good place to watch for wildlife and follow the boat traffic in Frenchman Bay. During the summer, peregrine falcons are often conspicuous, with the chicks loudly announcing the return of either parent to the nest. In addition to the falcons, bald eagles and other raptors frequent the thermals around Champlain Mountain. With a good pair of binoculars, it is also possible to spot harbor porpoises, harbor seals, and minke whales plying the waters of Frenchman Bay. The views of the bay are breathtaking, as you sit 1,058 feet above sea level while less than a mile from the water. From here, you can see the Porcupine Islands and Bar Harbor to the north, Egg Rock and the Schoodic Peninsula to the northeast, the Cranberry Isles to the south, and the other mountains of Mount Desert Island to the west.

To begin your descent, look for the Champlain North Ridge Trail at the summit cairn. Follow the trail north, toward Bar Harbor and the Porcupine Islands. This trail has good views to the east and north as it descends moderately over smooth granite ledge. It stays on open ledge for most of its mile-long traverse of Champlain Mountain's north ridge and enters the forest shortly before ending at the Park Loop Road.

Turn left and follow the Park Loop Road. You will soon come to an active beaver pond with views of both Huguenot Head and Champlain Mountain. The beaver are most active at night, but you can often see them from the road at dawn and dusk. This is also a good spot to look for warblers, phoebes, and flycatchers and to photograph the abundant waterlilies.

At 0.75 mile from the Champlain North Ridge Trail, turn left toward Sieur de Monts Spring. Turn left again in about 200 yards. In 300 more yards, turn right on Route 3 for a short walk to the parking area.

TRIP 11
PEMETIC MOUNTAIN AND BUBBLE POND

NPS Rating: Strenuous, then moderate and easy
Distance: 4.1 miles round-trip
Elevation Gain: 950 feet
Estimated Time: 2.5 hours
Map: AMC's Acadia National Park Discovery Map: E7, D8

This hike takes some effort at first but leads to some of Mount Desert Island's most spectacular views.

Directions

From the Acadia National Park Visitor Center, drive south on the Park Loop Road for 5.2 miles. Be sure to continue straight at the intersections marked Sand Beach and Cadillac Mountain. The Bubble Pond parking area will be on your left. The parking area is stop B on the Island Explorer Jordan Pond route (route 5). *GPS coordinates*: 44° 21.006′ N, 68° 14.456′ W.

Trip Description

At 1,247 feet, Pemetic Mountain is the fourth highest on Mount Desert Island and affords some excellent views of Cadillac Mountain, Jordan Pond, and the Atlantic Ocean. Beginning and ending at Bubble Pond, a picturesque glacial pool nestled between Pemetic and Cadillac mountains, this hike climbs the northeast face of Pemetic via the Pemetic North Ridge Trail. The long hike above treeline on the south ridge of Pemetic is nicely complemented by an easy walk along the carriage road on the western shore of Bubble Pond.

The Pemetic North Ridge Trail starts at the south end of the Bubble Pond parking area. After crossing the carriage road, follow the Pemetic North Ridge Trail to the right. The trail to the left is the Cadillac West Face Trail. The trail quickly crosses back over the carriage road before starting its climb to the summit.

The trail climbs moderately through a forest of mixed hardwoods and conifers before it becomes a steep climb through a forest of pure hemlock.

A carriage road lines one side of Bubble Pond, making for a pleasant and leisurely hike.

Due to the thick hemlock canopy, the forest floor here is devoid of undergrowth except for spruce saplings and the occasional striped maple. The climb stays steep and the footing gets rougher as the elevation increases.

The trail crosses a few open ledges with views of Cadillac Mountain. Lowbush blueberry and sheep laurel are common through here. After going in and out of the trees several times, the trail leaves the forest for good at its junction with the Pemetic Northwest Trail, 1.1 miles from the trailhead. The Pemetic Northwest Trail is to the right and leads to the Bubble Rock parking area. Follow the Pemetic North Ridge Trail, which turns left, climbs over open ledge, and reaches the summit of Pemetic Mountain in another 0.1 mile.

From the summit of Pemetic (*pemetic* is the Wabanaki word for "gently sloping land"), there are views in all directions. To the northeast are Bubble Pond and Cadillac Mountain. To the south are the Atlantic Ocean and the Cranberry Isles. Jordan Pond is directly below the mountain to the west, and the summits of Penobscot and Sargent mountains rise up directly behind the pond. Eagle Lake is to the north.

Continue south on the Pemetic South Ridge Trail, which is marked by cairns and blue blazes on the bare rock. The south ridge of Pemetic is gently sloping exposed granite, making for an extended walk with views in all directions. The views end at 1.9 miles, where the Pemetic South Ridge Trail forks to the right. Follow the Pemetic East Cliff Trail left into the trees. The trail makes a short, steep descent before becoming a moderate footpath through a northern hardwood forest.

At 2.2 miles, the trail intersects the Bubble and Jordan Ponds Path. Turn left onto this path, which makes an easy descent of 0.3 mile to a carriage road. Follow the carriage road left for 1.6 miles back to the Bubble Pond parking area. Along the way, the carriage road follows the western shore of Bubble Pond. Views across the pond are of the steep west slope of Cadillac Mountain, which includes a large boulder field that rises from the southeast corner of the pond. While on the carriage road, remember that you are now sharing the trail with horses and bikes.

TRIP 12
ACADIA AND SAINT SAUVEUR MOUNTAINS

NPS Rating: Strenuous
Distance: 3.7 miles round-trip
Elevation Gain: 1,050 feet
Estimated Time: 3.0 hours
Map: AMC's Acadia National Park Discovery Map: E5, F5

See the only fjord on the East Coast of the United States.

Directions
The parking area for the Acadia Mountain Trail is on the west side of Route 102, 3.3 miles from the intersection of Routes 102 and 198 in Somesville. The parking area is an unscheduled stop on the Island Explorer Southwest Harbor route (route 7), between Somesville (stop D) and Echo Lake (stop E). *GPS coordinates*: 44° 19.319′ N, 68° 19.972′ W.

Trip Description
Acadia and Saint Sauveur Mountains form the western wall of Somes Sound, providing a symmetrical counterpart to Norumbega Mountain on the east side of the sound. Although these peaks are both under 700 feet in height, this is a strenuous hike that starts at around 150 feet and drops back down almost to sea level between Acadia and Saint Sauveur. Both the summit of Acadia Mountain and the ledges of Eagle Cliff offer excellent views of the sound.

The Acadia Mountain Trail begins with a set of stone steps directly across the road from the parking area. At 0.1 mile, the Saint Sauveur Trail leads to the right. You will be returning via this trail in a few hours. At this point, turn left to continue on the Acadia Mountain Trail, which meanders through a forest of pine and spruce with an understory of blueberries and sheep laurel. At 0.2 mile, the trail crosses a dirt fire road and then begins climbing steeply over granite ledges and stone stairs.

The trail quickly reaches its first reward, an area of open ledges with views to the south and west of Echo Lake, Beech Mountain, and Saint Sauveur Mountain. At 0.8 mile from the parking area, the trail reaches Acadia Mountain's summit, a beautiful flat area of pitch pine, blueberry, and pros-

Acadia Mountain is best known for its views of Somes Sound, but it also offers clear views of other mountains, such as Beech Mountain.

trate juniper. The trail continues east over granite, in and out of pine, to a point where the mountain drops almost straight down to Somes Sound. From here, you get excellent views of the eastern mountains and the whole of Somes Sound, its deep waters bordered by steep mountains, making it the only fjord on the East Coast of the United States. The sound was carved by the Wisconsin Glacier between 15,000 and 25,000 years ago. The water in the sound reaches depths of almost 200 feet.

To continue on this hike, follow the Acadia Mountain Trail to the right as it descends very quickly through beautiful pitch-pine forest. At 1.5 miles, the trail levels out at Man o' War Brook. A side trail leads left to where the brook cascades over rock directly into Somes Sound. During the seventeenth and early eighteenth centuries, when Down East Maine was hotly contested territory between the French and British, Mount Desert Island was a dangerous place to visit for ships of either side. According to legend, this made Somes Sound a haven for pirate ships, which would sail up next to the cascade at Man o' War Brook to fill up with freshwater.

Soon after the brook is a trail junction. Take the right fork, heading toward the Man o' War Brook Road and Saint Sauveur Mountain. In another 100 yards, the road leaves the trail to the right and the Valley Cove Trail leads left to Valley Cove. Continue straight on what is now called the Valley Peak Trail. From here, the trail climbs steeply through a mixed conifer forest of white pine, red pine, cedar, spruce, and fir before reaching the open ledges of Eagle Cliff. Eagle Cliff rises 500 feet straight up from Valley Cove, a very protected part of the sound where boats often drop anchor to wait out bad storms. From here, you get a good view of Flying Mountain and the estates of Northeast Harbor across Somes Sound.

At a trail junction on the cliff, turn right to head toward the summit of Saint Sauveur. In another 0.1 mile, you will reach a second trail junction. Turn right again for a 50-yard walk to the wooded summit of Saint Sauveur, which was known as Dog Mountain before becoming part of the national park. The forest here is a fairly thick stand of pitch pine, while blueberry bushes fill in the understory and turn a spectacular fire-engine red in late fall.

From the summit it is 1.3 miles back to the parking area on Route 102. The rest of the hike is a moderate descent of the north ridge of Saint Sauveur. Just 0.3 mile below the summit, the Ledge Trail enters from the left. Continue straight both here and at the next trail junction as the trail makes it way through a rocky forest of pine, cedar, and spruce. As the trail flattens out, it reaches a junction with the Acadia Mountain Trail. From here, the parking area is 0.1 mile to the left.

TRIP 13
PENOBSCOT AND SARGENT MOUNTAINS

NPS Rating: Strenuous
Distance: 5.3 miles round-trip
Elevation Gain: 1,300 feet
Estimated Time: 3.5 hours
Map: AMC's Acadia National Park Discovery Map: E7, D7

Take a challenging hike to two of Acadia's highest peaks, with long stretches on open ledges with spectacular views.

Directions

From the Acadia National Park Visitor Center, drive south on the Park Loop Road for 7.3 miles. Be sure to continue straight at the intersections marked Sand Beach and Cadillac Mountain. The Jordan Pond parking area will be on your right. The parking area is stop C on the Island Explorer Jordan Pond route (route 5) and stop F on the Loop Road route (route 4). *GPS coordinates*: 44° 19.332' N, 68° 15.121' W.

Trip Description

The cliffs of Penobscot Mountain rise steeply from the western shore of Jordan Pond and provide habitat for one of Acadia's nesting pairs of peregrine falcons. This hike provides an alternative to the Jordan Cliffs Trail, which is often closed due to the nesting falcons. Sargent Mountain is the second-highest peak on Mount Desert Island, and its flat, wide-open subalpine summit provides some of the island's best views of Somes Sound, the Cranberry Isles, and the western mountains.

This hike starts on the Spring Trail, located behind and to the left of the Jordan Pond House. The trail crosses a carriage road in about 50 yards. Cross the stream on the other side of the carriage road where there is a trail junction. The trail to the left is the Asticou and Jordan Pond Path. This hike continues straight on the Spring Trail.

The trail rises and falls gently through the mixed hardwood and conifer forest to the west of Jordan Pond. After crossing another brook, the trail begins a steep ascent up a well-built set of rock steps. These steps are a good

The gradual ascent to the summit of Sargent Mountain will continually cross a stream and also pass the picturesque Waterfall Bridge.

example of how proper trail maintenance can prevent severe erosion on a trail that receives a lot of use. Just before crossing another carriage road, the Spring Trail turns left at its junction with the Jordan Cliffs Trail. After crossing the carriage road, the trail begins a very steep ascent up the cliffs of Penobscot Mountain. There are a few iron rungs on this section of the hike as the trail squeezes through narrow cracks in the granite cliff face. About 0.5 mile from the Jordan Pond House, the Spring Trail ends at the Penobscot Mountain Trail, where you should turn right.

The Penobscot Mountain Trail soon emerges from the trees as it makes a moderate ascent of the south ridge of Penobscot Mountain. The walk up the south ridge is over open granite ledges with good views of most of the mountains in the park and of the Atlantic Ocean. The environment is subalpine, with prostrate trees and plants from the heath family like sheep laurel and rhodora. Lowbush blueberries are very common along this trail.

Looking north from the summit (1.6 miles from Jordan Pond), you will see Sargent Pond and the summit of Sargent Mountain. The summit is a good place to watch for ravens and hawks riding the thermals of air warmed by the sun-baked granite peaks. You should be able to spot the peregrines if they are nesting on Jordan Cliffs. The small but swift-flying sharp-shinned hawk can also be seen here. Hawk watching in Acadia is particularly good in the fall on a sunny day that follows several days of storms. After hunkering down in the wet weather, the hawks are eager to find thermals and ride the winds out of the northeast.

Continuing north from the summit, the trail descends quickly to the col between Penobscot and Sargent Mountains. At this col, the Deer Brook Trail enters from the right. Stay to the left and you will soon reach Sargent Pond. Sargent Pond is fairly typical of ponds in the sprice-fir forests of Maine—a bowl of water surrounded by spruce forests with blueberry bushes and rhodora clinging to its banks. From the pond, the trail rises moderately to a junction with the Sargent Mountain South Ridge Trail.

Turn right on the Sargent South Ridge Trail. From here, the trail ascends very gradually for 0.8 mile to the summit of Sargent Mountain. This part of the hike is reminiscent of the Table Land plateau on northern Maine's Mt. Katahdin, although at a much lower elevation. The summit of Sargent is surrounded by an extensive area of relatively flat, open terrain filled with sedges, wildflowers, and stunted versions of spruce, cedar, and birch. On the way to the summit, two more trails come in from the left. Continue straight at these junctions to keep on track for the summit cairn. The views from the summit are excellent.

To return to the Jordan Pond House, there are two choices. If the weather is dry and you don't mind very steep descents, follow the Sargent East Cliff Trail southeast for a steep 0.7 mile descent to the Deer Brook Trail, where you should turn left. In wet weather, you can avoid the Sargent East Cliff Trail by walking back down the Sargent South Ridge Trail to the Penobscot Mountain Trail and turning left toward Sargent Pond. After passing by Sargent Pond again, the trail rises to meet the Deer Brook Trail. Turn left on the Deer Brook Trail, which goes down toward Jordan Pond. This trail descends steadily and has very rough footing over wet rocks and tree roots. The trail follows a stream, which overflows onto the trail after heavy rains.

At 0.6 mile from the Penobscot Mountain Trail (or 0.1 mile from the Sargent East Cliff Trail,) the Deer Brook Trail reaches a carriage road. Turn right on the carriage road for an easy 1.5-mile walk back to the Jordan Pond House. Shortly after leaving the Deer Brook Trail, the carriage road passes through a boulder field below Jordan Cliffs. There are good views of the pond and the Bubbles from here. The rest of the walk is through northern hardwood forest. At the only intersection, stay to the left.

TRIP 14
THE WESTERN MOUNTAINS— MANSELL AND BERNARD

NPS Rating: Strenuous, with ladders on the Perpendicular Trail
Distance: 4.2 miles
Elevation Gain: 1,350 feet
Estimated Time: 3.5 hours
Map: AMC's Acadia National Park Discovery Map: F4

The views are limited, but the climb to the highest peaks on the western side of Mount Desert Island is physically rewarding.

Directions

From the center of Southwest Harbor, go west on Seal Cove Road. Take the first paved road on the right, Long Pond Road. Follow Long Pond Road through a residential area until it ends at the south end of Long Pond. There is a small parking area to the right of the pumping station. There is no Island Explorer stop at this parking area. The closest stop (2.0 miles away) is Echo Lake (stop E) on the Southwest Harbor route (route 7). *GPS coordinates:* 44° 18.898′ N, 68° 21.210′ W.

Trip Description

This is a hard hike with few views. It is a great chance, however, to enjoy a seldom-used trail through a mature spruce forest that was untouched by a large fire in 1947 that burned several thousand acres on the eastern side of Mount Desert Island. This hike starts at the southern end of Long Pond and climbs Mansell Mountain via the Perpendicular Trail, which features an amazing stretch of stone staircases. Unlike the rest of the higher peaks on Mount Desert, the summits of both Mansell (938 feet) and Bernard Mountain (1,071 feet) are wooded, obscuring the view.

From the parking area at the southern end of Long Pond, follow the western shore of Long Pond on the Long Pond Trail, which starts behind the pumping station. After 0.2 mile, turn left on the Perpendicular Trail. This trail rises quickly, angling over a boulder field on the east face of Mansell.

Because of their heavily wooded summits, Bernard Mountain and Mansell Mountain have restricted views but offer a rewarding hike nonetheless.

The 704 stone steps built by the Civilian Conservation Corps in 1933 and 1934 give the trail a spiral-staircase look. The craftsmanship of this stretch of trail is excellent and rivals that of the Ladder Trail on Dorr Mountain. From the boulder field, views open up of Long Pond, Southwest Harbor, and the Cranberry Isles.

The trail levels off for a while as it works its way through a mixed forest dominated by spruce and cedar. The trail resumes its steep climb and, shortly before the summit of Mansell, reaches an overlook with perhaps the best views of the hike. A sign marks the short path on the right that will take you to a granite ledge high above Long Pond. From here, there are good views of Beech Mountain; Cadillac Mountain; the towns of Southwest Harbor, Bass Harbor, and Bernard; the Cranberry Isles; and the Atlantic Ocean.

From here, you'll reach the wooded summit of Mansell after 0.1 mile of gradual climbing. The trail goes west, through a spruce forest that tops the west ridge of Mansell. At junctions with the Mansell Mountain Trail and the Razorback Trail, continue hiking straight. The trail crosses a granite ledge that affords views across Great Notch to Bernard Mountain, as well as views west and north of Blue Hill Bay, Pretty Marsh, and Bartlett Island. After the

Razorback Trail, the trail descends steeply for 0.3 mile into Great Notch, a narrow passage between the summits of Bernard and Mansell. From here, the Great Notch Trail leaves to the left and descends quickly to the Cold Brook Trail and eventually the south end of Long Pond. The Long Pond Trail leaves to the right and makes a gradual and lengthy descent to the western shore of Long Pond.

To continue this hike, go straight (west) and begin the steep climb to the summit of Bernard, which is 0.6 mile from Great Notch. After the steepest part of the climb, an overlook on the left has limited views to the east and south of Mansell Mountain, Southwest Harbor, and the Atlantic Ocean. Shortly after this overlook, the trail crosses the wooded Knight's Nubble before descending 0.1 mile to Little Notch and a junction with the Sluiceway Trail. Continue straight on what is now called the Bernard Mountain Trail and make a short but steep climb to the Bernard Overlook, which has limited views north and west to Bartlett Island and over Blue Hill Bay to Blue Hill.

Like that of Mansell, the summit of Bernard Mountain is a viewless spruce forest, thick and mossy but also quiet and secluded. The Bernard Mountain Trail makes a gradual descent through this forest, which is one of the highest spruce forests on the coast of Maine. From the summit to the Western Mountain Fire Road, it is 1.7 miles. At the only trail junction (with the West Ledge Trail), turn left to stay on the Bernard Mountain Trail. As the trail descends, the forest becomes increasingly diverse as hardwoods and pines fill the spaces not occupied by spruce. At times the trail is steep, but the footing is good. After crossing a stream, the trail ends at a parking area on Western Mountain Road.

Hike up the road for a short distance to where another road leads to the left. Take this left, and you will soon find yourself in a cul-de-sac. On the right side of this cul-de-sac, look for a sign marking the Cold Brook Trail, which leads east toward the southern end of Long Pond. This trail is a relatively flat trail through mixed forest. Continue straight at intersections with the Razorback and Mansell Mountain Trails. The Cold Brook Trail ends at the Long Pond Trail on the southern shore of Long Pond, completing the loop you started several hours ago. From here, the parking area is 0.1 mile to the right.

TRIP 15
PEAK-BAGGERS' DELIGHT—BALD PEAK, PARKMAN MOUNTAIN, GILMORE MOUNTAIN, AND SARGENT MOUNTAIN

NPS Rating: Strenuous
Distance: 4.0 miles
Elevation Gain: 1,500 feet total
Estimated Time: 3.5 hours
Map: AMC's Acadia National Park Discovery Map: E6, E7

This difficult hike goes over four peaks, including Sargent Mountain, Acadia's second-highest point.

Directions

For this hike, park at the Norumbega parking area on Routes 198/3, 1.5 miles north of Northeast Harbor. The Hadlock Brook Trail is directly across the street. The parking area is an unscheduled stop between Gate House (stop D) and MDI High School (stop C) on the Island Explorer Brown Mountain route (route 6). *GPS coordinates*: 44° 19.558′ N, 68° 17.489′ W.

Trip Description

With the potential to summit four peaks in less than 4.0 hours, this hike can be tiring but enjoyable. Starting on Route 198 north of Northeast Harbor, this hike loops up and over Bald Peak and Parkman, Gilmore, and Sargent mountains. Sargent, at 1,379 feet, is the second-highest peak on Mount Desert Island and has one of the more interesting summits, with a large plateau-like area full of subalpine vegetation such as mountain sandwort, mountain cranberry, and alpine club moss. While lower than Sargent, the other three peaks on this hike all have open summits with good views. The return trip from the summits follows the cool waters of Maple Spring as it courses down the southeast flank of Sargent Mountain through a forest with large trees and a small gorge.

Begin this hike on the Hadlock Brook Trail, which starts on the eastern side of Route 198, directly across the road from the Norumbega parking lot. Hike past the junction with the Parkman Mountain Trail and then turn left

The summit of Bald Peak is the first summit conquered on this four peak hike.

onto the Bald Peak Trail 0.3 mile from the road. The Bald Peak Trail crosses a carriage road and ascends moderately through a forest of cedar and spruce. After crossing a second carriage road, the trail climbs more steeply, breaking out of the trees and quickly providing views of Norumbega Mountain, Upper Hadlock Pond, and the islands at the mouth of Somes Sound.

More steep hiking brings you to the summit of Bald Peak, 0.8 mile from the parking area. The great views here are similar to those you will have on Parkman and Gilmore Mountains. The other peaks on this hike are visible to the north and east, while Penobscot and Cedar Swamp Mountains are to the east and south. The views do not end with the surrounding peaks, however, as on a clear day you can see beyond Mount Desert Island and its environs to Isle au Haut, Blue Hill, and the Camden Hills to the west.

After you enjoy the views, Parkman Mountain is next. Follow the trail northwest and down into the col between Bald Peak and Parkman Mountain. The descent is steep but only 0.1 mile long. At 0.2 mile from Bald Peak, turn right on the Parkman Mountain Trail for the short hike to the summit of Parkman. From here, turn right on the Grandgent Trail and head east toward Sargent Mountain. The trail descends moderately, then steeply, through a forest of spruce and birch, and comes to the low point between Parkman and Gilmore in 0.3 mile. Here the trail crosses the Giant Slide Trail before making a short but steep climb to the summit of Gilmore Mountain.

You can soak up more of the same great views on Gilmore before continuing toward Sargent Mountain. Follow the Grandgent Trail, which heads north from the summit for a short distance before turning east and descending moderately into a mixed forest of spruce, cedar, birch, and maple. You soon come to the col between Gilmore and Sargent. After crossing a brook, the blue-blazed Grandgent Trail reaches an intersection with the Maple Spring Trail. Continue left on the Grandgent Trail.

The climb up Sargent on the Grandgent Trail is steep and the footing is rough in places, but the forest here is interesting with its mixture of spruce, fir, cedar, and hardwoods. The entire hike from Gilmore to Sargent feels wilder than other hikes on Mount Desert Island, because the area is relatively difficult to reach by Acadia National Park standards. As the Grandgent Trail emerges from the trees, more views of Somes Sound and beyond appear. The summit of Sargent Mountain is attained 0.7 mile from Gilmore Mountain.

The summit of Sargent is surrounded by an extensive area of relatively flat terrain filled with sedges, wildflowers, and stunted versions of spruce, cedar, and birch. The views from the summit are excellent. Over the Bubbles and Jordan Pond is Cadillac Mountain to the east. Somes Sound and the western mountains are to the west. Somes Sound, with mountains on both sides and a V-shaped bottom that is 200 feet deep, is the only fjord on the entire East Coast of the United States. On clear days you can see as far as Isle au Haut, 20 miles to the southwest, and the Camden Hills.

For the return trip, turn right (south) on the Sargent South Ridge Trail. It is an almost flat walk above treeline for 0.3 mile to a trail junction, where you should turn right onto the Maple Spring Trail. The Maple Spring Trail descends moderately over open granite ledges for the first 0.3 mile before entering the forest for the rest of the hike. Rocks and tree roots make the footing on this trail rough for most of its length, creating a longer hike than you would expect. The trail is one of the few in the park that follow a stream, often crossing it during the descent. At 0.5 mile below the Sargent South Ridge Trail, turn left to stay on the Maple Spring Trail at its intersection with the Grandgent Trail. The trail passes the Giant Slide Trail in another 0.5 mile. Continue straight on the Maple Spring Trail as it enters a small but beautiful gorge before crossing under an attractive stone bridge that carries a carriage road. In this area, the trail is lined with large white pines, hemlocks, and cedars.

The Maple Spring Trail dead-ends into the Hadlock Brook Trail. Turn right for the final 0.4 mile to the parking area on Route 198.

NPS Rating: Strenuous, with a few ladders
Distance: 4.0 miles
Elevation Gain: 1,500 feet
Estimated Time: 4.0 hours
Map: AMC's Acadia National Park Discovery Map: D8

See spectacular views, a narrow gorge, and quiet forests on this difficult hike.

Directions
This hike starts at the parking area on the west side of Route 3, just past Sieur de Monts Spring at the north end of the Tarn, 2.2 miles south of Bar Harbor. The closest Island Explorer stop is at Sieur de Monts (stop B, about 0.25 mile from the Tarn) on Sand Beach route (route 3). *GPS coordinates*: 44° 21.508′ N, 68° 12.344′ W.

Trip Description
The first leg of this hike is very steep, gaining 1,100 feet in about a mile. The Ladder Trail's continuous series of stone steps makes much of the climb relatively simple, although strenuous. After reaching the summit of Dorr Mountain, this hike loops around the north ridge of Dorr, descending through a picturesque gorge that separates Dorr from Cadillac. The hike meanders through the forest near historic Sieur de Monts Spring before returning to the parking area near the Tarn.

From the south end of the Tarn parking lot, begin your hike by following the trail that skirts the north end of the Tarn, a pond gouged out by glaciers during the last ice age. After crossing the outlet of the Tarn, turn left onto the Kane Path, which follows the west side of the pond. The trail traverses the bottom of a large field of granite boulders plucked off the east face of Dorr Mountain by glaciers. Luckily for hikers, the builders of this trail managed to build an almost sidewalk-like trail through the boulder field using granite they found among the rubble.

The slippery and difficult Gorge Path runs in between Dorr Mountain and Cadillac Mountain.

Shortly after the Kane Path leaves the shore of the pond, turn right onto the Ladder Trail. From here, it is 0.9 mile to the summit of Dorr. The Ladder Trail is so named because of the three sets of iron ladders used to scale particularly steep sections of the trail. However, the trail might have been more appropriately named the "Hike of 1,000 Stairs." While the ladder sections of this trail are very short, there is a seemingly endless proliferation of impressive stone steps, which were built in 1893 and restored by the Civilian Conservation Corps in the 1930s.

The trail rises quickly through a mixed forest of paper birch, yellow birch, beech, oak, white pine, big-tooth aspen, and maple. After squeezing through a very narrow passage between a large boulder and the cliff face, the trail continues over iron ladders and stairs into a forest of pitch pine and scrubby red oak. The stairs end for good once the trail meets up with the Schiff Path, where you should turn left. The trail climbs up steep granite slabs (be extremely cautious on these in wet weather) during the next 0.3 mile, and the views really start to open up, with Frenchman Bay visible over Huguenot Head and Champlain Mountain.

Just below the actual summit, the trail reaches a junction with the Cadillac-Dorr Connector and the Dorr North Ridge Trail. Turn left to walk the final few hundred yards to the summit. Cadillac Mountain looms directly to the west and seems almost close enough to touch. Otter Creek and the Cranberry Isles are now visible, as is all of Frenchman Bay and the Schoodic Peninsula. At 1,265 feet, Dorr Mountain is the third-highest peak on Mount Desert Island.

For the next part of the hike, return to the trail junction just north of the summit. Turn left onto the Cadillac-Dorr Connector. The trail descends steeply 0.2 mile over Cadillac pink-granite boulders to the gorge between Cadillac and Dorr Mountains. Once the trail levels off, the A. Murray Young Path goes south, while the Gorge Path goes north to the Park Loop Road. Turn right onto the Gorge Path.

The Gorge Path takes an interesting route through the narrow, rocky gorge separating Dorr and Cadillac Mountains. The trail passes under steep cliff walls and descends moderately along a stream and past small cascades. The footing can be rough, but much of the trail has flat rocks strategically placed to improve the hiking. The trail crosses the stream often, and sometimes trail and stream coincide. Waterproof your boots before this hike! While the forest in here consists mostly of mixed hardwoods, there are also some impressive hemlocks that somehow survived a forest fire in 1947 that burned much of the surrounding forest.

About a mile from the Cadillac-Dorr Connector, the Gorge Path levels off and the Hemlock Trail enters from the east. Turn right onto the Hemlock Trail, which will lead you to Sieur de Monts Spring. After briefly rising to meet the Dorr North Ridge Trail, the Hemlock Trail runs into an old dirt service road, known as the Hemlock Road, which is now used as a hiking trail from Sieur de Monts Spring. Turn right on the road and then right again 0.3 mile later onto the Jesup Path, which is not marked by a trail sign. If you reach the Sieur de Monts parking area, you have gone too far. At a Park Service nature center building, the trail forks. Stay to the right. After crossing a road and a bike path, which both lead to the Abbe Museum, the trail continues through the woods to the Tarn. When you reach the Tarn, you have completed the loop. Turn left and head up the path to return to the Tarn parking area.

A Forest and a Wetland in One?

Wetlands and forests have both received considerable attention in recent years as vital habitats for sustaining the health of our planet, increasing species diversity, and providing a natural filtering system for drinking-water supplies. The forested wetland is a combination habitat often overlooked by scientists and amateur naturalists alike. Forested wetlands are usually small areas of forest, an acre or two in size, that have standing water for only part of the year. In Acadia National Park, trees such as the northern white cedar grow in these wetlands, and the ground is often covered with sphagnum moss.

While it can look like the rest of the forest on the surface, a forested wetland is a bonanza of biodiversity that provides habitat for a disproportionate number of threatened and endangered plants and animals. Forested wetlands are are a good place to look for unusual wildflowers like orchids in the spring and summer, and they are the most likely place in Acadia to find uncommon amphibians such as the four-toed salamander. Common plants include skunk cabbage, starflower, and partridgeberry. Common birds in a forested wetland include cedar waxwings, hermit thrushes, and northern saw-whet owls. Like other wetlands, forested wetlands are also important for regulating water flow in a forest and helping to recharge groundwater supplies.

Forested wetlands can be found throughout the park, especially on the western side of Mount Desert Island. They are common along the Long Pond, Western Mountain, and Hio Fire roads.

TRIP 17
CADILLAC MOUNTAIN

NPS Rating: Moderate
Distance: 7.0 miles
Elevation Gain: 1,500 feet
Estimated Time: 4.0 hours
Map: AMC's Acadia National Park Discovery Map: E8, D8

Take a relatively long hike over open ledges to the summit of Mount Desert Island's highest mountain. There are great views during most of this hike.

Directions
The trailhead for the Cadillac South Ridge Trail is just west of the entrance to Blackwoods Campground on Route 3, 5.6 miles south of Bar Harbor. The parking area is stop F on the Island Explorer Sand Beach route (route 3). *GPS coordinates:* 44° 18.810′ N, 68° 12.854′ W.

Trip Description
Although this hike is not a loop, the south ridge of Cadillac Mountain, with its open forests of pitch and jack pine, is worth experiencing twice in the same day. This hike starts on Route 3 near the entrance to Blackwoods Campground and makes a moderate, enjoyable climb to Cadillac's busy summit over a leisurely 3.5 miles. While the summit may not be the wildest spot in the park, with its gift shop and parking lot full of tourists, the south ridge of Cadillac is relatively quiet and full of excellent views.

The Cadillac South Ridge Trail starts on the north side of Route 3, about 50 yards west of the entrance to the Blackwoods Campground. It is legal to park on the shoulder of the highway. The first mile of this hike rises gently, then moderately, through a forest predominated by white pine and spruce. At the 1.0-mile mark, a spur path leads 0.1 mile to the right to an overlook called Eagle Crag, which has good views of Otter Creek and the Atlantic Ocean. This is a worthwhile destination for families staying at the campground who are not up for the full hike to the summit.

Cadillac Mountain's summit, at 1,528 feet, provides an excellent spot to watch the sunrise.

The spur path loops around to reconnect with the main trail after a total of about 0.2 mile. Turn right to head toward the summit. Almost immediately, the hike enters a forest of pitch pine spread over granite ledge, taking on an open, airy feeling. The occasional boulder among the gnarly and twisted trees contributes to the forest's look of a grown-up Japanese bonsai garden. Of course, this is a real forest, and wind and water are the gardeners. From here there are good views of the island and the surrounding waters for most of the way to the summit. The trail then passes though one of the few pockets of jack pine on the island just before it makes a short descent to the Featherbed.

The Featherbed is a boggy area 2.3 miles from the trailhead. This is one of the highest wetlands in the park. The trail crosses the Canon Brook Trail, which leads east to Dorr Mountain and west to Jordan Pond. Continuing straight on the Cadillac South Ridge Trail, the hike soon reaches its steepest climb. A trail junction 0.5 mile below the summit marks the Cadillac West Face Trail, which leads west to Bubble Pond. At this point, the trail nears the summit road before making its final ascent toward the summit.

Shortly before reaching the summit, the trail descends into a thick spruce-fir forest, which stands in marked contrast to the open pine forest of the last 2.5 miles. This forest grows in an area protected from the strong summit winds, and it collects just enough soil and water to allow the spruce-fir forest to thrive. The trail crosses a fire road and reaches the summit parking area just below the actual summit, which is marked by a set of interpretive signs describing the views extending in all directions of Frenchman Bay, the Schoodic Peninsula, the islands to the west, and even Mount Katahdin 115 miles to the north.

Sixteen species of hawks, eagles, and falcons live in or migrate through Acadia. In the fall, Cadillac Mountain's location and elevation make it an excellent spot to watch for migrating raptors, especially when the wind is out of the north. Check with the park visitor center for information about hawk-watching programs run by park naturalists throughout September and early October.

To complete your hike, walk back down the trail to your car.

Twisted Pines

While hiking on Cadillac Mountain and most of the other rocky summits in Acadia, you will encounter beautiful stands of pitch and jack pine. Although these pines will grow to be as tall as 70 feet in ideal conditions, they usually top out at 20 or 30 feet in the exposed environment of Acadia's mountains. Harsh winds twist the trunks into gnarled, stunted, surreal shapes that make for a fascinating forest to hike through. The lack of fertile soil also creates an "open" forest, making it quite common to have good views out past the trees, even ones 30 feet tall. It is relatively easy to tell these pines apart by studying their needles. A pitch pine has 4-inch needles in bundles of three, while the jack pine's 1-inch needles come in bundles of two.

In Acadia, pitch pine is the more common of the two, but it is most often associated with the sandy pine barrens of southern New England and New Jersey. Jack pine is less common in Acadia, as it is a more northerly species that lives primarily in Canada. Both species are highly resistant to fire, and jack pine actually depends on fire to heat open its cones and release its seeds. Without fire, both species would gradually be replaced by hardwoods. In Acadia, pitch and jack pines colonize granite ledges where there is little soil and where they are usually joined by an understory of blueberries, sheep laurel, and sometimes scrubby oaks.

TRIP 18
NORTHEAST HARBOR TO EAGLE LAKE
VIA SARGENT MOUNTAIN

NPS Rating: Strenuous
Distance: 8.0 miles
Elevation Gain: 1,800 feet
Estimated Time: 5.0 hours
Map: AMC's Acadia National Park Discovery Map: E6, E7, D6, D7

You will find both wide-open ridge hiking and scenic shoreline walks.

Directions

To the Brown Mountain gatehouse: Follow Routes 198/3 for 0.5 mile north from Northeast Harbor. The parking area is stop D on the Island Explorer Brown Mountain route (route 6). *GPS coordinates*: 44° 18.681′ N, 68° 17.131′ W.

To Eagle Lake: From the intersection of Route 3 and Route 233 in Bar Harbor, take Route 233 west toward Cadillac Mountain. There are two parking areas for the carriage road in 2.1 miles, one on the right and one on the left. The parking area is stop B on the Island Explorer Brown Mountain route (route 6). *GPS coordinates:* 44° 22.648′ N, 68° 15.141′ W.

Trip Description

This is a great one-way trip that spends about half the time on open ridges populated with pockets of pitch pines. It also offers great views, particularly from Sargent Mountain and the North Bubble. It requires spotting a car or riding the Island Explorer bus at either end of the trip. In addition to climbing Sargent Mountain and the North Bubble, this hike crosses the summits of Cedar Swamp Mountain and Conners Nubble, passes the north shore of Jordan Pond, and parallels most of the western shore of Eagle Lake. Starting at the Brown Mountain gatehouse in Northeast Harbor (E6 on the map), you will use the carriage road system and the following trails: Sargent South Ridge Trail, Jordan Cliffs Trail, Deer Brook Trail, Jordan Pond Path, Bubbles Divide Trail, and the Bubbles Trail. This description follows the hike from south to north, but this hike can just as easily be hiked from north to south.

From the Brown Mountain parking area, follow the carriage road 0.1 mile to post 18 and turn right. Turn right again at post 19 (0.3 mile), and then turn left onto the Sargent South Ridge Trail at 0.8 mile. The trail climbs moderately through spruce forest and open areas populated with lowbush blueberry and sheep laurel; enjoy the views to the south and west. At 1.7 miles, you'll reach ledges with big views to the east. Good views continue for the next 0.2 mile, at which point you'll reach the summit of Cedar Swamp Mountain. (To reach the actual summit, take the 75-yard side trail to the summit cairn.)

After Cedar Swamp Mountain, the trail descends back into the forest and Birch Spring, where you cross the Amphitheatre Trail. Continue straight and begin the moderate climb to an intersection with the Penobscot Mountain Trail. From here it is an easy climb over open ridge, past the Hadlock Brook Trail and Maple Spring Trail (both enter from the left) to the summit of Sargent Mountain, about 3.5 miles from the Brown Mountain parking area. The summit of Sargent Mountain (1,379 feet) is a broad, windswept plateau with spectacular views in all directions and flora matching the alpine world of New England's much higher summits: three-toothed cinquefoil, mountain sandwort, and rock-hugging, heart-shaped paper birch.

From the summit, turn right onto the Jordan Cliffs Trail and make the steep descent to the Deer Brook Trail, 0.4 mile below the summit. Turn left onto the Deer Brook Trail and continue descending over a rough trail filled with rocks and tree roots for 0.2 mile. You'll cross a carriage road, then, in another 0.2 mile, you'll reach the northern shore of Jordan Pond; turn left on the Jordan Pond Path. A flat, 0.2-mile shore walk brings you to the Bubbles Divide Trail, where you should turn left and make the steep climb over a pink-granite boulder field. At 0.3 mile above the pond, the Bubbles Trail leads right to the summit of South Bubble. (If you feel like a detour, take the short side trip to the summit of South Bubble and Bubble Rock.) Continue straight for 0.1 mile and then turn left onto the northern section of the Bubbles Trail.

A short but steep climb brings you to the summit of North Bubble, where there are good views of Sargent and Penobscot mountains. Continuing beyond the summit, you'll be rewarded with extensive views to the east of Cadillac Mountain and Eagle Lake before descending into the trees and reaching a carriage road, 0.6 miles below the summit. The trail crosses the road and makes another quick climb to the top of Conners Nubble, which has good views in all directions.

Conners Nubble is only a stone's throw from Eagle Lake; it is common to hear loon calls and see circling osprey while sitting on the summit. The trail continues over the summit and down to the lake, reaching the Eagle Lake Trail in 0.4 mile. Turn right for a 100-yard walk to a carriage road, and then turn right again on the carriage road for an easy walk through spruce woods next to the lake. Stay straight at post 9 and you will reach the Eagle Lake parking lot 1.3 miles from the North Bubble Trail and 8.0 miles from the Brown Mountain parking area. It is an 11-minute ride on an Island Explorer Bus (route 6) back to Brown Mountain, or a 5-minute ride to Bar Harbor.

TRIP 19
BAR HARBOR TO JORDAN POND VIA DORR, CADILLAC, AND PEMETIC MOUNTAINS

NPS Rating: Strenuous
Distance: 10.0 miles
Elevation Gain: 2,900 feet
Estimated Time: 6.0 hours
Map: AMC's Acadia National Park Discovery Map: C8, D7, D8, E7

This lengthy hike starts with an easy walk from downtown Bar Harbor before bagging three of Acadia's four highest peaks.

Directions
Park anywhere in Bar Harbor. There are public lots on Rodick Street and at the municipal pier at the end of Main Street. The hike will start at the corner of Main Street and Mount Desert Street at the town green (see Bar Harbor map at the back of this book).

Directions to Jordan Pond Parking area: From the Acadia National Park Visitor Center, drive south on the Park Loop Road for 7.3 miles. Be sure to continue straight at the intersections marked Sand Beach and Cadillac Mountain. The Jordan Pond parking area will be on your right. The parking area is stop C on the Island Explorer Jordan Pond route (route 5) and stop F on the Loop Road route (route 4). *GPS coordinates:* 44° 19.332′ N, 68° 15.121′ W.

Trip Description
This is a great trip no matter where you are staying on the island, but it is particularly enjoyable if you are staying in Bar Harbor because you can begin your hike right from your hotel door. By using the new Great Meadow Loop Trail, you can go from town sidewalks to the park's trail system in just a few minutes. The trip then ascends Dorr, Cadillac, and Pemetic mountains before ending at Jordan Pond. This hike is very strenuous and includes a very steep descent on the west side of Cadillac that can be dangerous in wet

Frenchman Bay is the busy harbor of Acadia National Park and is popular with fisherman and scenic cruises alike.

weather. Keep your pack light (but well stocked with safety gear, of course— see the list at the beginning of this chapter), and keep an eye on the weather. Over the course of this hike, you will use the following trails: Great Meadow Loop Trail, Hemlock Road, Jesup Path, Homans Path, Schiff Path, Emery Path, Cadillac-Dorr Connector, Cadillac South Ridge Trail, Cadillac West Face Trail, Pemetic North Ridge Trail, Pemetic South Ridge Trail, Bubble and Jordan Ponds Path, and Jordan Pond Path. You will need to spot a car or use the Island Explorer bus system (route 5) to complete this trip.

To start this hike, you need to find the beginning of the Great Meadow Loop Trail on Cromwell Harbor Road. The easiest way to do this is to walk up Ledgelawn Avenue from Mount Desert Street (three streets west of the town green). About 0.6 mile from Mount Desert Street, turn right onto Cromwell Harbor Road. The trail will be on the left side of the road in a few hundred yards, just east of a large cemetery. The Great Meadow Loop Trail parallels the cemetery in the woods for 0.2 mile before it crosses a stream and a reaches a road. Turn right onto the road; after about 100 yards the trail reenters the woods across the street. The trail crosses the road again in another

0.4 mile and then parallels the Park Loop Road and a golf course for about 0.3 mile, where you should turn left, crossing the Park Loop Road and following the Hemlock Road, an abandoned woods road now used as a hiking trail. The trail skirts the edge of Great Meadow, a marshy wetland popular with birders. At 0.2 mile from the Park Loop Road, turn left at a trail junction onto the Jesup Path.

After a 0.4-mile walk through a beautiful grove of maples and paper birch, you'll reach another junction with the Hemlock Road, a few hundred yards from the parking area at Sieur de Monts Spring. Turn right onto the dirt road and then make a quick left onto Homans Path. Up until this point, the hike has consisted of about 2.0 miles of leisurely flat walking, but that's all about to change, as you will now climb Dorr Mountain. Homans Path, a recently restored historic trail, makes a steep climb that is made a little easier by switchbacks lined with beautiful pink-granite steps—the new trail work here is impressive. You quickly rise to views of Great Meadow and Frenchman Bay, reaching the Emery Path, 0.3 mile above the Hemlock Road and 2.3 miles from Bar Harbor.

The Emery Path continues the steep climb over switchbacks, passing Kurt Diedrich's Climb in 0.2 mile, where you should continue straight (taking the right fork) on what is now called the Schiff Path. In another 0.6 mile, turn right to stay on the Schiff Path at its intersection with the Ladder Trail. The trees get sparser and the views bigger as you climb, eventually topping out at a trail junction on the north ridge of Dorr Mountain 1.3 miles from the Homans Path. Turn left and make the 150-yard walk to the 1,270-foot summit of Dorr Mountain, which has excellent views in all directions. To continue the hike, return to the trail intersection below the summit and turn left toward Cadillac Mountain on the Cadillac-Dorr Connector.

The Cadillac-Dorr Connector makes a short, steep descent to the notch between Dorr and Cadillac, where the A. Murray Young Trail leads left and the Gorge Path leads right. Continue straight on the Gorge Path and make the steep 0.5-mile, 500-foot climb to the summit of Cadillac Mountain. Cadillac Mountain is the tallest in Acadia, and the views are superb. Expect to share your experience with a few hundred others, though, as there is a road to the summit. There is also a gift shop, where you can refill your water bottles or buy a sports drink and a candy bar. Two summits down, one to go.

From Cadillac Mountain, this trip next heads to Bubble Pond, a picturesque glacial tarn nestled between Cadillac and Pemetic mountains. From the summit, look for the Cadillac South Ridge Trail, which is just east of the gift shop. Follow this trail through the spruce forest near the summit and then down 0.5 mile to the Cadillac West Face Trail, where you should turn right. The next 0.7 mile is a very steep descent over granite ledge and boulders. *Caution:* it can be dangerous in wet weather and uncomfortable with a heavy pack. However, the views of Bubble Pond and Pemetic Mountain are spectacular. When you reach Bubble Pond, turn left onto a path that follows the north shore of the pond to the Pemetic North Ridge Trail. Turn right and cross the carriage road and begin your climb up Pemetic Mountain.

The trail makes a steep climb (600 feet in 0.5 mile) through conifers to a good view of Bubble Pond and the cliffs of Cadillac's West Face towering above the water. After the initial climb, the hiking gets easier, going gently up (and sometimes down) in and out of the woods. At 1.1 miles above the pond, the Pemetic Northwest Trail leads right to the Bubbles; continue straight for an easy 0.1-mile walk over bald granite to the 1,234-foot summit of Pemetic Mountain, where there are good views in all directions, especially out toward the Cranberry Isles.

From the summit, continue hiking on what is now called the Pemetic South Ridge Trail as it traverses the wide-open granite south ridge of the mountain. At 0.8 miles from the summit, turn right to stay on the Pemetic South Ridge Trail, which makes a moderate descent into spruce forest, reaching the Pond Trail 1.4 miles below the summit. Turn right onto the Bubble and Jordan Ponds Path and follow it across the Park Loop Road to the shores of Jordan Pond in about 0.5 mile. Turn left onto the Jordan Pond Path for a scenic walk next to the pond on your way to the Jordan Pond House and the end of your hike.

Cairns

Cairns are conical-shaped piles of rocks used to mark hiking trails above treeline. With Acadia's open summits, cairns are numerous and play an important role in keeping hiking traffic confined to the intended trails. This in turn helps to prevent erosion of what little soil exists above treeline and to prevent the destruction of important plants and animals that need the rocks for shelter. Cairns are also an important safety feature on trails, as they help keep hikers from getting lost, particularly in bad weather.

The cairns in Acadia seem to take on a life of their own, growing over time—and even reproducing! Many park visitors find it irresistible to add a rock to a cairn or build their own. This is a problem for two reasons: First, trail maintainers build cairns to direct hiking traffic along specific routes. Adding a cairn can work against this route building, increase trail erosion, and get hikers lost. Second, moving rocks above treeline disturbs delicate microhabitats that exist because of the soil and moisture that collect around the rocks. The flora and fauna that survive in these microhabitats usually perish when the rocks are removed.

Park naturalists ask that you admire the construction of cairns during your visit to Acadia, but please leave them as you find them.

Cairns should be left as is for ecological and safety reasons.

TRIP 20
EASTERN SIDE TRAVERSE—
SAND BEACH TO NORTHEAST HARBOR

NPS Rating: Strenuous, with ladders on the Beehive Trail
Distance: 11.0 miles
Elevation Gain: 2,500 feet
Estimated Time: 6.5 hours
Map: AMC's Acadia National Park Discovery Map: E6, E7, E8, E9,
   D8, D9

**This traverse of the eastern half of Mount Desert Island visits
some of Acadia's best-known features and follows some of the
park's quietest trails.**

Directions
To Sand Beach: From downtown Bar Harbor, drive south on Route 3 for 2.1
miles and turn right at the Sieur de Monts entrance to the Park Loop Road.
Follow the signs for Sand Beach. The Sand Beach parking area is on the left,
3.25 miles south of the Sieur de Monts entrance. The Bowl Trail is across the
road from the parking area. The parking area is stop C on the Island Explorer
Sand Beach route (route 3), and stop D on the Loop Road route (route 4).
GPS coordinates: 44° 19.783′ N, 68° 11.058′ W.

To the Brown Mountain gatehouse: Follow Routes 198/3 for 0.5 mile
north from Northeast Harbor. The parking area is stop D on the Island
Explorer Brown Mountain route (route 6). *GPS coordinates:* 44° 18.681′ N,
68° 17.131′ W.

Trip Description
Sand Beach, Champlain Mountain, and Jordan Pond are some of our favorite
places in Acadia, and this hike takes you to all of them and more. You will
need to spot a car or use the Island Explorer bus system to avoid turning this
trip into a 22-mile out-and-back epic, but it's definitely worth the extra logistical effort. Focus your eyes on eastern side of your Acadia National Park
Discovery Map and look for the parking area at Sand Beach in grid E8. From
this starting point, the hike works its way over the Beehive, Champlain

A hiker climbs the iron rungs of the Beehive.

Mountain, and the south ridge of Cadillac, and then down to Jordan Pond and over to the Brown Mountain gatehouse, just west of Northeast Harbor. It uses the following trails: Bowl Trail, Beehive Trail, Champlain South Ridge Trail, Beachcroft Trail, Kane Path, Canon Brook Trail, Bubble and Jordan Ponds Path, and Asticou and Jordan Pond Path.

If you get an early start from the Sand Beach parking lot, you can take a pre-hike dip in the cold waters of the Gulf of Maine by running down the steps at the southeast end of the parking lot to the beach before beginning the steep climb up the Beehive. To reach the Bowl Trail, walk to the Park Loop Road and follow it to the right for about 40 yards, where the trail begins across the road. After 0.2 mile on the Bowl Trail, turn right onto the Beehive Trail and make the short, steep climb up iron rungs to the summit and its views of the beach, Frenchman Bay, and the island's interior mountains.

Caution: This hike traverses the cliffs of the Beehive via iron rungs and ladders and is very dangerous in wet or icy weather. It is not recommended for people with a fear of heights or those hiking with small children. As an alternative, follow the Bowl Trail around to the backside of the Beehive.

From the summit, follow the trail northwest down to the Bowl (a beautiful, sheltered glacial tarn), continuing straight at an intersection with the Bowl Trail, 0.1 mile from the summit. After reaching the pond, the trail follows the shore to the left and soon reaches the Champlain South Ridge Trail, which continues to hug the shoreline before beginning a moderate climb up the pink-granite south ridge of Champlain Mountain. This ridge hike goes in and out of open pitch-pine forest with an understory of blueberries and sheep laurel. There are good views much of the way to the summit, which at 1,058 feet has spectacular views of Frenchman Bay and its islands. At this point, you have tackled about half your elevation gain for the day, but only about a quarter of your mileage.

From the summit, turn left on to the Beachcroft Trail and follow it around the summit of Huguenot Head and down a series of switchbacks sporting some very impressive stone trail work most of the way down to Route 3, across from the Tarn (0.8 mile below the summit of Champlain). Cross the street and follow the trail along the north edge of the Tarn to a trail intersection, where you should turn left onto the Kane Path. This trail leads south over boulders that practically lie in the Tarn, offering dramatic views of the cliffs across the pond as well as a look at the pickerel weed, small fish, and bullfrog tadpoles living in the pond. At 0.5 mile from its beginning at the north end of the pond, the Tarn Trail passes the Ladder Trail, which leads right to the summit of Dorr Mountain. In another 0.2 mile, the Canon Brook Trail enters from the left; continue straight on what is now the Canon Brook Trail (not signed).

The Canon Brook Trail continues in a southerly direction through hardwoods and past beaver ponds before turning right and beginning its climb up to the south ridge of Cadillac Mountain. The trail soon passes the Dorr South Ridge Trail on the right and then reaches an intersection with the A. Murray Young Path, 0.8 mile from the Tarn Trail. At this intersection, take the left fork, crossing the brook and following a sign that points to Eagles Crag. Here the trail begins a steep climb, paralleling and sometimes crossing the brook, which tumbles over ledges of pink Cadillac granite. This is a little-used trail that is enjoyably quiet but sometimes a little tricky to follow. About

2.3 miles from the Tarn Trail and 4.5 miles from Sand Beach, the Canon Brook Trail reaches the Featherbed, a small wetland on the south ridge of Cadillac Mountain.

If you are feeling strong and of a peak-bagging mind, take a right on the Cadillac Mountain South Ridge Trail for a 2.5-mile round-trip side hike to the summit and its heavy dose of civilization. Otherwise, from the Feather-bed, continue hiking west on what soon becomes the Bubble and Jordan Ponds Path. You are almost immediately treated to spectacular views of Pemetic Mountain and the Cranberry Isles from atop steep cliffs. The next 0.5 mile is a very steep and rocky descent to a stream crossing. After this stream crossing, it as an easy 1.5 miles of hiking to Jordan Pond. Along the way, you will cross a carriage road, the Pemetic East Cliff Trail, the Pemetic South Ridge Trail, and the Park Loop Road, and hike through beautiful groves of spruce, pine, and cedar. Just continue straight at all of these intersections. When you reach Jordan Pond, turn left on the Jordan Pond Path for a short walk to the Jordan Pond House.

At the Jordan Pond House, you will find restrooms and refreshments (upstairs in the gift shop). You can also ask for a table and enjoy a meal or tea and popovers. This is also a regular stop on Island Explorer route 5, so if you are feeling a little tired or daylight is waning, you can end your hike here. Otherwise, look for a path that leads into the woods directly behind the re-strooms. This path crosses a carriage road and Jordan Stream before reaching the Asticou and Jordan Pond Path, where you should turn left. This trail has no drama or views, but instead provides crowd-free, primarily easy hiking through some of the most beautiful spruce woods on the island. Some of the older spruce are more than 20 inches in diameter and are a great example of what many of the trees in Acadia must have looked like before the forest fire in 1947.

About 1.0 mile from the Jordan Pond House, the trail crosses the carriage road (twice) and the Penobscot Mountain Trail. Soon it crosses Harbor Brook and the Harbor Brook Trail; continue straight. In another 0.3 mile, follow the right fork, where the Elliot Mountain Trail leads left for Eliot Mountain. In another 0.3 mile, turn right onto the Sargent South Ridge Trail and make the 150-yard climb to a carriage road. Turn left onto the carriage road for a 0.8-mile walk to the Brown Mountain gatehouse, taking care to turn left at posts 19 and 18. From this parking lot, you can catch an Island Explorer Bus (route 6) for a 5-minute ride into Northeast Harbor for some fine dining and shopping or take the 20-minute ride into Bar Harbor, where you can switch to a bus bound for Sand Beach and the beginning of the hike (route 3).

Tourism and the Creation of Acadia National Park

During the first half of the nineteenth century, Mount Desert Island was a quiet place, home to subsistence farmers and fishermen. Things started to change in the 1850s as visiting artists and journalists began to tell the world about the beauty of Mount Desert Island. The most prominent of these early visitors were painters of the Hudson River school such as Thomas Cole and Frederic Church. Their dramatically lit renditions of landscapes such as Eagle Lake, the Beehive, and the Porcupine Islands lured visitors from the big cities on the East Coast. These early visitors, known as "rusticators," rented rooms from local farmers and fishermen and ate simple meals with their hosts.

Of course, as word got out about Mount Desert Island's simple life, salty spruce-scented air, and mild summer climate, tourism grew substantially. By 1870, steamers began landing in Southwest Harbor, and tourists soon made their way to Bar Harbor. By 1871, Bar Harbor had eleven hotels and was visited by four steamers a week. Daniel Rodick built the largest of the hotels, the Rodick House, which by 1882 could hold more than 600 guests. Magazines such as *Harper's* began calling Bar Harbor a "fashionable spa," and soon tourists from around the world were spending their summers on Mount Desert Island.

The 1880s saw the beginning of the building of summer "cottages" by America's wealthy elite. These estates of 50 or more rooms, complete with ten to fifteen servants, were the summer residences of families such as the Rockefellers, Astors, Fords, Morgans, and Carnegies. At one point, there were as many as 90 of these estates. Wealthy families also bought up huge pieces of the most desirable pieces of real estate on Mount Desert Island. For example, J. P. Morgan owned Great Head and Sand Beach, which he gave to his daughter in 1910. The wealthy summer residents also contributed generously to the towns on the island, greatly improving sanitation and building libraries and hospitals. It was this spirit of philanthropy that would lead to the establishment of Acadia National Park.

In 1901 Charles Eliot, president of Harvard and a summer resident of Northeast Harbor, became concerned that the invention of the portable sawmill was going to bring about the demise of the tranquil beauty that existed on Mount Desert Island. He asked Charles Dorr, a wealthy Bostonian and fellow summer visitor to Mount Desert Island, to help him preserve the best of the island. Dorr convinced other summer residents, such as John S. Kennedy and George Vanderbilt, to help him start a nonprofit organization whose sole purpose was "to acquire by devise, gift, or purchase, and to own, arrange, hold, maintain, or improve for public use lands in Hancock County, Maine, which by reason of scenic beauty, historical interest, sanitary advantage or other like reasons may become available for such purpose." So began the Hancock County Trustees of Public Reservations.

With George Dorr at the helm, the Trustees acquired substantial pieces of Mount Desert Island, including the summit of Cadillac Mountain and Otter Cliffs. Dorr worked tirelessly for years to persuade landowners to donate land to the Trustees. By 1913, 6,000 acres had been acquired, and in 1916 the land was given to the federal government for the creation of Sieur de Monts National Monument. Dorr continued to acquire land for the park, and in 1919 the national monument became Lafayette National Park, the first national park east of the Mississippi River. Dorr was hired as the park's first superintendent and is generally thought of as the father of Acadia National Park, which became the park's official name in 1929. Acadia now protects 46,000 acres on Mount Desert Island, the Schoodic Peninsula, and Isle au Haut, and is the only national park in the United States for which all of the land was donated to the government.

2

Biking in Acadia National Park

DURING MUCH OF THE TWENTIETH CENTURY, the Rockefeller family donated large amounts of time, money, and land in an effort to make Acadia
and Mount Desert Island a nature paradise for future generations to enjoy.
Perhaps the greatest Rockefeller legacy is the network of carriage roads John
Rockefeller Jr. had built during the 1920s and 1930s. These roads were built
originally so that walkers and horse-drawn carriages could enjoy the island's
backcountry without the disturbing noise and pollution of automobiles.
Horses and walkers still use the carriage roads, but now these roads get most
of their traffic from bicycle riders. The roads follow easy grades and blend
into the contours of the hills in a way that makes them seem a natural part
of the landscape, and their crushed-gravel surface makes an excellent base
for riding. Built by local craftsmen, the roads traverse a series of intricate
stone bridges that cross streams, gorges, and the Park Loop Road while providing visitors with the greatest viewing pleasure possible. With no single-
track mountain-bike trails to speak of (bikes are not allowed on hiking trails),
Acadia is not a place for hard-core mountain biking. However, the carriage
roads, as well as the dirt fire roads on the western side of the island, provide
an excellent way to experience the park on two wheels. Trips range from flat
1-hour rides through mature spruce forest to steep half-day climbs with
spectacular views of the surrounding peaks, lakes, and bays.

Biking the carriage roads is a wonderful way to explore the natural beauty
of Mount Desert Island's eastern district. Fifty-seven miles of these roads
take you to the scenic splendor of places like Jordan Pond, Eagle Lake, and

Day Mountain. Passing through a variety of natural habitats, they create the opportunity for extensive nature study and wildlife watching. Magnificent bridges provide views of waterfalls and mountain vistas, and the roads make occasional climbs to reveal stunning views of the Atlantic Ocean and the rest of Maine. You can explore the western part of the island—with its cool, quiet boreal forests—on a series of dirt fire roads. These fire roads are a great way to see the natural habitats of Mount Desert Island as they were before the great fire of 1947.

Trip Times and Ratings
While we think the bike trip times we list are useful for planning, your times undoubtedly will be different from ours. Our times are based on our experience as average riders. Obviously, the times can vary based on the weather, the physical fitness level of your group, and how much gear you bring with you. Also, the times we list do not include breaks, so if you plan to stop often and take in the scenery, your times will be longer.

Trip ratings vary based on the length of the trip and the elevation gain. Most trips in Acadia are fairly short and easy from a road-biking standpoint, but the elevation gains can make a trip seem much longer.

Safety and Etiquette
Its mild summer climate makes Acadia an enjoyable and relatively safe biking destination. Of course, bad weather or poor planning can spoil any biking adventure. Before heading into Acadia's backcountry, consider the following tips:
- Select a trip that is appropriate for everyone in the group. Match the ride to the abilities of the least capable person in the group.
- Plan to be back at the trailhead before dark. Determine a turn-around time and stick to it even if you have not reached your goal for the day.
- Check the weather. Acadia's carriage roads and fire roads are safe places to be during wet weather, but riding can be less enjoyable in a steady rain or when there are strong winds. Give yourself more time to stop in the rain, as wet brakes do not work as well as dry ones.
- Bring a pack with the following items:
  ✓ Water: Bring 1 or 2 quarts per person depending on the weather and the length of the trip.

✓ Food: Even for a short trip, it is a good idea to bring some high-energy snacks like nuts, dried fruit, or snack bars. Bring a lunch for longer trips.

✓ Map.

✓ Extra clothing: rain gear, sweater, hat.

✓ Headlamp or flashlight, with spare batteries and lightbulb.

✓ Sunscreen.

✓ First-aid kit.

✓ Pocketknife.

✓ Basic bike-maintenance tools and a spare inner tube.

- Wear appropriate footwear and clothing. Legwear should be tight fitting: loose pants can get stuck on pedals and in the gears of a bike, causing nasty accidents. Bring rain gear even in sunny weather, since unexpected rain, fog, or wind is possible at any time in Acadia. Avoid wearing cotton clothing, which absorbs sweat and rain, making for cold, damp riding. Polypropylene, nylon, fleece, silk, and wool are all good materials for keeping moisture away from your body and keeping you warm in wet or cold conditions.

- The best bikes to use on the carriage paths in Acadia National Park are hybrid-style bikes with tires that are 35mm wide.

In addition to practicing the no-impact techniques described in this book's introduction, it is also a good idea to keep the following things in mind while bike-riding:

- Call the Park Service to confirm that the carriage roads are open. In the spring, the roads are often closed because they are too wet to handle traffic of any kind. It can cost thousands of dollars to repair one tire rut, so if the roads are closed, please stay off them.

- Bikes are not permitted on hiking trails or on the carriage roads to the south of Jordan Pond and east of the Stanley Brook Road.

- Always wear a helmet.

- When on paved roads or the dirt fire roads where cars are allowed, wear bright colors and follow the same rules of the road you follow while driving a car.

- Ride slowly and in control—and be able to stop quickly. Gravel surfaces are loose, and quick stops are dangerous.

- Do not obstruct the road by riding (or resting) three or four abreast.
- Yield to hikers.
- Yield to horses and walk your bike past them. Sometimes they can get spooked by a bicycle speeding past them.
- When passing, politely inform the person you are passing by saying "On your left" or "On your right."
- Try not to disturb other bike riders and hikers. While you may often feel alone in the wilderness, wild yelling or cell phone usage will undoubtedly upset another person's quiet backcountry experience.
- When you are ahead of the rest of your group, wait at all road junctions. This avoids confusion and keeps people in your group from getting lost or separated from one another.
- Obey National Park Service rules and signage regarding bike restrictions on the paths south of Jordan Pond and east of Stanley Brook Road.

Rating: Easy
Distance: 4.0 miles
Elevation Gain: 350 feet
Estimated Time: 1.25 hours
Map: AMC's Acadia National Park Discovery Map: E6

This relatively easy ride goes to a 40-foot waterfall and Upper Hadlock Pond.

Directions
For this trip, park at the Parkman Mountain parking area on Routes 198/3, 1.8 miles north of Northeast Harbor. The parking area is an unscheduled stop between Gate House (stop D) and Mount Desert Island High School (stop C) on the Island Explorer Brown Mountain route (route 6). *GPS coordinates*: 44° 19.898′ N, 68° 17.653′ W.

Trip Description
This trip may be short, but it packs in views of the Cranberry Isles, rides through sweet-smelling spruce forests, and visits one of Acadia's biggest waterfalls. The carriage roads on this ride pass over Maple Spring and Hadlock Brook on two of the magnificent granite bridges that are synonymous with Acadia's carriage-road system. Except for one short steep section, the grades are reasonable and the pedaling easy. The trip finishes with a ride along the afternoon-sun-soaked eastern shore of Upper Hadlock Pond, which provides a good habitat for a variety of waterfowl.

From the Parkman Mountain parking area, follow the sign that points toward post 13. At post 13, turn left for a steep climb through a beautiful spruce forest. To the south, Upper Hadlock Pond and the Cranberry Isles come into view shortly before you reach post 12, at 0.4 mile from the parking area. This is the steepest part of this trip. At post 12, turn right. At 0.8 mile, you come to the Hemlock Bridge, which rises high above Maple Spring, a beautiful pine- and hemlock-lined stream that tumbles down to Upper

Bikers on this trip will pass one of the largest waterfalls in the park, Hadlock Brook Waterfall.

Hadlock Pond from just below the summit of Sargent Mountain. Only a hundred yards or so beyond the Hemlock Bridge is Waterfall Bridge, with its single arch spanning Hadlock Brook. Like many of the bridges on the carriage roads, viewing turrets entice you to stop and soak in the sights and sounds of nature. To the left of the bridge, Hadlock Brook tumbles 40 feet over Cadillac granite, carrying the soothing sounds of rushing water past the bridge to the valley below.

Beyond Waterfall Bridge, the carriage road parallels the south ridge of Cedar Swamp Mountain, making a long, gradual descent that will have you wishing that all biking were this easy. As you coast through the dark green of a spruce forest, the calls of chickadees and nuthatches fill the air as the pungent smell of the North Woods wafts over you. Just before reaching post 19, at 2.2 miles, you'll pass through a grove of northern white cedar. Named arborvitae, Latin for "tree of life," the northern white cedar's bark and foliage are high in vitamin C. Tea made from northern white cedar foliage was used to prevent scurvy among the crew of French explorer Jacques Cartier in 1535. The tree was introduced as an ornamental in Europe the following year. It tends to grow in wet, acidic soils covered with a thick layer of sphagnum moss, creating a forested wetland that is the ideal habitat for rare orchids. Birds that live in a cedar stand include northern saw-whet owls, alder flycatchers, hermit thrushes, cedar waxwings, Canada warblers, and black-throated green warblers.

At post 19, turn right, and then turn right again at post 18. A fairly level ride brings you to Upper Hadlock Pond at 3.0 miles. In the afternoon, the sun shines on the eastern shore of the pond, which is only a few yards to the west of the carriage road. It is a peaceful spot to take a break and watch for the ducks that live on the pond. Norumbega Mountain rises steeply beyond the west side of the pond, its thick spruce-fir forest looking like an impenetrable covering. As the road makes its way around the northern end of the pond, it crosses a small stream over a modest bridge made of large granite blocks. While not as large or dramatic as the taller and longer bridges of the carriage-road system, this small bridge and others like it display the same intricate craftsmanship. After the bridge, the road begins a 150-foot climb back to post 13. Turn left at this intersection to complete your journey.

Rating: Easy
Distance: 4.0 miles
Elevation Gain: 100 feet
Estimated Time: 1.0 hour
Map: AMC's Acadia National Park Discovery Map: G5, G6

This easy ride for families follows a dirt road in prime bird-watching habitat.

Directions

From Southwest Harbor, follow Route 102 south. At the intersection with 102A, bear right to stay on 102. In another 1.4 miles, the Hio Fire Road will be on your left, just before crossing the Bass Harbor Marsh. The closest Island Explorer stop (about 1 mile) is the Tremont School stop (stop M) on the Southwest Harbor route (route 7). *GPS coordinates*: 44° 15.227' N, 68° 20.363' W.

Trip Description

The Hio Road is an unused dirt fire road near Seawall Campground that traverses a spruce-fir forest near a large bog called the Big Heath. Birds more common in Canada than coastal Maine inhabit the woods along this road, which is relatively flat and has a good riding surface for most of its length. Although there are a few very short rough spots, kids will enjoy this trip. Since it is short, you can take your time with this trip, watching and listening for birds, exploring vernal pools for frogs and salamanders, and enjoying flora like rhodora, bog laurel, and skunk cabbage. You can also add a short ride to the Atlantic Ocean at Seawall.

This is an out-and-back trip that can be started either from Route 102 or from the group camping area in Seawall Campground. This description assumes you will start from Route 102.

From the east side of Route 102, the Hio Road starts out near Bass Harbor Marsh, which has excellent views of Bernard, Mansell, Beech, and Acadia

Mountains. The road immediately enters the spruce-fir forest that will be the dominant feature for the entire ride. This forest attracts northern bird species such as boreal chickadees, gray jays, black-backed woodpeckers, and spruce grouse. At 0.8 mile, you cross a small stream that flows through a northern white cedar swamp toward the Big Heath. In April skunk cabbage is the first herbaceous (nonwoody) plant to appear in large quantities, sprouting through a layer of fuzzy green sphagnum moss.

The Big Heath is one of Acadia's largest bogs. Bogs usually form in glacial depressions that were at one time lakes or ponds. Over time the lake fills with accumulated plant material that decays slowly. What results is a layer of peat that can be as deep as 40 feet and often floats on top of water. For this reason, bogs are a less-than-pleasant place to walk through. If you attempt to pass through a bog, consider yourself lucky if all you lose is a boot or two. This slowly decaying plant material creates a highly acidic and nutrient-poor environment that makes it difficult for plants to survive. Insectivorous plants such as sundew and pitcher plants survive there by trapping insects and consuming their nutrients. Other plants that tend to grow in bogs are evergreen shrubs such as Labrador tea, sheep laurel, bog laurel, and orchids. Black spruce, larch, and white cedars are the types of trees that usually manage to survive in the acidic soil of a bog. Birds you might find in the Big Heath include Lincoln's sparrow, northern water-thrush, and palm warblers.

Two miles from Route 102, you reach the end of Hio Fire Road. Through the gate is the group camping area at Seawall Campground. From this end of the campground, it is about a 0.4-mile ride over pavement to the Atlantic Ocean. There is a picnic area on a natural seawall overlooking the ocean. The 10-foot-high cobblestone seawall is impressive as it winds its way along the coast for about a mile.

TRIP 23
WITCH HOLE POND AND PARADISE HILL

Rating: Easy
Distance: 4.4 miles
Elevation Gain: 350 feet
Estimated Time: 1.25 hours
Map: AMC's Acadia National Park Discovery Map: C7

This great trip for families goes past beaver ponds and bogs to excellent views of Hulls Cove and Frenchman Bay.

Directions

From the intersection of Route 3 and West Street in Bar Harbor, head west on the West Street Extension for 0.7 mile, then turn right onto Duck Brook Road. The parking area is on the right in 0.6 mile. There is no Island Explorer stop for this parking area, which is about 1.5 miles from the Bar Harbor village green. *GPS coordinates*: 44° 23.499′ N, 68° 14.130′ W.

Trip Description

Witch Hole Pond is a beautiful remote lake surrounded by colorful bogs and filled with beaver lodges. This bike ride takes you past more beaver activity than any other trip in this book. We saw numerous dams and lodges as well as recent tree cuttings. A great view from Paradise Hill also reminds you that the ocean is only a few thousand feet away. This is an easy trip with only a few short gradual climbs, making it a perfect choice for families with small children. It is also very convenient to downtown Bar Harbor, as you can ride your bike to the carriage road from town. Of course, this easy access does draw the crowds in midsummer, so you may want to get an early-morning start on this trip in order to enjoy the peacefulness of Witch Hole Pond.

Begin your trip by crossing Duck Brook Bridge, an impressive triple-arch structure built in 1929. The views from the bridge of Duck Brook and Acadia's mountains are especially spectacular in the fall. Stone steps lead down from the bridge to Duck Brook, where the sound of the rushing stream can make it seem as though you are miles from civilization. Once you cross the bridge, turn right at post 5 to make your way toward Witch Hole Pond. After

Frenchman Bay can be see while riding on Paradise Hill.

0.7 mile and a short gradual uphill section, you will come to a beaver pond with a small dam and lodge. Beavers are most active at night, but you can sometimes catch a glimpse of them in the early morning.

In the spring, this is a good place to listen for the drumming of ruffed grouses. The 17-inch-long ruffed grouse is the common partridge in New England, and it is well suited to Acadia's mixed woodlands. To attract females, a male will perch on a favorite "drumming log" and beat its wings in an accelerating drum roll. This drumming sounds like a distant helicopter or tractor engine starting up. The beaver pond is also an ideal breeding area for insects, which attract all kinds of small songbirds such as swamp sparrows and flycatchers. This seemingly small and insignificant pond bustles with activity on a warm, sunny day.

After about a mile from Duck Brook Bridge, Witch Hole Pond appears on your left, with views of Youngs and McFarland mountains providing a backdrop for the pond. You will see that beavers have dammed the inlet to the pond, creating an extensive marshy area to the right. Witch Hole Pond itself has at least three large beaver lodges, which are up to 6 feet tall. With the marsh and pond both surrounded by bogs and mixed woodlands, this is a good place to look for the large variety of ducks that can be seen in Acadia, such as mallards, black ducks, wood ducks, and blue-winged teals. Witch Hole Pond is also big enough to support a good population of fish, which draw both ospreys and fly-fishermen.

After passing between Witch Hole Pond and the marsh, the carriage road comes to post 3. Turn right to head up Paradise Hill. At this point, it is possible to turn left to avoid the extra mile required to summit Paradise Hill, but the views of Hulls Cove and Frenchman Bay are well worth the extra effort. The climb up to the summit is gradual and relatively short, about 0.4 mile from post 3. From the summit, you can see beyond the deep blue waters of Frenchman Bay toward the hills of the Schoodic Peninsula and the rest of eastern Maine. As you loop back toward Witch Hill Pond, continue straight at post 1 (turning to the right would take you to the park visitor center). You return to Witch Hole Pond at post 2, where you will want to turn right and explore the bogs surrounding the southern end of the pond. Stunted spruce and white pine attempt to grow in the acidic soil, which is held together by sphagnum moss.

A long but very gradual uphill section brings you through more mixed woodlands peppered with beaver activity. Just before reaching post 4, you come upon Halfmoon Pond on your right, which has a small beaver lodge in its center. There are good views here of Youngs Mountain. At post 4, bear to the left for the final mile of this trip. Sheep laurel and rhodora are common on the roadside here. Both plants have beautiful pink blossoms in late May and early June. At post 5, turn right to cross over Duck Brook Bridge and return to your car.

TRIP 24
SEAL COVE POND—WESTERN MOUNTAIN LOOP

Rating: Easy
Distance: 5.0 miles
Elevation Gain: 150 feet
Estimated Time: 1.25 hours
Map: AMC's Acadia National Park Discovery Map: F3, F4

This easy ride goes through a boreal forest frequented by moose.

Directions
From Route 102 in Southwest Harbor, drive east on Seal Cove Road. After 3.5 miles, turn right on a dirt Park Service road. After 0.4 mile, there will be a sign for Western Mountain Road. Turn right. After another 0.5 mile, there will be a sign for Seal Cove Pond. Follow this sign to the left. You are now on Western Mountain Road. The road ends at Seal Cove Pond in another 0.7 mile. There is no nearby Island Explorer stop for this parking area, which is about 4 miles from Southwest Harbor. *GPS coordinates*: 44° 17.513' N, 68° 23.536' W.

Trip Description
The system of fire roads around Acadia's western mountains provides about 10.0 miles of bike-riding opportunities. The roads are all similar in character: dirt and gravel auto roads that pass through a dark yet enchanting boreal forest. Views are nonexistent, but that only adds to the feeling of wilderness in what could pass for Maine's North Woods. This trip begins and ends at Seal Cove Pond, which is home to herons, loons, and bald eagles. The rest of the trip loops through tall spruce and past biologically interesting cedar bogs. This is an easy trip that leaves plenty of time for a paddle on Seal Cove Pond or a hike up the West Ledge Trail, which provides almost instant views of Blue Hill Bay and the Atlantic Ocean. Cars are allowed on this road, and while traffic is light, you still need to observe the rules of the road.

From the Seal Cove Pond parking area, ride up the hill on Western Mountain Road. This short, steep section is the hardest climb of the trip. In this area, the road passes through a small stand of hardwoods, with beech and maple trees lining small rushing streams. By the time you reach the West Ledge Trail, the makeup of trees begins to change as you enter the boreal forest. The West Ledge Trail leads 1.6 miles to the summit of Bernard Mountain (hiking only). This strenuous trail makes a great side trip, as it leads hikers to the island's best views of Blue Hill Bay.

Continue straight on Western Mountain Road until you reach an intersection at 0.7 mile. Turn right, following the sign that points to Seal Cove. At 1.2 miles, you will reach another intersection, where you should turn left. (Turning right will lead you to a dead-end in only a few hundred yards.) Just before reaching Seal Cove Road at 1.6 miles, you enter a stand of tall red spruce and the forest takes on a primeval feel. Keep your eyes open for moose! At Seal Cove Road, turn left.

The hard dirt surface of Seal Cove Road makes for easy riding. Despite being a dirt road, Seal Cove Road is a popular road for those driving between Southwest Harbor and Seal Cove. Ride single file for safety. The road passes through more spruce forest, although some deciduous trees like birch and downy serviceberry have taken over the disturbed areas along the road. Common along streams, downy serviceberry, with its showy white flowers, was nicknamed "shadbush" by early colonists because it blooms at the same time shad swim upstream to spawn. At 2.0 miles, a small family cemetery from the nineteenth century can be seen among the trees on the left. When visiting the cemetery, remember to follow the Leave No Trace ethics discussed in this book's introduction (see page xx); in particular, leave what you find.

At 3.1 miles, you will reach another intersection, where you should turn left to return to Western Mountain Road. At 3.5 miles, turn left again, following the sign for Seal Cove Pond. At 4.1 miles, the boreal forest is interrupted on the left by a northern white cedar bog, with its carpet of sphagnum moss hosting such hardy plants as partridgeberry and starflower. Sphagnum wetlands like this add a boost to the biodiversity of Acadia, providing habitat for rare orchids and uncommon animals such as the four-toed salamander.

At the next intersection, go straight to complete the final 0.7 mile back to Seal Cove Pond.

TRIP 25
LONG POND FIRE ROAD

Rating: Easy
Distance: 5.5 miles
Elevation Gain: 250 feet
Estimated Time: 2.0 hours
Map: AMC's Acadia National Park Discovery Map: E3, E4

Take an easy ride on a dirt road to a secluded cove on Long Pond.

Directions
Head south on Route 102 in Somesville. Turn right at the flashing yellow light onto Pretty Marsh Road/Route 102. After 4.9 miles, park at the Pretty Marsh Picnic Area, which will be on your right. The Long Pond Fire Road is on the east side of the road about 0.1 mile south of the picnic area. There is no nearby Island Explorer stop for this trip. *GPS coordinates*: 44° 19.845′ N, 68° 24.249′ W.

Trip Description
Long Pond is the largest body of freshwater on Mount Desert Island. On a calm day its deep blue waters reflect the rounded shapes of Acadia's mountains in like a mirror. The pond itself is a busy place in summer, with motorboats and personal motorized watercraft sharing the water with canoes and kayaks (see Trips 40 and 44). This trip on one of Acadia's dirt fire roads brings you to a secluded cove on the bay formed by the pond's Southern Neck peninsula. Thick evergreen forests line the entire length of the road, adding to the feeling of seclusion on Mount Desert Island's "quiet side." This trip also has good wildlife-viewing opportunities, as it visits a boggy beaver pond and passes through some of the island's best moose habitat.

Begin your trip on the Long Pond Fire Road, just south of the Pretty Marsh Picnic Area. This dirt road is open to cars during the summer and fall, but traffic is light. It is a fairly level ride for the 1.8 miles to Long Pond, with a only a few short ups and downs. The forest is boreal, dominated by spruce and fir. There are a large number of small boggy areas where northern white cedar or alders grow. Vernal ponds—temporary pools of water where amphibians breed—are also common, making this an interesting trip in spring. Pickerel and wood frogs make use of these small vernal pools to mate and lay eggs. Softball-sized clumps of gelatinous eggs can be found floating free in the pools or attached to sticks or other debris. You will certainly hear the calls of these frogs as you pedal your way toward Long Pond. Smaller egg clumps are probably those of salamanders that also use small temporary pools of water to breed.

From the shore of Long Pond, you get good views across the water to Cadillac Mountain. The bay to your right is formed by the peninsula of land called Southern Neck. The bay on the left is formed by Northern Neck. All of the shoreline on the Southern Neck side of the pond is part of Acadia National Park, making it seem much wilder than most of the pond, which is home to many summer cottages. Mallards, loons, and mergansers are common on the lake, and ospreys and bald eagles often soar high above it looking for fish. Northern white cedar bogs are common along this part of the shoreline, with sphagnum moss carpeting the forest floor and pitcher plants surviving in the nutrient-poor soil by capturing and digesting insects.

After leaving the shoreline of Long Pond, the fire road soon reaches a fork, where you should bear right. Still in a forest of spruce and fir, you are experiencing the forested island much as it was before the forest fire in 1947. This part of the island, with its thick forest peppered with bogs, is home to many of the moose in the park. Moose are about 6 feet tall and can weigh as much as 1,200 pounds. Only males have antlers, up to 6 feet across. Moose are not terribly dangerous, but it is a good idea not to approach them, as they have been known to trample people when angry. If a moose puts its ears back or starts to move toward you, just retreat and it will probably leave you alone. If you do not see moose around Long Pond, you are still likely to see their tracks in the road. Look for prints shaped like deer hooves but much larger, between 3.0 and 6.5 inches in length.

At 2.5 miles, a road on the right leads about 100 yards to Duck Pond, a small, boggy pond that appears to have been flooded by beaver at one point. The sun-bleached trunks of scores of long-dead spruce stand in much of the pond, which is bordered by rhodora and blueberry shrubs. Pitcher plants and sundews grow from the bed of sphagnum moss that lines the shore. This is a good place to watch birds, with the pond and forest edge joining to form a habitat where you can see warblers, flycatchers, wrens, sparrows, wood ducks, hawks, and even bald eagles perching in the tall white pines circling the pond.

At 3.5 miles, the Great Notch Trail (hiking only) leads to the summits of Mansell and Bernard Mountains on the left. In another 100 yards, turn left at the T intersection. The road continues through spruce-fir forest and cedar swamps, passing by Seal Cove Pond on the left and Hodgdon Pond on the right at 4.1 miles. At 4.4 miles, turn left onto the narrow paved road, which leads to Route 102 at 4.5 miles. Turn right on 102 to ride the final mile of the trip. Route 102 is not an extremely busy road, but it is narrow and the shoulder is soft, so you will need to be cautious while riding this final stretch.

TRIP 26
AMPHITHEATER LOOP

Rating: Moderate
Distance: 5.5 miles
Elevation Gain: 350 feet
Estimated Time: 2.0 hours
Map: AMC's Acadia National Park Discovery Map: E6, E7

Ride through an enchanting evergreen forest with streams lined with pink-granite stones.

Directions
For this trip, park at the Brown Mountain gatehouse parking area on Routes 198/3, 0.5 mile north of Northeast Harbor. The parking area is stop D on the Island Explorer Brown Mountain route (route 6). *GPS coordinates*: 44° 18.681′ N, 68° 17.131′ W.

Trip Description
The Amphitheater is a narrow valley that is walled in by the steep sides of Penobscot and Cedar Swamp mountains. Its cool streams and forests are the perfect place to escape summer's heat, and the carriage roads rise just high enough above the trees to give you good views of the ocean. This trip takes you from the Brown Mountain gatehouse on Route 198 around the southern end of Cedar Swamp Mountain and into the Amphitheater before heading south along the west side of Penobscot Mountain. Like the other carriage roads, this piece of Mr. Rockefeller's work features gentle grades, majestic bridges, and sweeping curves that seem to melt into the hillsides.

From the south end of the parking lot just north of the gatehouse, pedal up the fire road, which leads about 50 yards to the carriage road. At post 18, turn right and make your way through the forest of tall red spruce. The road climbs quickly to post 19 (0.3 mile), where you should take another right. After about a mile, views begin to open up to the south. In the fall, hardwoods in the foreground create a beautiful contrast to the dark green spruce that cover the hills between you and the Cranberry Isles. The forest is so thick that it hides any signs of civilization, despite the fact you are looking past Route 3 and the town of Northeast Harbor.

The road makes a gentle descent below the trees where it reaches post 20 at 1.3 miles. Turn left toward the Amphitheater. The road makes a graceful left turn toward Cedar Swamp Mountain in order to hug the contour of the mountain. In the forest above the road are car-sized boulders covered in green, gray, and brown lichens. The ride eventually turns into a downward coast until you reach the Amphitheater Bridge at 1.8 miles. Built in 1931, the Amphitheater Bridge is 235 feet long, the longest in the carriage-road system. Turrets are used as viewing platforms for looking at the small waterfall, which is part of Little Harbor Brook. The bridge's single arch was built in order to frame the waterfall from below. Characteristic of his love for nature, Rockefeller insisted that a 20-foot pine and a 20-foot hemlock both be left standing after construction.

The bridge sits at the head of the Amphitheater, which was named for its shape. The steep walls of Cedar Swamp and Penobscot Mountains rise above and around the northern end of the valley, which gradually widens as it falls toward the ocean. Apparently, the early visitors who named the Amphitheater pictured giants sitting on the sides of the mountains watching some grand event out on Bear Island. As you continue south on the carriage road, you can get a look back at the mountains that form the Amphitheater. The road falls slowly through a mosaic forest of white pine, spruce, maple, beech, and birch. At 2.5 miles turn right at post 21, and turn right again at post 22 in another 0.5 mile. To the left of post 22, the carriage road enters private property where bikes are not allowed.

At 3.2 miles, the road parallels and soon crosses Little Harbor Brook, a small but beautiful stream lined with pink Cadillac granite. The small bridge that crosses the brook is a peaceful place to listen to bird song and rushing water as you rest up for the steep climb that follows. The climb continues until you reach post 20 at 4.2 miles. During the climb, you get views of the east side of Cedar Swamp Mountain, which you traversed at the beginning of the trip. Looking at the mountain, it is impossible to discern where the carriage road travels. Once at post 20, turn left to retrace your route back to the parking area. Turn left again at posts 19 and 18 to complete the 5.5-mile loop.

TRIP 27
ECHO LAKE TO SEAL COVE POND

Rating: Moderate
Distance: 12.0 miles
Elevation Gain: 400 feet
Estimated Time: 2.0 hours
Map: AMC's Acadia National Park Discovery Map: E5, F4

Ride through spruce woods from Echo Lake to Seal Cove Pond.

Directions

From the intersection of Routes 102 and 198 in Somesville, drive 4.2 miles south on Route 102, where you should turn right on the road to Echo Lake and AMC Echo Lake Camp. Parking is at the end of this road in 0.7 mile. This parking area is stop E on the Island Explorer Southwest Harbor route (route 7). *GPS coordinates*: 44° 18.898′ N, 68° 20.210′ W.

Trip Description

This trip takes advantage of the new Western Mountain Connector, a multi-use trail that allows for easy bike access between the Echo Lake swimming area and Seal Cove Pond (and the hiking trails up Bernard and Mansell Mountains). The ride is primarily on dirt roads through thick spruce-fir forests, with one short single-track jaunt and about 1.5 miles on pavement (which you will appreciate on the steepest uphill of the trip). You can do this trip as an out-and-back ride of about 10.5 miles, but we have described it as a loop of 12.0 miles to add some variety to the ride. The 400 feet of elevation gain is spread out pretty evenly over the course of the 12.0 miles, making for only a few short steep climbs.

From the parking area, ride back up toward Route 102 for 0.3 mile and turn right onto Lurvey Spring Road, a gravel fire road that soon enters a thick, green mossy forest of tall spruce trees. This road sets the tone for much of the trip, as this boreal forest is common on the western side of Mount Desert Island and will be the main habitat for most of the ride. The trees are tall and straight, with not much growing in the understory except for ferns, blueberries, and bunchberries. The gravel surface is easy riding and

Echo Lake is a popular swimming spot, possibly because it is freshwater and warmer than the ocean beaches.

the terrain is gently rolling, two features common to all of the fire roads used on this trip. Shortly before reaching the end of Lurvey Spring Road at 1.6 miles, an unmarked fire road comes in from the right; continue straight.

Lurvey Spring Road ends at Long Pond Road, but you can now cross Long Pond Road and ride on the Western Mountain Connector. This easy single-track gravel trail passes some municipal buildings before heading downhill through more quiet spruce woods on its way to a right-hand turn onto a double-track road, 0.4 miles from Lurvey Spring Road. The Western Mountain Connector is one of several village connector trails built in Acadia this decade as part of an effort to make it easier to gain access to the park without a lot of driving. Other connector trails include the Great Meadow Loop and Schooner Head Path in Bar Harbor.

After the right-hand turn onto the double–track road, the Western Mountain Connector makes a short climb up to the Western Mountain Road and a parking area known as Gilley Field (2.4 miles from Echo Lake). At Gilley Field, there are trailheads for trails that go to Long Pond and Bernard and Mansell mountains. These trails make great hikes, but bikes are not allowed. To ride to Seal Cove Pond, follow Western Mountain Road to the left, taking care to stay left at a fork 0.1 mile from Gilley Field. Like Lurvey Spring Road, Western Mountain Road is a gravel fire road that makes for easy riding over gently rolling hills through a beautiful forest of spruce and fir trees. It is a 2.8-mile ride from Gilley Field to Seal Cove Pond—just stay straight at two intersections, 1.3 and 2.1 miles past Gilley Field. There is a nice view of Seal Cove Pond from the end of the road. It is a quiet place, home to loons and visited by bald eagles. (For more about Seal Cove Pond, see Trip 40.)

To begin the return trip, turn around and ride back up the Western Mountain Road for one of the longer uphill stretches of the trip. In 0.7 mile, turn right on a side road that leads to Seal Cove Road. About 1.6 miles from Seal Cove Pond, you'll reach Seal Cove Road, where you should turn left. Though still in the park with that fire-road feel, Seal Cove Pond is a main route between Southwest Harbor and Seal Cove, so keep your eyes open for auto traffic. At 0.6 mile after turning onto Seal Cove Road, you pass a small old cemetery in the woods; the road then turns to pavement and goes through a more residential area before reaching Long Pond Road at 4.4 miles from Seal Cove Pond.

To finish the trip, turn left onto Long Pond Road and make the steep climb up the 0.8 mile to Lurvey Spring Road. Turn right to follow Lurvey Spring Road back to Echo Lake. Hot and sweaty after your ride? Go for a swim at Echo Lake Beach, next to the parking area. It has the warmest swimming water on Mount Desert Island.

TRIP 28
AUNT BETTY POND LOOP

Rating: Moderate
Distance: 6.0 miles
Elevation Gain: 300 feet
Estimated Time: 1.5 hours
Map: AMC's Acadia National Park Discovery Map: D7

This ride offers the possibility of seeing beaver and the certainty of having good views of Sargent Mountain and Eagle Lake.

Directions

From the intersection of Routes 3 and 233 in Bar Harbor, take Route 233 west toward Cadillac Mountain. There are two parking areas for the carriage road in 2.1 miles, one on the right and one on the left. The parking area is stop B on the Island Explorer Brown Mountain route (route 6). *GPS coordinates*: 44° 22.648′ N, 68° 15.141′ W.

Trip Description

This trip begins at the northern end of Eagle Lake. It quickly veers away from the lake to visit Aunt Betty Pond and Gilmore Meadow, both of which offer good opportunities to see wildlife. A steep climb through cool evergreens is rewarded with a downhill coast to the western shore of Eagle Lake, with its stunning views of Cadillac Mountain, Pemetic Mountain, and the Bubbles. This trip can easily be combined with the Eagle Lake Loop (Trip 29) or the Giant Slide Loop (Trip 34).

If you park on the north side of Route 233, turn left on the carriage road, which soon passes under Route 233. Go straight at post 6. If you park on the south side of Route 233, go right on the carriage road and turn left at post 6. From either direction, about 100 yards past post 6, turn right at post 9 to head toward Aunt Betty Pond. The road makes a moderate climb to views of Cadillac, Pemetic, and Sargent mountains before heading downhill for more than a mile on its way to Aunt Betty Pond. At 2.4 miles from the parking area, you'll reach the pond, which is surrounded by the dark green of spruce and the light green of white pine. There are at least two active beaver lodges in the pond; they are visible on the shore opposite the carriage road. Since beaver are nocturnal, your best chance of seeing them is at dawn or dusk.

At 2.8 miles, you reach post 11 and Gilmore Meadow. Gilmore Meadow is formed by a small stone dam at the bridge to the left of post 11. You can see a narrow, meandering channel in the center of the meadow as tall grasses fill in the rest of this freshwater wetland. Lincoln and swamp sparrows, sedge and marsh wrens, flycatchers, and warblers all feed on the insects that proliferate here in spring and summer. There is also an excellent view to the south of Sargent Mountain, the second-tallest mountain in Acadia. Turn left at post 11 for a short downhill before beginning a steep climb that crosses several streams and tops out at post 10, which is 3.9 miles from the parking area.

Turn left at post 10 and again at post 8. The carriage road heads moderately downhill until it reaches the western shore of Eagle Lake, which it follows for the remainder of the trip. At 110 feet deep, Eagle Lake is one of the deepest lakes on Mount Desert Island, and its cold water provides the ideal habitat for cold-water fish like salmon and trout. Loons, mergansers, and cormorants ply the lake's surface looking for fish. Bald eagles and ospreys fish from the tall spruce and pines circling the lake, and belted kingfishers can be heard chattering away between attempts at catching fish.

At 6.0 miles, you'll reach post 6 and the end of your trip.

TRIP 29
EAGLE LAKE LOOP

Rating: Moderate
Distance: 6.0 miles
Elevation Gain: 350 feet
Estimated Time: 2.0 hours
Map: AMC's Acadia National Park Discovery Map: D7

This great ride for families goes through rich woodlands, with good views from Eagle Lake.

Directions
From the intersection of Routes 3 and 233 in Bar Harbor, take Route 233 west toward Cadillac Mountain. There are two parking areas for the carriage road in 2.1 miles, one on the right and one on the left. The parking area is stop B on the Island Explorer Brown Mountain route (route 6). *GPS coordinates*: 44° 22.648′ N, 68° 15.141′ W.

Trip Description
Except for one long, gradual uphill stretch, this ride is relatively easy on the legs. It begins at the northern end of Eagle Lake, with its spectacular views of Cadillac and Pemetic Mountains. This trip circles the lake in a counterclockwise direction in order to complete the climb up the west side of Conners Nubble at the beginning of the trip. This makes for an easy ride for the rest of the loop. While the views from higher up are limited on this trip, the mixture of beautiful forests makes for a very scenic ride. As with Witch Hole Pond, Eagle Lake is very accessible to Bar Harbor and can be crowded during busy weekends, but the lake's undeveloped shoreline gives it a good wilderness character.

If you park on the north side of Route 233, turn left on the carriage road, which soon passes under Route 233. Go straight at post 6. If you park on the south side of Route 223, go right on the carriage road and turn left at post 6. About 100 yards past post 6, stay to the left at post 9. The carriage road makes a long and steady ascent for much of the 2.1 miles to post 8. The forest alternates between tall spruce, tall white pine, and mixed hardwoods, occasionally providing views through the trees down to Eagle Lake.

Eagle Lake is the second-biggest lake on the island after Long Pond, and its deep, cold waters provide good habitat for salmon and trout. Osprey can often be seen circling above the lake while hunting for fish. In the forest, you are more likely to see and hear chickadees, juncos, and thrushes, and the noisy chattering of red squirrels. When you reach post 8, you have completed most of the climbing on this trip. Stay to the left and enjoy the ride back down to the shoreline of the lake, first through sweet-smelling spruce forest and then through a stand of large maple and beech.

As you round the southern end of the lake, you will notice that the forest opens up. Tall hemlocks grow here, shading the ground so well that very little light reaches the forest floor, making it hard for shrubs and small trees to grow. The eastern hemlock is one of the more beautiful conifers in the Northeast, with its rich brown bark and feathery green-and-white needles. A hemlock's needles are flat and soft like those of a fir tree, but they are much shorter, only about half an inch in length. Unlike fir trees, which live only 70 to 100 years, eastern hemlocks can live to be 400 years old and grow to be 70 feet tall. They often grow in pure stands in cool, moist valleys and ravines like the one at the southern end of Eagle Lake. These pure stands are often pockets in the midst of a larger northern hardwood forest, creating an edge habitat within the forest that has a higher number of species than the habitat away from the edge.

Approximately 3.8 miles from the parking area, you'll come to post 7. Stay to the left and continue through a marshy area where the trees are smaller and closer together and views open up toward Cadillac Mountain. In the spring, you can hear wood frogs making their quack-like mating call here. They are hard to find with their brown coloring, but if you scan the small vernal pools near the road for moving shapes about 2 inches long, you should find some. After crossing a stream lined with white birch and sugar maples, the carriage road makes a short ascent before it makes a fairly level return to the parking area. Beautiful stone retaining walls line the Cadillac Mountain side of the road. Just before the parking area, a mosaic forest of hardwoods and softwoods provides a good opportunity to look for pileated woodpeckers and yellow-bellied sapsuckers.

Early Human History of Mount Desert Island

Available archaeological evidence suggests that American Indians were living on Mount Desert Island at least 6,000 years ago. It is likely they were on the island even earlier, but Maine's wet coastal climate has caused any older evidence to decay into oblivion. Shell middens—deep heaps of discarded clam and mussel shells that also harbor stone tools and other artifacts—can be found throughout this part of coastal Maine. The Wabanaki lived throughout Maine and spent at least part of the year on Mount Desert Island, which they called Pemetic (Sloping Land). It was originally believed that the Wabanaki spent summers on the island and wintered inland. However, archaeological evidence suggests the opposite was true. Avoiding the brutally cold winters of inland Maine, the Wabanaki most likely wintered on the coast, living off fish and shellfish. In the summers they moved inland to take advantage of runs of Atlantic salmon. You can learn more about Maine's American Indian heritage at the Abbe Museum, located in the park at Sieur de Monts Spring, and in downtown Bar Harbor at 26 Mount Desert Street.

It is possible that Leif Ericson and his crew of Viking sailors in search of timber encountered Mount Desert Island around 1000 A.D. However, most of the known history of Mount Desert Island begins with the arrival of Europeans, who arrived after 1500. Sailing on behalf of France in 1524, Italian explorer Giovanni da Verazzano was the first European to make note of the island. However, Samuel de Champlain is generally given credit for "discovering" Mount Desert Island; in 1604, he ran aground near Otter Point. Champlain, who was mapping the area for the French, named the island L'Isle des Monts-Deserts (Island of the Desert Mountains). Maps of the region that predate his visit called the area La Cadie, a word that derives either from the area's resemblance to the Arcadia region of Greece or from the Wabanaki word for "where it is plentiful." Most of what was to become New France, from Down East Maine to Nova Scotia, would be known for many years as L'Acadie or Acadia.

The first permanent European settlement on Mount Desert Island was short-lived. In 1613, two French Jesuit priests, Father Biard and Father Masse, established a mission, possibly at Fernald Point, near the entrance to Somes Sound. They called their mission Saint Sauveur, now the name of the mountain just to the northwest of Fernald Point. The local Wabanaki, led by their chief, Asticou, welcomed the Jesuits' attempt to build a fort, plant corn, and baptize the natives. However, before the Jesuits finished building the mission, an English ship under the leadership of Captain Samuel Argall destroyed their fledgling settlement. For the next 150 years, this part of Maine became disputed territory as the French and English fought for control of North America. During this period, Mount Desert Island was used primarily as a landmark for passing ships, and some say as a hideout for pirates.

In 1688, French king Louis XIV granted 100,000 acres on the Maine coast to Antoine de Mothe Cadillac, who briefly settled on Mount Desert Island before moving on to found Detroit. While he bestowed upon himself the important-sounding title of Sieur de la Mothe Cadillac, the French explorer had little influence on the history of Mount Desert Island. Shortly after the American Revolution, however, Madame de Gregoire, Cadillac's granddaughter, asked the United States to give her the land from her grandfather's grant. Feeling friendly toward the French after their help in the war, the Massachusetts legislature agreed to uphold part of her claim and granted her rights to the entire eastern half of Mount Desert Island. Mount Desert Island is the only place in the United States outside of Louisiana where land titles can be traced back to the French crown. Madame de Gregoire and her husband settled at Hulls Cove in 1788, but they proved to be rather ill suited to the pioneer lifestyle. They gradually sold off their landholdings in order to support themselves, and their family grant was completely used up by the time of their deaths in 1810 and 1811.

The English began settling Mount Desert Island after their victory in the French and Indian War in 1759. In 1760, John Bernard, governor of Massachusetts, obtained a royal land grant on Mount Desert Island and attempted to secure his claim by offering free land to settlers. Abraham Somes and John Richardson of Gloucester, Massachusetts, took advantage of Bernard's offer and settled in what is now Somesville. Bernard lost his grant as a result of the American Revolution, but the early U.S. government granted his son the western half of the island at about the same time it deeded the eastern half to Madame de Gregoire. However, the grants of Bernard and de Gregoire had little effect on the settlers homesteading on the island, and by the middle of the nineteenth century, Mount Desert Island was thriving like much else of the Maine coast, with a diverse economy revolving around farming, lumbering, and fishing.

TRIP 30
BAR HARBOR TO OCEAN DRIVE LOOP

Rating: Moderate
Distance: 11.5 miles
Elevation Gain: 300 feet
Estimated Time: 2.0 hours
Map: AMC's Acadia National Park Discovery Map: C8, C9, D9, E9

This moderate road bike ride goes from Bar Harbor to scenic Ocean Drive.

Directions

This trip starts at the Village Green in downtown Bar Harbor at the intersection of Mount Desert Street and Main Street. With the exception of the Loop Road and Schoodic routes, all Island Explorer routes stop at the Village Green. *GPS coordinates*: 44° 23.252′ N, 68° 12.257′ W.

Trip Description

This ride is the only one in this book to follow pavement, but the spectacular views are worth having to share the road with cars. This trip takes you from Bar Harbor to the Schooner Head Overlook's dramatic view of the Atlantic Ocean. It also visits Sand Beach, Ocean Drive, and the Tarn, a glacially carved pond beneath the steep cliffs of Dorr Mountain. The elevation gain is minimal for the length of the ride, making it easy to complete this loop in less than an hour, but we encourage you to take your time and drink in the ocean views and fresh salt air. Please note that the section of this trip on the Park Loop Road is one-way.

Starting from the Village Green in Bar Harbor, follow Route 3 (Main Street) south, away from the harbor. The ride passes the outskirts of Bar Harbor on the way to Schooner Head Road at 1.2 miles, where you should turn left. Less busy than Route 3, Schooner Head Road passes the Jackson Lab (a world-renowned supplier of lab mice) and then enters woodlands filled with paper birch and home to numerous white-tailed deer. At 3.5 miles from the Village Green, you'll cross the outlet of a large beaver pond with excellent views of the cliffs on Champlain Mountain.

Waves wash over cobble-stones in a cove below Ocean Drive.

Shortly after the beaver pond, you'll reach an intersection where a right brings you to the Park Loop Road. You'll be going that direction soon, but first turn left for a 0.1-mile ride to the Schooner Head overlook and a great view of the open ocean. If you need a break from riding, you can walk down the 0.25-mile-long trail to Anemone Cave, where at low tide you can climb into the cave and look for the namesake sea creatures that live there. After taking in the views from Schooner Head, turn around and ride to the Park Loop Road, where you must turn left. (This is the one-way section.) In about 0.5 mile, you will pass the parking area for Sand Beach on the left (bath-rooms can be found here); the road then makes a short climb up to the pink-granite ledges that help make Acadia famous. This is the Ocean Drive section of the Park Loop Road, and you will be compelled to get off your bike and explore the ledges. Here you'll have views of crashing surf, distant islands, and seabirds like guillemots and eiders. Thunder Hole and its towers of sea

Ocean Drive follows the coast from Bar Harbor to Schooner Head.

spray during big seas are the best-known attraction of Ocean Drive (at mile 5.2), but in our experience, any of the ledges or the intervening cobble beaches are worth a visit, especially if you want a little solitude.

At 0.6 mile past Thunder Hole, you should turn right off the Park Loop Road, onto Otter Cliff Road (unmarked). In 0.2 mile, there is a picnic area with bathrooms on the left, but the majority of Otter Cliff Road is an uneventful though pleasant ride through woods and past a few houses, reaching Route 3 at mile 7.7 of the trip (1.9 miles from the Park Loop Road). Turn right and follow Route 3 for the 3.8 miles back to the Village Green. Along the way, you may want to stop and explore the northern shoreline of the Tarn, a glacial pond tucked beneath the cliffs of the east face of Dorr Mountain. Just beyond the Tarn, you can turn left for a short ride to Sieur de Monts Spring and check out the Wild Gardens of Acadia (a native wildflower garden) and the Abbe Museum (American Indian history).

TRIP 31
BAR HARBOR TO JORDAN POND VIA EAGLE LAKE

Rating: Easy
Distance: 8.3 miles
Elevation Gain: 200 feet
Estimated Time: 2.0 hours
Map: AMC's Acadia National Park Discovery Map: C8, C7, D7, E7

Take an easy, scenic bike ride from Bar Harbor to Jordan Pond.

Directions

To Bar Harbor town pier: From the intersection of Mount Desert Street and Main Street, head north on Main Street, which dead-ends at the pier after 0.25 mile. With the exception of the Loop Road and Schoodic routes, all Island Explorer routes stop at the Village Green, which is about 0.25 mile from the town pier. *GPS coordinates:* 44° 23.484′ N, 68° 12.283′ W.

To Jordan Pond Parking area: From the Acadia National Park Visitor Center, drive south on the Park Loop Road for 7.3 miles. Be sure to continue straight at the intersections marked Sand Beach and Cadillac Mountain. The Jordan Pond parking area will be on your right. The parking area is stop C on the Island Explorer Jordan Pond route (route 5), and stop F on the Loop Road route (route 4). *GPS coordinates:* 44° 19.332′ N, 68° 15.121′ W.

Trip Description

The ride to Jordan Pond is an easy, rewarding trip that starts in Bar Harbor, follows the carriage roads at the Duck Brook Bridge, and proceeds past Eagle Lake on its way to the Jordan Pond House. Even people without their "biking legs" should be able to ride this mostly flat route without having to get off and push. It is a great ride anytime, but we think it makes an ideal first experience for those new to the carriage-road system, particularly if you are staying in or near Bar Harbor. You can rent a bike from an outfitter in town and ride off, getting to the carriage roads in about 15 minutes. If you feel strong after the 2.0-hour ride to Jordan Pond, you can make this an out-and-back trip. Otherwise, you and your bike can get a ride back to Bar Harbor on an Island Explorer bus (route 5); check at the visitor center for a current schedule.

From the parking area at the town pier in Bar Harbor, ride west on West Street, which parallels the bay. In 0.6 mile, you will cross Route 3 and continue straight until you reach Duck Brook Road at 1.3 miles, where you should turn right. In another 0.6 mile, you will reach the carriage roads at Duck Brook Bridge, which will be on the right. Ride over the beautiful granite bridge (complete with viewing turrets) and turn left at post 5. (For a longer ride, combine this trip with Trip 23, Witch Hole Pond.) About 1.0 mile from the bridge, turn left at post 4 and ride another mile to Eagle Lake, where you will quickly pass posts 6 and 9; continue straight at both intersections. Most of the elevation gain of this ride is during the next 2.1 miles as you first parallel the lake before climbing around Conners Nubble on the way to post 8.

Turn right at post 8 and then turn left at post 10 in another 0.2 mile. From here it as an easy 2.5-mile ride to the Jordan Pond House. On the way, you'll pass the Deer Brook waterfall at the northern end of Jordan Pond and have excellent views of the pond and the Bubbles as the carriage road breaks out into the open under the cliffs of Penobscot Mountain. Just before reaching the end of the ride, you will want to continue straight at posts 14 and 15, and turn left at post 16. You will then come to the Park Loop Road, with the Jordan Pond House just a few hundred yards to the left.

TRIP 32
DAY MOUNTAIN

Rating: Moderate
Distance: 8.0 miles
Elevation Gain: 500 feet
Estimated Time: 2.5 hours
Map: AMC's Acadia National Park Discovery Map: E7, E8, F7

This moderate ride goes to great views of the Atlantic Ocean and the islands to the south and west of Mount Desert Island.

Directions

From the Acadia National Park Visitor Center, drive south on the Park Loop Road for 7.3 miles. Be sure to continue straight at the intersections marked Sand Beach and Cadillac Mountain. The Jordan Pond parking area will be on your right. The carriage road for this trip begins next to the Jordan Pond gatehouse, across the road from the Jordan Pond House. The parking area is stop C on the Island Explorer Jordan Pond route (route 5), and stop F on the Loop Road route (route 4). *GPS coordinates*: 44° 19.332′ N, 68° 15.121′ W.

Trip Description

Day Mountain is the only peak in Acadia that you can climb via the carriage roads. When John D. Rockefeller Jr. was having the carriage roads constructed, he originally decided against building them over mountaintops. He agreed to this road because Day Mountain is a relatively small peak, 583 feet tall, and it was possible to build the road so that it was not visible from any other peaks. Bikers visiting Acadia National Park are glad he made this decision. This trip is an enjoyable one, as you climb above the trees to sweeping vistas of the open Atlantic and the islands to the south and west of the park.

Begin this ride by heading east on the carriage road next to the Jordan Pond gatehouse, across the Park Loop Road from the Jordan Pond House. Rockefeller had the prominent New York architect Grosvenor Atterbury design the Jordan Pond gatehouse, which was constructed in the early 1930s. It was designed along the lines of a European hunting lodge in the French

Day Mountain is the only mountain in Acadia that provides a carriage road to the peak, making for an excellent bike route.

Romanesque architectural style. Another gatehouse was built near Lower Hadlock Pond outside of Northeast Harbor. These gatehouses were built to provide a place for attendants to live while manning the gates that would allow carriages in but not automobiles. The gatehouses are no longer occupied, and the gates are closed to motorized traffic except for Park Service maintenance vehicles.

The first 0.25 mile is a nice downhill coast before the road begins a long, gradual ascent. After passing above Wildwood Stables, the carriage road reaches post 17 at 1.2 miles. Turn right and cross the Triad-Day Bridge. Completed in 1940, this was the last of the carriage-road bridges to be built. Across the bridge, you will come to post 37. Turn right to circle around the west side of Day Mountain. You will need to watch your speed on the long downhill stretch here in order to maintain control and avoid accidents with horses or other bikes. At 1.8 miles you will reach post 38, where you should continue straight through a forest of spruce, fir, birch, and maple. From post 38, the road begins its gradual ascent toward the summit of Day Mountain. On your left you will see a low but beautiful retaining wall made of bowling-ball-sized boulders of pink granite.

At 2.5 miles, turn left at post 36 to ride the final 1.5 miles up to the summit. As you gain elevation, spectacular views open up of the Atlantic Ocean to the east and the Cranberry Isles to the south. The climb is steady but moderate, and long stretches of the carriage road are well above the trees, so the views are constant while you ride. At 3.7 miles, you'll reach the summit, which has excellent views to the south of the Cranberry Isles, Duck Island, Isle au Haut, and the western mountains. With its quiet woods and good views, Day Mountain is a great place for a picnic lunch.

Return down the carriage road to post 36, where you should turn left. You will have to watch your speed again on the descent, as there are many tight corners. Between post 36 and post 37 are more good views of the Atlantic before you drop down for good into the shade of the cool forest. When you reach post 37, you are back at the Triad-Day Bridge, which spans the Park Loop Road. Cross the bridge and turn left at post 17. About 100 yards past post 17, take the right fork in the road, as the left fork is used as an access from Wildwood Stables. From here, retrace your route back to the Jordan Pond House.

Rating: Moderate
Distance: 9.0 miles
Elevation Gain: 500 feet
Estimated Time: 2.5 hours
Map: AMC's Acadia National Park Discovery Map: E7, E8, D7

Take in the dramatic scenery of Jordan and Bubble Ponds on this moderate ride.

Directions

From the Acadia National Park Visitor Center, drive south on the Park Loop Road for 7.3 miles. Be sure to continue straight at the intersections marked Sand Beach and Cadillac Mountain. The Jordan Pond parking area will be on your right. The carriage road for this trip begins across the street from the Jordan Pond gatehouse. The parking area is stop C on the Island Explorer Jordan Pond route (route 5) and stop F on the Loop Road route (route 4). *GPS coordinates*: 44° 19.332′ N, 68° 15.121′ W.

Trip Description

Jordan Pond is arguably the most scenic pond in Acadia National Park, with its deep blue waters reflecting the steep cliffs of Penobscot Mountain and the graceful curves of the Bubbles. Bubble Pond is smaller and more intimate, with dramatic scenery of its own as the steep west face of Cadillac Mountain rises above its eastern shoreline. This is one of the longer rides in the carriage-road system, but its grades are never steep. For this reason it makes a great day trip for a family with older children who are comfortable spending the day on bikes. Of course, following your ride you can recharge your system with tea and popovers at the Jordan Pond House.

Begin this trip by turning onto the carriage road across the street from the Jordan Pond gatehouse. Turn right at post 16 and go straight at post 15. At 0.3 mile, a small bridge crosses the outlet to Jordan Pond as the carriage road climbs up to post 14 at 0.5 mile, where you should continue straight. The road continues its upward trek through a mixed forest until Jordan Pond and the Bubbles come into view at 1.25 miles. The road crosses a huge rock slide where giant boulders line the steep east face of Penobscot Mountain.

George Dorr, the first superintendent of Acadia National Park, feared that constructing a road through such a treacherous rock slide was a risky proposition. John Rockefeller Jr. and his contractor managed to assure Dorr that no one would get hurt, and they were allowed to proceed. The views from this stretch of the carriage road are fantastic. The pond is about 150 feet below the road, and you can see the Bubbles as well as the entire south ridge of Pemetic Mountain. You can also look straight up at Jordan Cliffs, home to one of Acadia's nesting pairs of peregrine falcons.

As you reenter the forest, you are rewarded with a crossing of Deer Brook Bridge. This bridge, with its pair of tall, narrow arches, gives you a close-up view of Deer Brook as it cascades in a waterfall over large slabs of pink granite. The Deer Brook Trail, on the south side of the bridge, makes its way up to Sargent Pond and Sargent and Penobscot Mountains (see Trip 13). After the falls, the ride levels out as you pass the north end of Jordan Pond and head toward Eagle Lake. At 2.5 miles, turn right at post 10. At 2.7 miles, turn right again at post 8. At this point, you are about 500 feet up to the west of Eagle Lake behind a small peak called Conners Nubble. At 3.2 miles, you'll cross a hiking trail that you can use to walk quickly up to the summit for a nice view of Eagle Lake.

After passing Conners Nubble, the road makes a long descent to the southern end of Eagle Lake, which is surrounded by thick spruce forest. This forest is a great place to look for finches such as red crossbills, white-winged crossbills, pine siskins, and common redpolls. Except for redpolls, all these finches breed in the park, but their numbers are highly variable. These finches of the boreal forest tend to migrate in waves depending on the severity of the weather and the abundance of the seed crop, so their numbers in any one area can change greatly from year to year.

At 4.5 miles, turn right at post 7 to ride toward Bubble Pond. You will cross the Park Loop Road at 4.8 miles and pass by the northern end of Bubble Pond. You then cross a bridge that seems to cross nothing but forest. The bridge was built to cross the Park Loop Road, which was subsequently relocated because it passed too close to the pond. Bubble Pond Bridge was constructed of compressed rock, as opposed to the granite blocks used for the rest of the bridges in the park. After crossing the bridge, the road turns left and follows the shoreline of Bubble Pond. Pemetic Mountain rises steeply to the west. Across the pond to the east is the steep west face of Cadillac

Jordan Pond and the Bubbles are among the most popular destinations in the park.

Mountain. Cedar and paper birch grow on the shoreline as well as on the ledges on Cadillac. During the spring and fall migrations, you can see hawks, eagles, falcons, and vultures riding the thermals above Cadillac. Turkey vultures are known to use the huge boulders at the southeastern end of the pond as a resting spot. They blend in well with the gray rocks, so you may need binoculars to spot them.

As the road continues past the pond, it passes through a variety of forest types: spruce-fir, northern hardwood, cedar. In the northern hardwood forest, you will notice irregularly shaped and dying beech trees; they are infected with a blight that is a combination of a fungus and a scale and was introduced by European beech trees imported in the nineteenth century. While bad for the trees, the blight does benefit the insects that feed on the dying trees as well as the woodpeckers and flickers that feed on the insects. Nonetheless, the loss of a large number of American beech trees would be devastating to the forest animals that depend on beechnuts for food. Scientists are still unsure as to the long-term effects of this blight on the beech forests of North America.

After rounding the southern end of the Triad, go straight at post 17 (7.7 miles). The road then climbs for 0.5 mile as it traverses the west side of the Triad behind Wildwood Stables to views of the Cranberry Isles. From here it is an easy coast back down to the Jordan Pond gatehouse.

Acadia's Mosaic Forest

"Mosaic" is a term Acadia's naturalists use to describe much of the forest on the eastern half of Mount Desert Island. It is a forest with a high diversity of tree species that does not fit into the normal forest-habitat categories (e.g., northern hardwoods or boreal). This mosaic forest came about after the great fire of 1947. Before the fire, a boreal forest of red spruce and balsam fir covered most of the island. The thick canopy of the spruce and fir trees made it nearly impossible for other trees to grow. With the spruce-fir canopy gone, sun-loving trees such as birch, aspen, and maple were able to take root. White pine also grew quickly, while spruce and fir saplings sprouted from the stumps of trees killed in the fire. The result is a forest that is part boreal, part northern hardwoods.

With a new forest of deciduous trees, Acadia became a different place. Visually, Acadia now experiences the brilliant fall foliage displays that make New England famous. Wildlife concentrations are also different. Beaver, which eat birch and aspen, are much more common in the park now compared to 60 years ago. Their presence has created an increase in wetland habitats, which in turn has attracted more river otters. These additional wetlands nurture fish, crayfish, and amphibians that attract not only otters but also birds such as great blue herons and kingfishers. The forest itself provides good habitat for a myriad of songbirds, including yellow warblers, scarlet tanagers, and northern orioles, as well as pileated woodpeckers and ruffed grouse. White-tailed deer numbers are up, as the deer feed on acorns and the twigs of young birches and aspens.

TRIP 34
GIANT SLIDE LOOP

Rating: Difficult
Distance: 8.5 miles
Elevation Gain: 600 feet
Estimated Time: 2.5 hours
Map: AMC's Acadia National Park Discovery Map: E6, D6, D7

This ride goes over rushing mountain streams to spectacular ocean and mountain views.

Directions

For this trip, park at the Parkman Mountain parking area on Routes 198/3, 1.8 miles north of Northeast Harbor. The parking area is an unscheduled stop between Gate House (stop D) and MDI High School (stop C) on the Island Explorer Brown Mountain route (route 6). *GPS coordinates*: 44° 19.898′ N, 68° 17.653′ W.

Trip Description

This trip begins with a long ride over relatively flat terrain to the northwest of Parkman and Sargent mountains. It then visits a beautiful meadow with views of the mountains before beginning a long, steep climb up the north side of Sargent Mountain. The 600-foot climb is well worth the effort, though, as views open up all the way to the Camden Hills, 30 miles away. With wetlands, streams, and several different forest types, this trip also provides excellent opportunities for nature study.

Starting at the Parkman Mountain parking area, follow the carriage road to the left, away from post 13. The 3.3 miles to post 11 is almost all downhill, following a gentle grade through a dark green evergreen forest. The road crosses several small streams tumbling down from Sargent and Parkman Mountains. As you get closer to post 11, wetlands begin to appear on the left and the forest changes, with deciduous trees such as northern red oak, maple, and birch taking over the flat valley floor. Northern red oak is the northernmost oak in the eastern United States, and its range extends well into Quebec and Ontario. While it is most often associated with the oak-hickory forests to the south and west of Maine, in northern New England and Canada northern red oak can be found in northern hardwood forests. Like most oaks, it can grow to be tall and stately, producing bumper crops of acorns every three or four years.

At post 11, you reach Gilmore Meadow, a freshwater wetland with a great view of Sargent Mountain. The meadow, with its narrow meandering channel, surrounded by a wet, grassy swamp, is a great place to look for small birds such as sparrows, flycatchers, and warblers. Turn right at post 11 for a short downhill coast before beginning the steepest climb in the carriage-road system. The road enters a mixed evergreen and hardwood forest, passing through a grove of hemlocks as it makes several stream crossings over a series of uncharacteristic concrete and wooden bridges. At 4.4 miles, you will reach post 10, where you should turn right.

The steep climb continues as you wind your way up the north face of Sargent Mountain. At 4.9 miles, you reach Chasm Brook Bridge. Built in 1926, this bridge provides a welcome resting point where you can listen to the rushing water of Chasm Brook as it cascades over a 40-foot waterfall. The road continues up the mountain using switchbacks to make the climb more amenable. As you get higher, the hills of northern and eastern Maine come into view. Climbing still, you'll see Blue Hill and Acadia's western mountains to the west. At 6.3 miles, the road crosses the Sargent Northwest Trail and then levels out.

As you round the north side of Parkman Mountain, you get wide-open views of Somes Sound and all of Maine to the west. The road stays in the open for much of its way down from Parkman Mountain. Pitch pines and white pines cling to the rock ledges amid clumps of blueberry bushes and lichen. At 8.1 miles, turn right at post 12. Turn right again at post 13, at 8.4 miles. The parking area is on the left in another 0.1 mile.

TRIP 35
AROUND THE MOUNTAIN LOOP

Rating: Difficult
Distance: 12.0 miles
Elevation Gain: 1,000 feet
Estimated Time: 4.0 hours
Map: AMC's Acadia National Park Discovery Map: E6, E7,
    D6, D7

**This ride has it all: three waterfalls, mountain and ocean
views, and seven major bridge crossings.**

Directions

From the Acadia National Park Visitor Center, drive south on the Park Loop
Road for 7.3 miles. Be sure to continue straight at the intersections marked
Sand Beach and Cadillac Mountain. The Jordan Pond parking area will be on
your right. The carriage road for this trip begins across the street from the
Jordan Pond gatehouse. The parking area is stop C on the Island Explorer
Jordan Pond route (route 5) and stop F on the Loop Road route (route 4).
GPS coordinates: 44° 19.332′ N, 68° 15.121′ W.

Trip Description

It is not clear which mountain the person who named this loop had in mind,
for it actually loops around six: Penobscot Mountain, Cedar Swamp Mountain, Bald Peak, Parkman Mountain, Gilmore Peak, and Sargent Mountain.
It begins and ends next to the deep blue waters of picturesque Jordan Pond.
For 12.0 miles, it rises and falls through almost every forest type in the
park, passes steep cliffs and waterfalls, and climbs to dramatic views of the
areas surrounding Acadia National Park. It is long by carriage-road standards and gains more elevation than any other loop in the park. Neverthe-
less, strong riders can still complete it in less than half a day. However, it is
easy to spend the entire day studying the details of nature and soaking in
the long-distance views.

Begin this trip by turning onto the carriage road across the street from
the Jordan Pond gatehouse. Turn right at post 16 and go straight at post 15.

At 0.3 mile, a small bridge crosses the outlet to Jordan Pond, as the carriage road climbs up to post 14 at 0.5 mile, where you should turn left. A short but steep climb brings you to the modest West Branch Bridge, with its single tall, narrow arch spanning a small stream tumbling down Penobscot Mountain. After climbing 1.2 miles, you will reach the 230-foot-long Cliffside Bridge, which has the style of a fortress from the Middle Ages. Two large viewing turrets invite you to look out at Pemetic and Day Mountains, as well as the Triad. Maples and other hardwoods dominate the foreground, while spruce and fir trees cling to the distant mountains.

As you round the southern end of Penobscot Mountain, you come to post 21, where you should continue straight toward the Amphitheater. The road gently rises through a mosaic forest, and views of the rounded ridges that make up the Amphitheater soon come into view. At 2.2 miles, you'll reach the head of the Amphitheater and the 235-foot-long bridge that crosses the small gorge there. Walking down a trail at the west end of the bridge will take you down to Little Harbor Brook, where you can look through the arch in the bridge to a small waterfall.

Continuing past the bridge, turn right at post 20 for a gradual climb up to views of the Cranberry Isles. As you ride toward post 19, notice the variety of lichens that grow on the rocks lining the road. Green target lichen grows in concentric rings. Brown-and-black rock tripe looks like lettuce gone bad. Reindeer lichen grows in bunches, its greenish-white branches looking like antlers. It is actually eaten by reindeer and caribou in the arctic environments where they live. There are also large clumps of rhodora, an evergreen shrub that grows in bogs and other areas with acidic soils. When you reach post 19, at 3.6 miles, turn right.

At 5.0 miles, you'll reach a pair of magnificent bridges that span Hadlock Brook and Maple Spring. Waterfall Bridge looks out at Hadlock Brook as it tumbles over 40 feet of granite. Hemlock Bridge spans Maple Spring, which is lined with tall hemlocks and white pines. An enchanted-forest feeling creeps in as you ride over these intricate bridges through tall trees surrounded by the sounds of water and bird song. The road then climbs to views of Upper Hadlock Pond and the Cranberry Isles at post 12 (5.5 miles). Turn right to begin one of the longest climbs in the carriage-road system.

The carriage road goes up for most of the next 1.8 miles, reaching an elevation of 800 feet. The road traverses the western shoulder of Parkman Mountain, rising through a forest of pitch pine on its way to extensive views

The Around the Mountain Loop actually goes around six mountains.

to the west and north. Somes Sound, the only fjord in the eastern United States, can be seen just to the west of the road, with Acadia, Beech, and Bernard Mountains rising up to the west of the sound. As you get higher and round the northern end of Sargent Mountain, the wind gets a little stronger and the air a little colder. At this point, the views open up to include Mount Desert Narrows and northern Maine.

Once you pass the Sargent Northwest Trail, at 7.3 miles, you are rewarded with a long, winding downhill coast that will take you back to Jordan Pond. It is easy to pick up a lot of speed on this stretch. Try to control your speed, because it is fairly likely that someone will be stopped on the road, hidden behind a curve. You will have good views of Eagle Lake on the way down. Notice how the forest is sharply demarcated between spruce-fir and paper birch. Spruce-fir forests dominated the island before the great fire of 1947. After the fire, pioneer species such as aspen, birch, and other hardwoods grew back in place of the spruce and fir. In this area, thin soil has made it hard for trees to return, and the paper birch that are growing are very thin and spindly. By identifying the different forest types, it is easy to see where the fire did its damage.

At 8.7 miles, you'll cross a small bridge over Chasm Brook, which falls about 40 feet over the rocks to the south of the bridge. At 9.2 miles, go straight at post 10. A slight incline brings you to another waterfall and the Deer Brook Bridge at 10.0 miles. The north end of Jordan Pond begins to come into view through the trees on the left. Continuing south, you will break out into the open as you pass through a massive rock slide on the east face of Penobscot Mountain. Here you will have a great look at Jordan Pond, the Bubbles, and Pemetic Mountain. Looming above you are Jordan Cliffs. At 11.3 miles, bear left at post 14, which completes the loop. To finish your trip, stay to the left at posts 15 and 16.

TRIP 36
AROUND THE MOUNTAIN II

Rating: Difficult
Distance: 18.7 miles
Elevation Gain: 900 feet
Estimated Time: 5.5 hours
Map: AMC's Acadia National Park Discovery Map: D7, D6, E6, E7

This long ride goes through gorgeous forests and past scenic ponds.

Directions

From the intersection of Routes 3 and 233 in Bar Harbor, take Route 233 west toward Cadillac Mountain. There are two parking areas for the carriage road in 2.1 miles, one on the right and one on the left. The parking area is stop B on the Island Explorer Brown Mountain route (route 6). *GPS coordinates*: 44° 22.648′ N, 68° 15.141′ W.

Trip Description

This ride follows the outer edge of the carriage road system for most of its length, making it a long ride, but without the extensive or difficult uphill sections that are found on other rides in this book. Then again, 18.7 miles of riding on gravel roads that do climb 100 feet every now and then does require a day's worth of exertion, so bring plenty of food and water to keep your energy levels high. We describe this trip as it starts at Eagle Lake, but you can just as easily start at Parkman Mountain, Jordan Pond, or Bubble Pond. In addition to Eagle Lake, Jordan Pond, and Bubble Pond, this ride also visits Aunt Betty Pond and it crosses many of the magnificent stone bridges found on the carriage roads, including the 230-foot-long, fortress-like Cliffside Bridge. To trace out the route for this trip, start at the north end of Eagle Lake (grid E7 on the AMC map) and follow it to these carriage road intersections: 6, 9, 11, 13, 12, 19, 20, 21, 14, 15, 16, 17, 7, and back to 6.

If you park on the north side of Route 233, turn left on the carriage road, which soon passes under Route 233. Go straight at post 6. If you park on the south side of Route 233, go right on the carriage road and turn left at post 6. From either direction, about 100 yards past post 6, turn right at post 9 to head toward Aunt Betty Pond. The road makes a moderate climb to views of Cadillac, Pemetic, and Sargent mountains before heading downhill for more than a mile on its way to Aunt Betty Pond. At 2.4 miles from the parking area, you'll reach the pond, where beavers make their home and conifers fill the surrounding forests. In another 0.4 mile, you will reach Gilmore Meadow and post 11. After taking in the views of Sargent Mountain, turn right and enjoy an easy ride through beautiful softwood and hardwood forests. At 6.1 miles, you will reach post 13, where you should turn left for a short, relatively steep climb to post 12 at 6.5 miles. Turn right.

At 6.9 miles, you will reach Hemlock Bridge and then Waterfall Bridge, two of our favorite bridges in the carriage-road system. Hemlock Bridge rises high above a small gorge populated with tall hemlocks, while waterfall bridge gives an unobstructed view of Hadlock Brook as it cascades beautifully over pink granite. After Waterfall Bridge, the carriage road bends to the south for a long, gradual descent paralleling the south ridge of Cedar Swamp Mountain. At 8.3 miles, turn left at post 19 and then left again at post 20 (9.3 miles). It is a relatively easy ride from here to the Amphitheatre Bridge at 9.8 miles. At 235 feet with an arch that spans 50 feet, this is the longest bridge on any of the carriage roads.

The carriage road then bends to the right and follows a contour on the west side of Penobscot Mountain, providing good views of unbroken forests and the ocean in the distance. At 10.5 miles, turn left at post 21. You will soon reach Cliffside Bridge, where you can take a break in one of the viewing turrets that look out over the forests and mountains to the east. At 11.5 miles, turn right at post 14. Continue straight at post 15 and then turn left at post 16 at 12.0 miles. You will cross the Park Loop Road shortly after. If you need a break or want to recharge on the shores of Jordan Pond, turn left and follow the road a few hundred yards to the Jordan Pond House, where there are restrooms, bike racks, a gift shop, and restaurant. If you opt to skip Jordan Pond, continue straight across the Park Loop Road and pass the elaborate gatehouse on the left.

Easy riding brings you to post 17 at 13.2 miles, where you should continue straight, unless you have the energy for a ride up Day Mountain (see Trip 29). The carriage road then skirts around the east side of the Triad and

Kids enjoy the Around the Mountain Loop as it contains less elevation change than the other bike roads and offers a smoother ride.

Pemetic Mountain and closely follows the western shore of Bubble Pond, which has good views of the cliffs on the west face of Cadillac Mountain. At the north end of the pond, you will cross the Park Loop Road and reach post 7 at 16.4 miles. Turn right, cross Bubble Brook, and enjoy the views of Eagle Lake as you follow its eastern shore on the way back to the parking area and the end of the ride.

Road Biking Trips

While bike-riding enthusiasts flock to Acadia's gravel carriage-road system, those who enjoy biking the pavement can find several enjoyable trips around the island. The following is a brief description of bike-riding trips on the roads in and around Acadia National Park.

The Park Loop Road (19 miles)

From Bar Harbor, take Kebo Road 1.2 miles to the Park Loop Road. The ride must be completed in a clockwise direction, since much of the road is one-way. This trip will take you to many of the park's highlights, including Champlain Mountain, Sand Beach, Otter Cliffs, and Jordan Pond.

Western Side, Routes 102/102A (26 miles)

Following Route 102 around the western side of Mount Desert Island gives you the opportunity to visit Long Pond, Bass Harbor Head Light, Seawall, Echo Lake, and the town of Southwest Harbor. From Somesville, follow Route 102 south, turning right at the blinking yellow light. Route 102 basically loops around this side of the island. Pass the little town of Tremont and turn right onto Route 102A, heading toward Bass Harbor and Seawall. Just before reaching Southwest Harbor, you reconnect with Route 102, which you can follow north back to Somesville.

Schoodic Peninsula (12 miles)

From Route 186 in Winter Harbor, follow Moore Road south along the very scenic coastline of the Schoodic Peninsula. As you pass the picturesque scene of lobster boats in Bunker's Harbor and then Birch Harbor, turn left on Route 186 to return to Winter Harbor.

Swans Island (16 miles)

An enjoyable 40-minute ferry ride from Bass Harbor takes you to Swans Island. Its 16 miles of roads provide plenty of opportunity for spending your day exploring the hills and valleys of the island's 7,000 acres. Hockamock Head Lighthouse is probably the most popular attraction on the island, with rural countryside and ocean views making up the bulk of the scenery.

These road trips are a great way to get out of your car and see Acadia up close, but remember that you are sharing the road with cars, which travel at speeds up to 55 miles an hour. Wear a helmet and bright colors and follow the same rules of the road you follow while driving a car.

3

Quietwater Paddling in Acadia National Park

EXPERIENCING ACADIA'S QUIET INLAND WATERS from a canoe or kayak is a great way to get a new look at the beauty of Mount Desert Island. From the grand vistas of Eagle Lake to the quiet comfort of Little Long Pond, all of these paddles are suitable for families and solo paddlers alike. These trips also provide excellent wildlife-watching opportunities: loons and ducks and occasionally bald eagles, ospreys, and river otters all can be spotted in Acadia's inland waters. While we did omit a few of the island's smaller ponds, this chapter is a fairly complete description of the quietwater paddling available in Acadia National Park. The following trips take you from serene paddles through waterlilies to dramatic cliff-side paddling to meandering explorations in a bird-filled marsh.

Paddling Times and Distances

The distances listed on our trips basically assume you will follow the shoreline of the pond for most of the trip. Trips will be shorter in distance if you paddle directly from point A to point B and back, but we expect that most people will like to explore the shoreline for at least part of a trip to look for animals, flowers, and resting spots. Paddling times can vary widely according to paddlers' experience, physical conditioning, and curiosity. We have tried to come up with the time it would take a paddler of average strength and experience to complete these trips with only one short rest break to eat a snack. If you have a group of very curious paddlers, expect your trips to take a bit longer.

Safety and Etiquette

While paddling on Mount Desert Island is a fairly safe activity, cold and deep waters combined with regularly changing weather conditions require certain safety precautions. To ensure a safe and comfortable paddling experience, consider the following safety tips:

- Know how to use your canoe or kayak. Of course, lakes and ponds like those in Acadia are the perfect place for inexperienced paddlers to learn, but if you are new to the sport, you should at least have someone show you some basic paddling strokes and impress upon you how best to enter and exit your particular boat. New paddlers should consider staying close to shore until they are comfortable with their paddling skills. Luckily, some of the most interesting aspects of the trips in this chapter are found close to shore.

- Turn around before the members of your party start feeling tired. Paddling a few miles after your arms are already spent can make for cranky travelers. All of the trips in this book start and end at the same location, so you can easily turn around at any time.

- Make sure everyone in your group is wearing a life jacket or personal flotation device (PFD). You are required by Maine law to have at least one PFD per person in your boat. We suggest that you actually wear your PFD while paddling. It is very easy to tip a canoe accidentally and, with Acadia's ponds reaching depths of 150 feet, it just makes sense to wear a PFD at all times. Children aged 10 and under are required by law to wear a Class I, II, or III PFD in the state of Maine.

- Pay close attention to the winds. Winds as gentle as 10 miles per hour can create some fairly large waves on all of the ponds on the island. Waves of 2 and 3 feet are not unusual on Eagle Lake, Long Pond, and Echo Lake. We even paddled in 1-foot waves on the fairly diminutive Jordan Pond. All of the ponds on the island run from north to south, making northerly or southerly winds even more problematic. Bring a windbreaker, as it can get cold in a canoe in the lightest of winds. Little Long Pond is probably your best bet on a windy day.

- Stay off the water if thunderstorms are nearby. Lightning is a serious danger to boaters. If you hear a thunderstorm approaching, get off the water immediately and seek shelter. For a current weather forecast, call the weather phone at local radio station WDEA: 207-667-8910.

- Bring the following supplies along with you to make the trip more comfortable. Why not, when you don't have to carry them on your back?
  - ✓ Water: Bring 1 or 2 quarts per person, depending on the weather and length of the trip.
  - ✓ Food: Even for a short paddle, it is a good idea to bring some high-energy snacks like nuts, dried fruit, or snack bars. Bring a lunch for longer trips.
  - ✓ Map and compass—and the ability to use them.
  - ✓ Extra clothing: rain gear, a wool sweater or fleece jacket, a wool or fleece hat.
  - ✓ Headlamp or flashlight, with spare batteries and lightbulb.
  - ✓ Sunscreen and hat: you will be at the mercy of the sun on a clear day.
  - ✓ First-aid kit.
  - ✓ Pocketknife.
  - ✓ Binoculars (for wildlife viewing).

In addition to the no-impact techniques described in this book's introduction, please keep the following things in mind while paddling:

- Give wildlife a wide berth. Lakes and ponds are much different from forests in that wildlife has less of an opportunity to hide from humans. The summer months see a lot of people in the water, and the ducks, herons, and loons waste a good deal of energy just swimming or flying away from curious boaters. If you spot wildlife, remain still and quiet and let the animals decide whether to approach you. Use binoculars if you want a closer view. In spring, steer well clear of loons nesting along the shore.
- Respect private property. Much of the land surrounding the waters of Acadia is private property. We have mentioned this fact in each of the trip descriptions, but take a map that shows the park boundaries. Do not land your boat on private property, and speak quietly when paddling near homes and cottages.
- Respect the purity of the water. Most of the ponds on Mount Desert Island are used for drinking water by the surrounding communities. If you need to relieve yourself, try to do so on land, at least 100 yards from the shoreline. Echo Lake is the only pond in the park where swimming is allowed.
- Sound carries a long way on the water, so try to keep your conversations quiet in order to not disturb other paddlers or nearby hikers.

You can thank the last ice age for your chance at quietwater paddling on Mount Desert Island. Ice sculpted the landscape into deep cold-water ponds that reflect the rounded masses of pink granite that give Acadia its mountainous allure. Glaciers plowed through rock, creating cliffs that reach down to the water's edge on Long Pond, Jordan Pond, and Echo Lake. They created the deep waters of Eagle Lake, which remain cold enough throughout the year to support such cold-water fish as trout and salmon, which in turn support ospreys and bald eagles. The ice also left shallow depressions like Seal Cove Pond and Little Long Pond, which harbor marshes filled with wading birds and waterfowl, painted turtles, and green frogs. Surrounded by enchanting scenery and abundant wildlife, you are sure to enjoy your time on the water!

TRIP 37
LITTLE LONG POND

Distance: 1.25 miles
Estimated Time: 1.0 hour
Map: AMC's Acadia National Park Discovery Map: F7

Take a short, easy paddle on one of Mount Desert Island's most picturesque ponds.

Directions

From Bar Harbor, drive south on Route 3 for 8.8 miles. Little Long Pond will be on your right. You can park on the wide gravel shoulder next to the pond. *GPS coordinates*: 44° 17.602′ N, 68° 15.316′ W.

Trip Description

Little Long Pond, with its gently sloping lawns and beautiful views of Penobscot Mountain, is an easy and quiet place to paddle that is suitable for the entire family. While the pond is only about 0.5 mile long, it still provides a surprising amount of solitude during early-morning paddles. Owned by the Rockefellers, the pond and the surrounding lawns are open to the public and seem to have been landscaped for leisure. The lawns are an ideal spot to have a picnic, take a nap, and listen to the sounds of Mount Desert Island. You can also enjoy an easy walk around the pond on a wide, grassy path.

The route for this paddle is very simple. Put in at the southern end of the pond, along Route 3. Paddle straight ahead for 0.5 mile to the north end of the pond and then return. Along the way, you will enjoy pink and white waterlilies and cattails hiding green frogs, mallards, and black ducks. The old boathouse on the eastern shore was built for John D. Rockefeller Jr. It is an impressive structure for such a small body of water. The marshlike northern end of the pond is home to an active beaver lodge. Beavers are nocturnal, but early in the morning and late in the afternoon you may see one or more swimming across the pond, carrying branches from a birch, maple, or willow tree. They store these branches underwater near their lodges and use them as food.

Beavers are not the only animals you might see here. Great blue herons wade near the shore, hunting for small fish, amphibians, and snakes. Belted kingfishers fly from tree to tree, making an occasional dive into the pond hoping to catch a fish. While on shore, watch and listen for the largest of New England woodpeckers, the pileated woodpecker. About the size of a crow, this black-and-white bird with a bright red crest on its head makes a loud *kuk, kuk, kuk, kuk, kuk* call. This woodpecker excavates large rectangular holes in trees as it searches for ants and termites to extract from the wood with its sticky tongue. Unlike the similar-looking but extinct ivory-billed woodpecker, the pileated woodpecker has adapted comfortably to second-growth forests near small towns and is now common in the woods of Maine.

Frogs and Turtles

While visiting the freshwater ponds, swamps, and streams in Acadia you may encounter frogs and turtles, from the diminutive spring peeper to the menacing snapping turtle. Seven species of frogs are known to live in Acadia. Five of those are relatively common: spring peeper, bullfrog, green frog, pickerel frog, and wood frog. The gray tree frog and leopard frog are less common. As many as six species of turtles live in the park, but only two, the snapping turtle and the eastern painted turtle, are common. While out there paddling or hiking near water, keep your eyes out for the following:

- Spring peepers are more likely to be heard than seen. Considered chorus frogs but also exhibiting characteristics of tree frogs, spring peepers fill the night air in spring with their loud chorus of frog song. They prefer small, often temporary bodies of water near trees. These tiny frogs are less than an inch long and are usually brown or gray with a dark "X" on their backs.
- Bullfrogs are the largest frogs in the United States, measuring 3.5 to 6.0 inches in length. They are either green or brown and gray with a green background. They can be found in lakes, ponds, bogs, and streams and have a voracious appetite, eating almost anything they can swallow, including small snakes.
- Green frogs are smaller than bullfrogs, measuring 2.25 to 3.5 inches in length. True to their name, they tend to be greenish brown; in rare cases, however, they may be blue. Green frogs tend to like shallower water than bullfrogs do, spending their time in brooks, small streams, and the edges of lakes and ponds.

- Pickerel frogs are 1.75 to 3.0 inches in length and have square spots arranged in two parallel rows down their backs. They often have bright yellow or orange coloring on their hind legs. Pickerels prefer the clear, cold waters of sphagnum bogs, rocky ravines, and meadow streams.
- Wood frogs are slightly smaller than pickerels but have an unmistakable "robber's mask," a dark patch around the eye. Wood frogs are generally brown, blending in well with leaf litter on the forest floor. They spend a lot of their time in moist woods, away from water.
- Snapping turtles reach lengths of 18.0 inches, weigh up to 50 pounds, and can live as long as 100 years. They are easily recognized by their large heads, beaklike mouths, long tails, and very rough brownish-black shell. Snappers are voracious omnivores, eating small invertebrates, fish, reptiles, small birds, mammals, and vegetation. They will live in any permanent body of freshwater and spend a good deal of their time partially submerged in mud and shallow water. Luckily for swimmers, they tend to pull in their heads when underwater, letting people step on them and pass by unknowingly. On land, they will bite if harassed.

Frogs have been found recently throughout the United States with severe physical deformities, most commonly having extra sets of legs. Scientists have discovered that one cause of these deformities is a parasitic flatworm. While it has yet to be proved, scientists believe that pollution may be an additional cause. Breathing through their moist skin, all amphibians may be especially susceptible to acid rain, airborne pollutants such as mercury, and endocrine-system-disturbing chemicals like dioxin and PCBs. Acadia's frogs have yet to show these deformities, but if you happen to discover one with more than four legs, you should report it to a park naturalist.

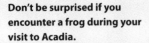
Don't be surprised if you encounter a frog during your visit to Acadia.

TRIP 38
ECHO LAKE

Distance: 1.5 miles
Estimated Time: 1.0 hour
Map: AMC's Acadia National Park Discovery Map: E5

This short paddle goes below towering cliffs and offers a chance to see peregrine falcons.

Directions

From Somesville, drive south on Route 102. At 2.7 miles from Pretty Marsh Road is a national-park sign on the right for Ikes Point. Turn right into the driveway, which leads to a parking area and the put-in. *GPS coordinates*: 44° 19.009′ N, 68° 20.082′ W.

Trip Description

Echo Lake is home to the Appalachian Mountain Club's Echo Lake Camp and Echo Lake Beach, the most popular place on the island to swim. At the southern end of the lake, Echo Lake Camp—with its comfortable tents, dining room, library, fireplace, and hot showers—is a great place to bring the family for the week. Next to it is sandy Echo Lake Beach, with warm waters, lifeguards, and changing rooms. Echo Lake itself runs up against Beech Cliff and Canada Cliff, which both rise 150 feet straight up from the water's edge. The north end of the lake is fairly populated with cottages, and Route 102 runs next to the eastern shore for about 0.5 mile. For these reasons, this trip explores the southern end of the lake.

Put your boat in at Ikes Landing, on the west side of Route 102. There is plenty of parking in this lot, as Echo Lake is popular with both paddlers and motorboats. From the put-in, paddle your boat straight across the lake and then turn left to follow the shore toward the cliffs of Beech Mountain. Keep the shoreline on your right for the remainder of this trip. The cliffs of Beech Mountain are home to one of the three nesting pairs of peregrine falcons in the park. Point your binoculars skyward to search for these most efficient and speedy fliers. While they may hunt occasionally for ducks or other birds on Echo Lake, the falcons often head out to the shorelines around Mount

Desert Island to hunt for seabirds. Common loons also frequent Echo Lake. While not endangered, these birds have been declining in number for most of this century. It is against the law in the state of Maine to harass loons, so please do not approach them. Hearing their haunting call is just as exciting as seeing them up close.

Like most of the other ponds and lakes on the island, Echo Lake was created by glaciers during the last ice age. Carving out the lake to a depth of 65 feet, the ice also created the cliffs of Beech Mountain. Water ahead of the glacier filled cracks in the rock and froze. Freezing and thawing continued, weakening the granite until the glacier moved over the mountain and plucked boulders off the mountainside, creating the cliffs. The glacier also deposited the sand at the southern end of Echo Lake, creating Echo Lake Beach. The beach is popular with families, so pay attention for stray swimmers.

After paddling past the beach and the AMC camp, follow the shoreline north. As you paddle back toward the put-in, you will encounter about 0.5 mile of undeveloped national-park shoreline, where you can pull over for a private lunch, a swim, or a quiet moment to yourself.

Echo Lake Camp

At the south end of Echo Lake, the Appalachian Mountain Club maintains Echo Lake Camp, a comfortable summer campground for families wishing to avoid the hustle and bustle of Bar Harbor. Accommodations are tents with board floors, beds, mattresses, pillows, and bedding. There is a shared bathhouse with hot showers as well as a library, recreation hall, dining room, and kitchen where your hosts will cook up your family-style meals. With access to Echo Lake outside your tent door, the camp provides rowboats, canoes, kayaks, and sailboats. Once a week the camp hosts a lobster picnic and clambake, and twice a week you have the opportunity to participate in trail maintenance.

Echo Lake Camp is usually open July 4 weekend through Labor Day. A one-week Saturday-to-Saturday stay is required. The camp is not appropriate for children under 4, and pets are not allowed. Despite these restrictions, tent space fills up quickly, so make reservations before April. For current rates and reservation information, visit the Echo Lake Camp website at www.amcecholakecamp.org.

TRIP 39
JORDAN POND

Distance: 2.5 miles
Estimated Time: 2.0 hours
Map: AMC's Acadia National Park Discovery Map: E7

Take an easy paddle on one of the most scenic ponds in Maine.

Directions
From the Acadia National Park Visitor Center, drive south on the Park Loop Road for 7.3 miles. Be sure to continue straight at the intersections marked Sand Beach and Cadillac Mountain. The Jordan Pond parking area will be on your right. *GPS coordinates*: 44° 19.332′ N, 68° 15.121′ W.

Trip Description
Jordan Pond has been a popular destination for visitors to Mount Desert Island ever since the first tourists started making their way to the island in the 1850s. One reason for this popularity is undoubtedly the Jordan Pond House, which has been serving afternoon tea at the south end of the pond since the 1870s. Of course, the incredible beauty of the area is just as big a draw. Jordan Pond, at 150 feet deep, is the deepest of Acadia's ponds and lakes, scraped out by the same glacier that gave the Bubbles their rounded appearance at the north end of the pond. The western side of the pond sits directly below Jordan Cliffs, a steep wall of granite on the east face of Penobscot Mountain. The long, sloping south ridge of Pemetic Mountain looms to the east. The pond is only about a mile long, making paddling trips here relatively short in duration. Of course that leaves plenty of time for tea and popovers at the Jordan Pond House.

The put-in for Jordan Pond is not at the restaurant but next to the Jordan Pond hiker parking area (located just to the north of the Jordan Pond House on the Park Loop Road). As you put in your boat on the eastern shore of the pond, you will be facing Penobscot Mountain and Jordan Cliffs. Blueberry bushes turn a fire-engine red in the fall on the side of Jordan Cliffs, which are home to one of Acadia's nesting pairs of peregrine falcons. As you paddle into the pond and turn to the right, you will be looking at one of the

**Look for loons on a paddle
around Jordan Pond.**

classic views in Acadia—Jordan Pond and the Bubbles. The Bubbles are a pair of rounded pink-granite peaks that are certainly bubble-like in shape. They are not particularly tall, reaching only 768 feet and 872 feet, but they add a distinctive and beautiful look to the pond's horizon. Like most of the features on Mount Desert Island, the Bubbles were shaped by glaciers during the last ice age, their pink-granite composition being stronger than the surrounding rock, which was scraped away and deposited farther south.

Jordan Pond is home to both common loons and common mergansers in the summer. Female mergansers have rust-colored heads, gray backs, red bills and red feet, while the males have white bodies, black backs, and greenish black heads. Mergansers nest around Jordan Pond, either in tree cavities or on the ground. Unlike loons, which share parenting responsibilities, male mergansers abandon the females while they are incubating the eggs.

Merganser chicks usually hatch by the Fourth of July, and those born in tree nests have to jump from the nesting cavity to the ground on their way to the pond. The female mergansers occasionally bring the fuzzy, cue-ball-colored chicks near the Jordan Pond Trail, which follows the shore for most of the pond.

As you paddle toward the northern end of the pond, the cliffs of South Bubble loom closer. The forest beneath the cliffs is a northern hardwood forest, filled with maples, birch, and beech that turn the mountainside a spectacular red, yellow, and orange in the fall. At the northern end of the pond is a small stream that is not navigable by canoe or kayak. The footbridge over the stream is for the Jordan Pond Path. If you feel like taking a short hike up South Bubble for an elevated view of Jordan Pond, park your boat here. About 50 yards to the right of the footbridge is the Bubbles Divide Trail, which leads 0.5 mile to the summit, a worthwhile side trip.

During the return trip the Jordan Pond House will be directly in front of you, while the hulking mass of Pemetic Mountain will be on your left.

TRIP 40
LONG POND—SOUTH END

Distance: 3.0 miles round-trip
Estimated Time: 2.0 hours
Map: AMC's Acadia National Park Discovery Map: F4, E4

This paddle goes beneath the steep cliffs of Beech and Mansell Mountains on the quiet end of Long Pond.

Directions
From the center of Southwest Harbor, go west on Seal Cove Road. Take the first paved road on the right, Long Pond Road. Follow Long Pond Road through a residential area until it ends at the south end of Long Pond. There is a small parking area to the right of the pumping station. *GPS coordinates*: 44° 18.009′ N, 68° 21.032′ W.

Trip Description
The southern end of Long Pond is nestled between the dramatic cliffs of Beech and Mansell mountains, granite walls hundreds of feet tall. This end of the pond is narrow (about 1,000 feet across) and quiet, as motorboats tend to stay at the larger, northern end of the pond. We found that we could not help but stop paddling from time to time to stare up at the mesmerizing cliffs and cedar-lined shoreline. At 4.0 miles long, this is the largest body of freshwater in the park and is home to loons, mergansers, and other waterfowl. Peregrine falcons nest on Beech Mountain and soar in the skies above the pond. Also known as Great Pond, Long Pond's shoreline has long been the home of summer cottages, much like the rest of Mount Desert Island, although here the homes are politely inconspicuous, often completely hidden from view.

The length of the pond and its north-south orientation can create some large waves at the southern end when the wind is out of the north. During north-wind conditions, the northern end of the pond is a better bet for paddlers (see Trip 44). The pond is used as a water source for the town of Southwest Harbor, so take extra care not to pollute. Swimming is not allowed in any part of the pond. Also, try to arrive early because parking is limited to

Fog rises off Long Pond during an early morning paddle.

about six or seven cars, and hikers climbing Mansell and Beech mountains also park here.

From the put-in at the end of Long Pond Road, begin your paddle by following the shoreline on your right. After passing a couple of private homes, you will be surrounded by Acadia National Park shoreline. The pond has a wild feeling here, as 30-foot-high granite cliffs drop straight into the water. These cliffs are the western shoulder of Beech Mountain, one of the more popular sites for hiking on the western side of Mount Desert Island (see Trip 8). Eventually the cliffs recede and the forest comes down to the water's edge, with northern white cedars forming an impenetrable wall of green, their lower branches reaching out over the water to collect as much sunlight as possible. With cliffs and cedars everywhere, it is difficult to land a boat, even a small kayak, on this side of the pond.

As the terrain starts to flatten out, you will soon see a small cottage on the right bank. At this point, paddle over to the western shore of the pond for the trip back. The western side of the pond is also thick with cedars, but there are a few places to land a boat and take a break. If you hear voices, they probably belong to hikers on the Long Pond Trail, which follows the shoreline from here back to the parking area. Near dusk and dawn, the shoreline of Long Pond is a good place to look for mink as they hunt for fish, frogs, snakes, and mice. About the size of ferrets, mink can swim underwater up to 100 feet and will occasionally pop their heads up out of the water near a canoe or kayak, providing a pleasant surprise for the boat's occupants.

As you paddle south along the western shore of the pond, the 700-foot-high cliffs of Mansell Mountain will dominate your field of vision. At its narrowest point, the pond is only 700 feet across, with cliffs on both sides. You can almost see the glacier squeezing through the huge granite mounds on either side of the pond, scraping clean the sides of the mountain and pushing bits of rock and dirt ahead into a terminal moraine, which is now the hill behind the parking area. You can thank the last ice age for providing you with the peaceful paddling and dramatic scenery. The cliffs end just prior to your return to the put-in.

Airborne Enemies: Bald Eagles and Ospreys

Bald eagles and ospreys are both conspicuous, but uncommon, residents of Acadia and the islands surrounding Mount Desert Island. While these large birds of prey are distinctly dissimilar in appearance, they share many common habits and habitats. These similarities often put them in proximity to each other and occasionally result in battles for prey and territory. Ospreys catch fish more than 50 percent of the time they try, and they rarely eat anything else. In contrast, bald eagles are less successful hunters and will feast on carrion every chance they get. They also follow and harass ospreys in an attempt to steal their catch. It was these habits that led Ben Franklin to observe, "I wish the bald eagle had not been chosen as the representative of our country. He is a bird of bad moral character; he does not get his living honestly. Besides he is a rank coward."

Although Ben Franklin may have disliked the habits of these huge birds, bald eagles are truly magnificent animals, soaring gracefully on thermals with an 8-foot wingspan and possessing beautiful and regal coloring. Adults mate for life and share in the parenting duties, raising broods of two chicks in huge nests that are used year after year. They nest in the tallest trees they can find—in Maine usually a white pine or spruce—near any large body of water that is sufficiently free of human disturbance. Older nests can weigh as much as a ton and will usually end up killing the trees in which they are situated. The birds do not grow their distinctive white tail and head feathers until they are 4 or 5 years old. Until that time, they are either mottled in appearance or have a completely brown coloring, resembling golden eagles. In Acadia, they nest on the smaller islands around Mount Desert Island but can be seen almost anywhere along the coast soaring high on thermals or perching on a tall tree where they can get a good view of their surroundings. In winter, some eagles will migrate south to congregate with other birds in areas of open water and concentrated food; others, however, remain in the park year-round.

Like bald eagles, the smaller ospreys prefer to nest in tall trees near water in relatively wild areas. They are somewhat more adaptable than eagles, often nesting closer to civilization on telephone poles or other tall artificial structures that give them an open view of the landscape. They are also more likely to nest next to small ponds that are rich in fish. Ospreys mate for life and, as with eagles, both parents raise the young. It is common to find eagles and ospreys nesting in sight of each other, which results in constant aerial battles. While the birds seldom hurt each other, ospreys will harass and dive at eagles flying in their vicinity. Groups of ravens, peregrine falcons, and other birds of prey will also harass eagles in order to get them to leave an area. These displays are quite exciting to watch and usually end with the eagle deciding to catch a thermal and fly to more peaceful surroundings.

Bald eagle populations declined consistently from the time Europeans arrived in North America until the 1940s as a result of persecution by hunters, fishermen, and farmers. Ospreys, on the other hand, managed to escape some of this persecution because farmers believed their presence kept away smaller falcons, such as merlins and kestrels, which preyed on domestic fowl. After World War II, both birds met considerable peril due to the widespread use of the pesticide DDT and other pollutants. These chemicals do not kill the birds, but they are stored in the birds' fatty tissues and eventually reach a level that creates reproductive problems. Eggs laid by birds with high concentrations of DDT had thin shells that often ended up being crushed during incubation. Since DDT was banned, the birds' reproductive success has improved in most of the country, although Maine bald eagles are still losing an inordinate number of chicks. It is speculated that this is due to the high amounts of chlorinated pollutants entering Maine watersheds as a result of the state's high concentration of paper-making facilities. Despite these problems, around 150 nesting pairs of bald eagles are now in Maine, and ospreys are relatively common in the state. The greatest threat to both birds is currently habitat loss.

It is possible to see bald eagles and ospreys in Acadia near the coast or one of the bigger lakes. Your best chance at seeing them is by getting out on the water, whether in a sea kayak or on one of the national-park nature cruises that leave from Bar Harbor. If you are kayaking, be aware that the Park Service prohibits the landing of any boat on an island with an active bald eagle, osprey, or seabird nest. (Check at the visitor center beforehand for a list of islands with active nest sites.) Also, whether you are boating or hiking, you should not approach within 0.25 mile of a nest. These birds are very wary of people and will abandon a nest if disturbed often.

Bald eagles nest on many of the smaller islands surrounding Mount Desert Island.

TRIP 41
SEAL COVE POND

Distance: 4.5 miles
Estimated Time: 2.5 hours
Map: AMC's Acadia National Park Discovery Map: F3

This paddle on the westernmost pond on Mount Desert Island offers the possibility of seeing waterfowl and bald eagles.

Directions
From Route 102 in Southwest Harbor, drive east on Seal Cove Road. After 2.1 miles, turn right on a dirt Park Service road. After 0.5 mile there is be a sign for Seal Cove Pond. Follow this sign to the left. You are now on Western Mountain Road. In 0.8 mile, follow the right fork in the road toward Seal Cove Pond. The road ends at the put-in in another 0.7 mile. *GPS coordinates*: 44° 17.513′ N, 68° 23.536′ W.

Trip Description
Like other ponds in Acadia, Seal Cove Pond is long and narrow and runs in a north-south direction. Geologically, however, it is different from most of the other large ponds in the park, as it is shallow and marshy. It also lacks the dramatic scenery of Echo Lake or Long Pond, as there are no cliffs to speak of and Route 102 runs along the western edge of the pond. However, there are plenty of reasons to paddle this pond. Its shallow waters provide a diverse habitat for waterfowl, making this an excellent spot to watch for ducks and wading birds. The eastern shore of the pond is densely forested and has some large spruce trees that provide good perches for bald eagles. There are also fewer boats here than in the rest of the park.

The drive into the pond on the narrow dirt road known as Western Mountain Road is perhaps the most remote drive on the island. This is a good place to watch for moose. The parking area at the end of the road is fairly small, so try to arrive early. From the put-in at the southeastern end of the pond, it is about 1.75 miles to the north end. Before heading north, however, take some time to explore the marshy southern end of the pond. Cattails, fragrant waterlilies, and pickerelweed creep in from the shoreline, providing hiding places for ducks, herons, and egrets. The small stream in the cove directly across from the put-in drains Seal Cove Pond into Seal Cove, only 0.5 mile away. Seal Cove, a picturesque little harbor filled with sailboats and lobster boats, is worth a visit. However, you will have to drive there, as the stream from Seal Cove Pond is not navigable.

Once you have explored the southern end of the pond, paddle past the put-in and toward the north end of the pond. Since the western shore is filled with houses, summer cottages, lawns, and driveways, the eastern shore is a much more interesting paddle. The eastern shore is also part of the national park, which makes it permissible to land your boat to take a break. The western shore and the island in the middle of the pond are private property. As you head north, the shoreline is less marshy than the southern end of the pond and takes on a rocky, forested character. The bird life is still interesting, as loons and cormorants hunt fish in the deeper waters of the pond and bald eagles sit patiently in the trees waiting for a fishing opportunity. The forest is thick with cedar, fir, spruce, birch, and maple. It is as wild as it looks, as no roads or trails trespass between the pond and the summit of Bernard Mountain, more than a mile to the east.

Good views of Bernard Mountain can be had from the northwestern end of the pond. From here you can see a lush and uninterrupted forest that is home to moose and black bear, ruffed grouse, and black-backed woodpeckers. While black-backed woodpeckers are common winter visitors, a few also live year-round and breed on Mount Desert Island. Although quite tame, they are rarely seen, but the thick evergreen forest to the east of Seal Cove Pond is the type of habitat they prefer. Both sexes can be identified by their black backs, wings, and tails, and the fact that they have only three toes. Males have yellow caps. These birds feed by peeling the bark off dead and dying spruce trees and eating the underlying beetles and other insects. The boggy cedar-and-spruce woods at the northeast end of the pond are a good place to sit quietly and watch for these birds.

TRIP 42
NORTHEAST CREEK

Distance: 5.0 miles round-trip
Estimated Time: 2.5 hours
Map: AMC's Acadia National Park Discovery Map: B5

This quiet paddle on a narrow creek travels through extensive wetlands and prime wildlife habitat.

Directions
From the Thompson Island Information Center, follow Route 3 east for 2.5 miles to the bridge over Northeast Creek. A small dirt parking area is immediately after the bridge on the right. Neither the creek nor the parking area is marked by signs. *GPS coordinates*: 44° 25.490′ N, 68° 19.625′ W.

Trip Description
This is the only paddling trip in this chapter that explores a moving body of water. Fortunately the current is negligible, as the creek drops a mere 5 feet from one end to the other. The meandering nature of Northeast Creek makes paddling here a completely different experience than canoeing one of Mount Desert Island's big glacial lakes or plying the waters of the wavy Atlantic in a sea kayak. Much of this trip is spent in the narrow channel of an extensive boggy area filled with wildlife and views of Acadia's mountains. Due to the open nature of the terrain for most of this paddle, windy days create some uncomfortable paddling here, but since this is an out-and-back trip, you can turn around and return to the put-in at any time.

To start this trip, park at the dirt parking area on the inland side of Route 3, just east of the bridge that crosses the creek. A path descends the short hill leading to the put-in. The put-in area, as well as all of the land bordering the creek, is private property. Please tread lightly at the put-in area, and plan your trip so that you do not need to land your boat once you are beyond the put-in. This creek has a small tidal influence, mostly confined to the portion of the creek on the Mount Desert Narrows side of the bridge.

Begin paddling on the inland side of the bridge and head toward the mountains. As you paddle south and east, you quickly leave the road and

Paddling along Northeast Creek provides a perfect opportunity for wildlife watching.

civilization behind. You are surrounded by private property, but you will only see one house and a few grassy lawns throughout your trip. The paddle makes its way through a mixed forest of maple, aspen, white pine, and oak. Keep your eyes open for white-tailed deer, black ducks, mallard ducks, and other waterfowl. You should watch also for the occasional large rock hidden just under the waterline for the first 0.75 mile.

After the creek turns sharply to the right, you leave the rocks and the woods behind. You have now entered Fresh Meadow, a boggy wetland of tall cattails, grasses and sedges. Here the vistas open up to include Cadillac and Sargent Mountains about 6 miles away to the south. Summer finds great blue herons hunting amid the cattails at the edge of the creek. The chatter of belted kingfishers can be heard on most days as they busily fly from perch to perch looking for fish. Lincoln's sparrows and swamp sparrows share the brushy surroundings with red-winged blackbirds and the occasional sedge wren.

About a mile from the put-in, Aunt Betsey's Brook enters on the right. In most conditions, Aunt Betsey's Brook is shallow and mucky and difficult to explore. This trip stays on Northeast Creek, which turns left and heads north for a short distance before resuming an easterly course. For the next mile, Northeast Creek continues to meander through Fresh Meadow and its marshy expanse. Quiet paddling in this remote section of the creek can pay off with a muskrat, beaver, or river otter sighting. Beaver and muskrats are vegetarians, eating young trees, shrubs, and other plants, while river otters feed on fish, frogs, salamanders, and snakes. Beaver and muskrats often swim at the surface of the water with their tails remaining underwater to be used as rudders. Otters, on the other hand, are more likely to be seen poking their heads out of the water in an attempt to get a better view of their surroundings.

After the creek flows past some higher land on the right bank, it turns right and heads due south for the final 0.5 mile of this trip. The creek narrows and becomes enclosed in an ever-increasing crop of cattails as it again nears civilization and the houses along Crooked Road. While you can turn around at any point on this trip, the end effectively becomes the spot where you can no longer navigate the cattails.

TRIP 43
EAGLE LAKE

Distance: 4.0 miles
Estimated Time: 3.0 hours
Map: AMC's Acadia National Park Discovery Map: D7

This moderate paddle on a scenic lake provides mountain views and goes past wild shorelines.

Directions
From the intersection of Routes 3 and 233 in Bar Harbor, take Route 233 west toward Cadillac Mountain. The parking area for Eagle Lake is at 2.1 miles on the left. *GPS coordinates*: 44° 22.648′ N, 68° 15.141′ W.

Trip Description
Eagle Lake is the largest lake on the eastern side of Mount Desert Island and is a popular spot due to its proximity to Bar Harbor. All of Eagle Lake is part of Acadia National Park, giving it a wild shoreline with none of the cottages and camps you find on most of the other lakes on the island. Its views of Cadillac and Pemetic mountains, as well as the Bubbles, are breathtaking. It is 4.0 miles around the edge of the lake, making it possible to spend a leisurely day taking in the scenery and watching for loons, mergansers, and ospreys. Carriage roads circle the lake and connect with hiking trails, creating the opportunity to spend the whole day in the area, paddling, hiking, and biking. Swimming is prohibited, however, since the lake is the water supply for Bar Harbor.

A paddling trip on Eagle Lake begins at the north end of the lake, at the Eagle Lake parking area on the south side of Route 233. Motorboats are allowed on the lake, but there is a 10-horsepower limit on motors. If you see motorized vehicles on the lake, they will most likely be slow-moving boats of fishermen dropping their lines into the 110-foot-deep water trying to hook the salmon and trout that thrive in the lake's cold water. These fish make up the diet of the common mergansers and common loons that nest around the lake. The fish are also what draw ospreys to the wild southern end of the lake. Ospreys are impressive fishermen, diving into the water talons first and emerging with a fish more than 50 percent of the time. It is no wonder bald eagles often spend their time harassing ospreys in an attempt to get them to drop their prey.

Paddling Eagle Lake can take as much or as little time as you want. The shoreline is wooded and rocky, with just a few coves and inlets to explore. Either follow the shoreline for a 4.0-mile paddle or paddle straight across to the southern end of the lake, 1.75 miles away. As on all of the lakes on Mount Desert Island, a wind out of the north can create some large waves at the southern end of the pond. On a windy day, keep in mind the fact that you will have to paddle against these waves on the return trip. At the southern end of the pond, directly opposite the put-in, is a shallow gravel area, which makes it easy to land your boat and take a break on shore. The Eagle Lake Trail can be found here. Hiking the trail to the right makes for a flat 0.5-mile walk along the southwestern shore of the lake. Following the trail to your left can connect you to the Jordan Pond Carry, which is a 1.1-mile footpath through northern hardwood forest that ends at the northeastern shore of Jordan Pond. These trails also connect with the extensive system of gravel carriage roads. For biking around Eagle Lake, see Trip 29. For details on the short hike up Conners Nubble on the west side of the lake, see Trip 1.

Whether you follow the shoreline back or paddle down the middle of the lake, see if your hearing is as keen as that of painter Thomas Cole, who first visited Eagle Lake in 1844. According to *Mount Desert Island and Acadia National Park: An Informal History*, by Sargent Collier, Cole named the lake for the bald eagles that soared over his easel, and he once remarked that at Eagle Lake "one may fancy himself in the forests of the Alleghenies, but for the dull roar of the ocean breaking the stillness." The ocean is 3 miles away.

Granite Domes and Glacial Lakes

The story of what is now Acadia National Park began about 500 million years ago at the bottom of an ancient sea called the Iapetus Ocean. In this prehistoric ocean, silt and volcanic ash accumulated at the rate of an inch every 100 years until the material was thousands of feet deep. This accumulated matter solidified into shales and tuffs before the heat and pressure associated with being deep within the Earth metamorphosed the rock into a dark gray or green schist composed of quartz, feldspar, and chlorite. This rock, now called Ellsworth schist, forms an incomplete ring around Mount Desert Island. It can be seen along the shore near the Thompson Island Picnic Area.

Around 400 million years ago, another round of silt accumulation formed a layer of sedimentary rock composed of sandstone and shale. Known as the Bar Harbor Formation, this rock is black to rusty brown and can be seen from the town pier in Bar Harbor, as well as around the Porcupine Islands and in Northeast Harbor. At about the same time, the Cranberry Island Series of sedimentary rock formed around the Cranberry Isles. This rock is lighter in color, with embedded rock fragments, and was formed by the sedimentation of volcanic ash.

These sedimentary and metamorphic bedrocks were an easily eroded covering that now makes up just a small part of the island. Between 380 million and 420 million years ago, the bulk of what is now Mount Desert Island literally bubbled up from deep within the Earth. At this time, North America was colliding with what is known as the Avalonian plate. This collision, called the Acadian Orogeny, created the mountains of Acadia and caused great movements of magma (molten rock) below the Earth's crust. Under Mount Desert Island, molten magma moved upward through the Earth's crust, consuming and altering the existing layers of bedrock. At one point a huge balloon of magma, 8 or more miles in diameter, worked its way upward. This magma eventually cooled into what is now known as Cadillac granite, the rock that makes up much of the island and all of the mountains. Its characteristic pink shading is due to a mineral called feldspar. Other minerals that are easily visible upon inspection of the granite are quartz, hornblende, and biotite.

As North America moved away from Europe and Africa, fissures occasionally formed in the crust. Molten black diabase rose from the Earth's mantle to fill these fissures. These diabase dikes can be seen in many places around Acadia. They are on mountain summits, such as Pemetic Mountain, as well as on the shoreline. The Schoodic Peninsula and Isle au Haut have some excellent examples.

While plate tectonics following millions of years of sedimentation are responsible for building the mountains and bedrock of Acadia National Park, it is the more recent phenomenon of glaciation that has shaped the park into its current form. Over the last 2 to 3 million years, New England has experienced 20 to 30 glacial cycles, each lasting about 100,000 years. Glacial periods take up about 80,000 years of that time, while interglacial periods last 15,000 to 20,000 years. During these glacial cycles, thick layers of ice up to a mile deep move over the landscape, breaking the weaker rocks and grinding them into sand and gravel. The dominant Cadillac granite in Acadia withstood this glacial grinding better than the weaker sedimentary and metamorphic rocks on Mount Desert Island. While the glaciers did not obliterate the granite, they were powerful enough to wear down Acadia's granite-topped mountains into the rounded shapes you see today.

The last ice age was named after the Wisconsin Glacier, which reached as far south as Long Island about 18,000 years ago. At this time, the ice had to be at least a mile thick, as it covered the entire 5,267 vertical feet of Katahdin in northern Maine. The ice was not stationary; it flowed toward the ocean as all water does, and it wore its way through rock, creating deep U-shaped valleys like the one between Dorr Mountain and Huguenot Head. Between Acadia and Norumbega mountains, the glacier dug so deep it created the only fjord in the eastern United States, Somes Sound. Most of the lakes and ponds on Mount Desert Island are also a result of glacial carving.

By 14,000 years ago, most of the ice had retreated from Mount Desert Island, leaving a treeless expanse of tundra surrounded by a constantly changing shoreline. As the glacial period ended, the ice melted, raising sea levels so that by 12,000 years ago, the shoreline of Mount Desert Island was much as it is now. Ice is heavy, however, and it had depressed the island by as much as 0.3 mile. With the ice gone, the land began to rebound. By 11,000 years ago, the land had rebounded faster than the sea was rising and Frenchman Bay and Blue Hill Bay were dry land. Ice continued to melt around the Earth's polar regions, and sea level finally rose to its current level about 8,000 years ago. By then, all the tree species now present in Acadia had colonized the island. Since that time, most of the shaping of Acadia's landscape has been done by pounding surf, wind and rain, and people.

TRIP 44
LONG POND—NORTH END

Distance: 7.5 miles round-trip
Estimated Time: 4.0 hours
Map: AMC's Acadia National Park Discovery Map: D4, E4

This long and popular paddle explores the wooded coves of Mount Desert Island's biggest lake.

Directions

The parking area for the Long Pond put-in is on Pretty Marsh Road, 1.5 miles west of Route 102 in Somesville. *GPS coordinates*: 44° 21.288′ N, 68° 21.794′ W.

Trip Description

If you do not have your own boat, this is the easiest place to paddle in Acadia, as the National Park Canoe Rental is just across the street from the put-in at the north end of Long Pond. (See Appendix D for a complete list of canoe outfitters.) With deep blue waters and scenic views of Beech, Bernard, and Mansell mountains, Long Pond is a beautiful place to paddle. You will not have the pond to yourself on a busy summer weekend, but there are plenty of quiet coves where you can find solitude and study the shoreline. This trip explores the northern end of the pond and its secluded coves, which are hidden by two peninsulas, Northern Neck and Southern Neck.

You begin the paddle at the boat launch on Pretty Marsh Road. The first 1.25 miles are a straight paddle up the narrow north end of the pond. The western mountains fill your views to the south, while the shoreline is lined by summer cottages. Boat traffic can get busy in this part of the pond, so stay near the shore and be prepared to ride the wakes of motorboats. The spit of land on your right is Northern Neck. As you come to the end of Northern Neck, the pond opens up to the right. At this point, Southern Neck is the narrow peninsula directly across from Northern Neck. Paddle your boat south toward Southern Neck. The shoreline of Southern Neck and all of the coves to the right of it are part of Acadia National Park.

This is the wildest part of Long Pond, with an undeveloped shoreline of white cedar, white pine, and balsam fir. Horsetail and fragrant waterlilies

A couple paddles on Long Pond toward Mansell Mountain.

add color to the pond in the shallows. Black ducks, mallards, and common mergansers are numerous throughout this area, and the forest is filled with the songs of thrushes and wood warblers. Twenty-three species of warblers and thrushes nest in Acadia, including the colorful yellow warbler and the ovenbird, with its unmistakable forest-filling song of *teacher, teacher, teacher, teacher, teacher.* In late fall, America's smallest duck, the bufflehead, arrives in small groups that entertain paddlers by popping up out of the water in all directions like black-and-white lobster buoys.

If you keep the shore on your left, eventually you will turn around and be heading north. As you enter the bay behind Northern Neck, the woods remain wild, though houses do begin to appear behind the trees. With a couple of islands and some marshy shoreline, this bay is worth exploring despite the summer cottages. From the westernmost part of the pond, you can even get a glimpse of Cadillac Mountain, 8 miles to the east. You can also look for small boggy areas filled with sphagnum moss and northern New England's most common carnivorous plants, sundews and pitcher plants. These plants trap insects and digest them with enzymes, feeding the plant with much-needed nutrients not available in the acidic soil of bogs.

By keeping to the shoreline on your left, you will emerge from the western side of Northern Neck and find yourself back in the main part of Long Pond. From here, the put-in is 1.25 miles to the left (north).

Loon or Cormorant?

While common loons and double-crested cormorants have very different markings, it is difficult to distinguish between the two in bright light because of their similar shapes. With a little practice, however, it is easy to tell the two birds apart by looking at their bills. A loon's bill is much thicker than a cormorant's, and loons tend to hold their bills level with the water. Cormorants strike a somewhat "snooty" pose, with their bills pointed slightly upward.

Common loons, with their haunting call, are among the most popular birds in North America. They are easily seen in the waters surrounding Mount Desert Island, particularly from early fall through spring. Loons that are not old enough to breed will often stay in the area year-round. In summer, mature loons nest on inland lakes and ponds, but during the rest of the year they feed in the ice-free waters of the Gulf of Maine. With their black heads, red eyes, black-and-white-striped neck, and black-and-white bodies, common loons are stunning birds. Occasionally red-throated loons, with their gray bodies and red throat patches, are also seen in the waters around Acadia.

Double-crested cormorants are very common in Acadia from spring through late fall. Except for their yellow bills and throat pouches, double-crested cormorants are black birds with an iridescent green or purple gloss. Like loons, cormorants are about the size of a goose and are excellent swimmers that are much more adept in the water than on the land. Cormorants lack the oils that other ducks and seabirds have to keep their feathers dry. Instead they perch on rocks, logs, and piers, and hold their wings up to dry. Great cormorants can also be seen in Acadia. They are larger than double-crested cormorants and have a white chin or throat patch.

Loons are present on both inland ponds and the open ocean in Acadia.

4

Sea-Kayaking the Waters of Mount Desert Island

ACADIA NATIONAL PARK IS AS MUCH ABOUT WATER as it is about mountains, with the cold waters of the Gulf of Maine creating rich food supplies for large numbers of seabirds and mammals. Sea kayaking in the bays and narrows around Mount Desert Island is like no other experience in the park, with dramatic scenery and wildlife sightings practically guaranteed. Taking a naturalist cruise or a whale watch is a great way to see Acadia from the water, but you get a much better look at the intricate details of the ocean ecosystem by sitting at the water level in a kayak. You also gain a lot more freedom to explore the myriad inlets and coves that make up the shoreline of Mount Desert Island and the other islands in Frenchman Bay, Blue Hill Bay, and Somes Sound. If you have never been in a sea kayak before, you can get a great introduction to the sport by taking a guided tour offered by one of the outfitters listed in Appendix D. (Taking a guided tour around the Porcupine Islands was our first experience in a sea kayak, and we have been hooked on ocean paddling ever since.) To get sufficient experience to paddle on your own, however, you should take a multiday sea-kayaking class.

Safety and Etiquette

Registered Maine Guides are excellent sources for kayaking information. The safety information in this chapter was compiled with the gracious help of Natalie Springel, former lead kayaking guide at Coastal Kayaking Tours, and Elizabeth Ehrenfeld, another longtime Registered Maine Guide. You can enjoy sea-kayaking in the waters around Mount Desert Island, but not without sufficient training and experience. At its warmest, the water temperature reaches the low 50s, and even at that temperature a submerged paddler can become hypothermic in minutes. The weather also can cause dangerous conditions, especially fog that can roll in off the ocean at any time, making strong navigation skills vital. Local outfitters will require you to prove your experience before renting you a kayak. In order to safely sea-kayak in Maine, you should have at least the following minimum level of experience:

- Previous paddling experience in a sea kayak.
- Knowledge of the basic paddle strokes: forward, reverse, sweep, skull, brace, draw.
- Knowledge of how to use a nautical chart and compass.
- Previous practice of self-rescues and two-person rescues, and knowledge of how to use a paddle float.

How do you get this experience? Some local outfitters in Bar Harbor and Camden, Maine, give multiday classes on sea-kayaking. Your local recreation department may offer introductory pool sessions in which you can practice self-rescues in a controlled environment. AMC and other outdoor clubs may offer kayaking workshops locally. Ask at the outdoors shops in your hometown if they know of any classes you can take locally. Sometimes the stores themselves have classes because they sell sea kayaks. Of course, you can always ask an experienced paddler you know if he or she is willing to teach you.

Before putting your boat in the water, you should always check the tide and weather forecasts. Tides are usually listed in local papers such as the *Bar Harbor Times*, the *Acadia Weekly*, and the National Park Service's *Beaver Log*. You can also buy official tide charts at local bookstores. Tides and weather forecasts can be heard on a National Oceanic and Atmospheric Administration (NOAA) weather radio. The NOAA weather forecasts are excellent for long-range forecasts, but for the best up-to-date Acadia weather information, call the weather phone for local radio station WDEA at 207-667-8910.

In addition to listening to the weather forecast, use your common sense and take a look at the conditions when you put your boat in the water. If you see whitecaps, it is probably too windy for a safe and pleasant paddle. Once the wind hits 10 knots, it can be exhausting to paddle for even an hour, causing you to constantly readjust your course in addition to fighting the wind and waves. Also, if it is foggy at your put-in, you should choose another trip. Besides causing navigational problems, fog can make you invisible to the many fishing and pleasure boats that travel through the area. Be aware of the weather forecast, as a sunny day in the Gulf of Maine can quickly turn into a foggy nightmare. What is convenient about kayaking around Mount Desert Island is that weather conditions, especially fog, can be very localized, and you can often drive to another part of the island and have a safe and sunny paddle. However, even in sunny conditions, it is advisable to keep your group in a tightly knit formation, as this makes you much more visible to boats. Even small ocean swells can make it hard for other boats to see you. As Elizabeth Ehrenfeld says, "Boaters on the Maine Coast call sea kayaks speed bumps." Lastly, you should never paddle alone.

Everyone in your group should have the following essential gear with them:

- Personal flotation device (PFD). Wear a PFD—that is, a life jacket—while sea-kayaking in Maine. If you end up in the water, a life jacket will allow you to save the precious energy you will need to stave off hypothermia. The few minutes of time a life jacket saves you while you try to get back into your boat can save your life. You should consider a PFD to be required equipment.
- Whistle, attached to the outside of your PFD.
- Spare paddle.
- Paddle float.
- Sprayskirt.
- Bilge pump.
- Lunch, snacks, and emergency food.
- Drinking water: Bring at least 1 gallon if you are out for the entire day.
- Sunglasses, sunscreen, and a hat.
- Appropriate clothing. Dress for the water temperature, not the air temperature. A wet or dry suit is highly recommended, but at the least wear synthetic materials and dress in layers. Neoprene or Gore-Tex gloves and booties are also good to have. Do not wear cotton. Even on an 80-degree day, a dunk in the 50-degree waters of the Gulf of Maine can cause hypothermia in minutes without the proper clothing.
- Dry bag to keep food and extra clothing dry.
- Binoculars for wildlife viewing.

You should also carry at least one set of each of the following for the entire group:

- Compass and charts.
- First-aid kit.
- Foghorn.
- Flare gun.
- VHF radio or cell phone, although cell phones do not work in all locations.

In addition to paying close attention to safety, kayakers in the waters around Mount Desert Island need to follow certain guidelines to avoid having a negative impact on the environment and local residents. First, it is important to respect private property and never land your boat near a house or on land marked No Trespassing. You should land your boat only in the national park or on other public lands, except for the few locations where it is acceptable to land on private property, which are listed in the individual trip descriptions in this chapter. You may want to discuss your trip with an outfitter or Park Service employee beforehand, to find out about possible changes in land status. Also, note that the Park Service prohibits the landing of a kayak on an island with an active eagle, osprey, or seabird nest.

Second, give wildlife a wide berth. Seals in particular are easily stressed by kayaks, possibly because kayaks are shaped like seals' main predator, killer whales. It is also possible that they have an inherited memory of when seals were hunted by men in kayaks. In any event, never approach seals in a kayak, particularly if they have hauled themselves out onto rocks, where they feel especially vulnerable. Try to stay at least 0.5 mile from basking seals. You should also enjoy eagle and osprey nests from a distance, trying to stay at least 0.25 mile away from an active nest. If any animal changes its behavior as you approach, you are too close.

Third, practice no-impact techniques both on and off the water. Pack out all of your trash, including toilet paper and solid human waste. Urinating below the high-tide line is the most effective way to ensure quick dispersal of urine. However, do not urinate in a tide pool, as this can have negative consequences on the delicate life there. Also, try to stay below the high-tide line at all times to minimize your impact on fragile island habitats. Please do not take rocks and shells home as souvenirs.

Finally, remember that fishermen are out there trying to make a living. Always let them have the right of way and try to stay out of their path. Do not go near lobster traps, and be as quick as possible while using local boat ramps. Theoretically, kayaks have the right of way when passing other boats. However, larger boats do not always see kayaks or are traveling too fast to change course quickly. Play it safe and move aside when possible.

This chapter highlights six possible trips that vary in length and difficulty. The islands in this part of Maine provide a great variety of scenery and wildlife habitat, and these trips explore many of them, from quiet, marshy coves to dramatic seaside cliffs and open ocean. The shorelines of Mount Desert Island and the surrounding smaller islands are a great place to study the intertidal zones of sea life present on rocky outcroppings. Students of geology will find the variety of rocks fascinating and will enjoy seeing evidence of volcanism, tectonics, and glaciation. Rocky ledges are interspersed with cobble and sand beaches, and in the shallows, low tide reveals mud flats that attract a variety of shorebirds and wading birds like sandpipers and great blue herons. Seals and porpoises frequent the spaces between islands, as do seabirds like loons, guillemots, and cormorants. Soaring overhead and nesting in island trees are ospreys and bald eagles, and watching it all are paddlers in their quiet kayaks.

TRIP 45
MOUNT DESERT NARROWS

Rating: Difficulty depends on weather conditions
Distance: 6.0 miles
Estimated Time: 3.0 hours
Map: AMC's Acadia National Park Discovery Map: B4, B5

This is a relatively sheltered paddle in shallow waters, with the chance to see seals, porpoises, and an eagle's nest.

Directions
From the Thompson Island Information Center, drive east on Route 3 for 4.0 miles, where you should turn left on Hadley Point Road. It is 0.6 mile to the end of the road, where there is plenty of parking. One problem here is that during full-moon high tides, this parking area can flood. *GPS coordinates*: 44° 26.608′ N, 68° 19.151′ W.

Trip Description
Weather and tide considerations: We recommend making this paddle during the hours around high tide. There are extensive mud flats near Thompson Island as well as in Thomas Bay and surrounding Thomas Island and the Twinnies. At low tide, these mud flats may be filled with feeding shorebirds, but they also drastically reduce the amount of paddling you can accomplish. The mud flats around Thompson Island make it quite difficult and unpleasant to land a boat there. Try to start your paddle at least 2 hours after low tide and plan to finish it at least 2 hours before low tide. The Acadia National Park Visitor Center can give you tide information. Occasionally a strong southwest wind can cause some unpleasant paddling conditions, but in general this is a good trip in windy conditions, as it is relatively sheltered. If you do not see whitecaps from Hadley Point, you should be all set. If you have strong navigational skills, this trip is a good choice in foggy weather, as there is not much boat traffic.

Mount Desert Narrows is the body of water that separates Mount Desert Island from the mainland. This paddle, which explores the narrows east of Thompson Island, is a good choice in strong winds. It also makes a great

Lucky paddlers may see a porpoise up close while paddling the Mount Desert Narrows.

sunset paddle. Wildlife such as harbor porpoises, great blue herons, and bald eagles can be found in this area of uninhabited islands, mud flats, and salt marshes. Beginning at Hadley Point, this trip follows the shoreline of Mount Desert Island past Northeast Creek to Thompson Island before circling back around Thomas Island and the Twinnies. Please note that Thompson Island and Hadley Point are the only landing spots on this trip. The remainder of the shoreline on Mount Desert Island is private property, as are the islands in the narrows.

From the put-in at Hadley Point, follow the shoreline to your left (west). The first mile or so of shoreline is wooded and rocky, with eelgrass becoming more prominent as you make your way toward Thomas Bay. Approximately 1.3 miles from Hadley Point, the Twinnies will appear on your right. These two islands, named for their similar size and shape, are uninhabited and provide an important nesting site for bald eagles. Please remember that it is illegal to disturb nesting eagles. On the return portion of this trip, you can paddle near the Twinnies and take a look at the nest from a safe distance. For now, continue to follow the shoreline of Mount Desert Island on your left. Marshes and mud flats dominate your surroundings as you enter Thomas Bay, with the outlet of Northeast Creek providing a rare look on Mount Desert

Island of an area where freshwater enters salt water. The marsh grasses and concentration of food in the form of mollusks, crustaceans, and small fish make this an area frequented by great blue herons, mallard and black ducks, and green-winged teals. To paddle up Northeast Creek, see Trip 39.

Continuing through Thomas Bay, you will run into a peninsula of land known as Israel Point. Paddle around Israel Point, keeping the shoreline on your left, and head toward Thompson Island, where you can see the bridge

Harbor Seals and Porpoises

While you need to take a whale-watching excursion to see dolphins and whales near Acadia, it is quite common to enjoy visits from harbor seals and harbor porpoises while kayaking the waters around Mount Desert Island. Of course, both seals and porpoises are mammals and need to breathe air, which means they have to show themselves at the surface every now and then. If you are lucky, they will do this near your boat. Never approach seals, especially when they are hauled out onto rocks or a beach, where they rest in relative safety. They are easily startled and waste precious energy swimming back and forth between the rocks and the water when disturbed by careless paddlers. Give them 0.5 mile of breathing room.

Seals are much more comfortable in the water than on land and may sometimes come near a kayak to check it out. However, whether you see seals in the water or not is very much up to them. The same can be said of harbor porpoises, which seem to go about their business with no regard to kayaks. If they need to swim near your boat to get where they are going, they will do so, but they will not hang around or display any curiosity whatsoever. Nonetheless, seeing the sleek black bodies and dorsal fins of a pod of porpoises within a few yards of your kayak is an exciting experience. Harbor seals appear in all of the waters around Acadia, including Somes Sound. Harbor porpoises are similarly distributed, although you are most likely to see them during a paddle in Mount Desert Narrows, in Bartlett Narrows, or in Frenchman Bay around the Porcupine Islands.

While kayaking, you will usually hear harbor porpoises before you see them. Their exhalation blow is a sharp, puffing sound that sounds almost like a sneeze and is probably responsible for the nickname "puffing pig." Usually in groups of two to five animals, harbor porpoises generally come up to breathe together, slowly arching their backs out of the water. While their undersides are white, you most likely will see only their black or dark gray backs. They are small for whales and porpoises, rarely exceeding 6 feet in length and weighing around 130 pounds. Harbor porpoises are found throughout the Northern Hemisphere in cold and subarctic coastal waters.

Like harbor porpoises, harbor seals are found throughout the Northern Hemisphere in cold coastal waters. They are year-round residents in the Gulf of Maine, where they feed on fish, crustaceans, and squid. Harbor seals have heads shaped much like a dog's, and they often poke their heads up out of the water to look around.

A young harbor seal rests on a Maine coast mudflat.

that connects Mount Desert Island with the rest of Maine. Thompson Island and about 0.5 mile of the surrounding shoreline on Mount Desert Island are part of Acadia National Park, and therefore it is acceptable to land your boat here to rest before heading into the deeper waters of Mount Desert Narrows. To start your return to Hadley Point, paddle past Israel Point toward the left side of Thomas Island, which is about 1.0 mile from Thompson Island. The Wabanaki apparently made use of Thomas Island, as there is evidence of a shell midden on the island. Shell middens are areas where American Indians discarded huge amounts of mussel and clam shells, as well as other refuse, over hundreds of years.

As you paddle around the northern (left) end of Thomas Island, you will enter the deeper waters of Mount Desert Narrows, where you are most likely to see harbor porpoises surfacing to breathe. Harbor porpoises and seals use the narrows as feeding grounds when the tides are highest. Traveling in pods of two to five animals, porpoises may come quite close to your kayak, as they feel no threat from the small boats. If you hear a porpoise blow, which sounds like a loud sneeze, stay still and soak in the magnificent sight of these sleek animals passing nearby. In addition to seals and porpoises, seabirds such as black guillemots, double-crested cormorants, and common loons are also found in the narrows.

As you pass Thomas Island, follow its shoreline to the right. At this point, the Twinnies come back into view. Using binoculars, look for a gray mass of branches—a bald eagle's nest—at the top of a large spruce. The birds often can be seen perching in the area, but please do not approach them or their nest too closely, as they are very wary of people and will abandon a nest site if disturbed often. Stay at least a 0.25 mile away from the nest site. To complete this wildlife-rich trip, paddle to the left of the more northerly of the Twinnies and then follow the shoreline of Mount Desert Island on your right for the final 1.2 miles back to Hadley Point.

TRIP 46
FRENCHMAN BAY AND THE PORCUPINE ISLANDS

Rating: Difficulty depends on weather conditions
Distance: 6.5 miles round-trip
Estimated Time: 3.0 hours
Map: AMC's Acadia National Park Discovery Map: C8, C9

This exciting paddle goes around the beautiful and wild Porcupine Islands.

Directions

From the intersection of Route 3 and West Street in Bar Harbor, drive east on West Street for about 0.3 mile. Turn left at the first street, which is Bridge Street. Drop your boat off on the Bar Harbor bar, and then park your car back on West Street. *GPS coordinates*: 44° 23.516′ N, 68° 12.592′ W.

Trip Description

Weather and tide considerations: Tide is a concern only at the put-in on the Bar Island bar. Do not expect to land your boat on the southern side of the bar during low tide because of extensive mud flats. This trip is not recommended during foggy conditions, due to heavy boat traffic in the area. Even during sunny weather, larger boats may have trouble seeing kayaks. This paddle has a fair amount of exposure to the open ocean and can be difficult in winds stronger than 10–15 knots from any direction. West winds in particular can make it slow going on the return leg of the trip. On windy or foggy days, consider paddling Trip 45 or Trip 49 instead.

Our first kayak trip in Acadia was a drizzly August ride through 5-foot swells around the Porcupine Islands in Frenchman Bay. Despite the wet weather and menacing seas, we were instantly hooked on the beauty of this place of 100-foot cliffs, seals, seabirds, and bald eagles. This trip passes near Bar Island and Sheep, Burnt, and Bald Porcupine, with a view of Long Porcupine thrown in for good measure. The mountains of Acadia provide the backdrop for some of the most scenic paddling on the Maine coast. This trip definitely should be undertaken only by experienced paddlers, as there are

A kayaker stands in Frenchman Bay while Sheep Porcupine rises in the background.

several open-water passages up to a mile long, fog can creep in at any time, and large swells can roll in from the Atlantic. If you lack experience with open-ocean paddling, consider joining a guided trip for a safe group exploration of the Porcupines.

Begin this trip at the put-in on the Bar Harbor bar, a gravel spit that connects Bar Harbor with Bar Island at low tide. You can drive a car on the bar at low tide or even hike across the bar to a short trail on the island. Take note that the bar does disappear underwater as the tide comes in, so park your vehicle back at the end of West Street. Start paddling on the left side of the bar and head for the eastern end of Bar Island. Paddle around the end of the island, turning right and following the northern shore. Daniel Rodick, whose fashionable Rodick House in Bar Harbor could accommodate more than 600 guests, bought Bar Island in the late 1800s. Eventually the island was sold to the Rockefeller family, who in turn donated it to Acadia National Park. Except for one year-round resident, Bar Island is now populated only by spruce and birch, herons and hawks.

Once you are on the north side of the island, the hustle and bustle of Bar Harbor disappear and you are immersed in the intricacies of the intertidal zones that are so apparent on Bar Island's rocky shore. Barnacles, periwinkles, and limpets share the rocks with seaweeds such as bladder wrack and Irish moss, while crabs, starfish, and sea urchins forage on and around the rocks. The intertidal shorelines around Mount Desert Island can be as exciting a habitat to explore as the high subalpine meadows of Cadillac or Sargent Mountains. You will notice that different plants and animals inhabit different layers of the intertidal zones depending on their requirements for light, water, and air.

When you reach the end of Bar Island, you face the first of three open-water crossings on this trip. Sheep Porcupine is straight ahead, approximately 0.3 mile away. Aim for the left side of the island. Sheep Porcupine is home to nesting bald eagles, so you will want to keep your eyes open for flashes of white among the dark green of the spruce trees that cover the island. Only adult eagles have the distinctive white heads and tails, but you are likely to see immatures in the area as well. Bald eagles that are less than 4 or 5 years old are brown with a varying amount of mottled white feathers. You will recognize them as eagles, though, as they are just as big as adults, with wingspans up to 8 feet. The Park Service has closed this island to foot traffic in order to give the eagles a better chance of successfully nesting. Stay at least 0.25 mile from the island.

During the crossing from Bar Island, you may also begin to see some of the other well-known wildlife that frequent Frenchman Bay, such as harbor seals and black guillemots. While not as popular as Atlantic puffins, which spend most of their time far off at sea, black guillemots are easily seen in Frenchman Bay and are just as fun to watch. Only about a foot long, these true seabirds are built like torpedoes, with their bright red feet trailing a black body with white wing patches. Also known as sea pigeons or pigeon guillemots, they are expert swimmers, feeding on small fish and crustaceans. Harbor seals seem more wary than guillemots, but you can occasionally look around and see them checking you out from behind. Other common animals in the bay are double-crested cormorants, common loons, harbor porpoises, gulls, and terns. Minke whales may also make an appearance in late summer.

Paddle around the north end of Sheep Porcupine, which was actually home to grazing sheep in the 1800s. The sheep are now gone and the forest has returned, as the island is now entirely a protected part of Acadia National Park. As you paddle around the northern end of the island, Burnt Porcupine comes into view. The crossing to Burnt Porcupine is about 0.5 mile in length, and it is fairly exposed to the seas coming in from the open Atlantic. A deep channel between the two islands is used extensively by boats, including the large catamaran known as the Cat, which travels between Bar Harbor and Halifax, Nova Scotia, at speeds up to 55 knots. Needless to say, steer clear of large vessels during this crossing, and if the fog is in, consider turning around and returning to Bar Harbor. Traveling in a compact group of kayaks can make you more visible to the larger boats and help reduce the possibility of an accident.

Burnt Porcupine is slightly larger than Sheep Porcupine, and its shoreline consists of a combination of cobble beaches, rocky shoreline, and high cliffs. Burnt Porcupine has been preserved by The Nature Conservancy, making it possible to enjoy the beauty of its thick spruce forest and dramatic coast from the seat of your kayak for years to come. Paddle around the north end of the island and you will eventually see a small island just off the western edge of Burnt Porcupine. This island is called Rum Key, and, though private, it is permissible to land on its cobble beach to take a break. Nonetheless, Rum Key is a fragile island environment, so try to remain on the rocks and below the high-tide line. From Rum Key you can see a receding set of islands to the southeast. The first two islands are Long Porcupine and Ironbound Island, the largest island in Frenchman Bay. The farthest island is not actually an island but the Schoodic Peninsula, the only portion of Acadia National Park on the mainland.

A longer day can be spent exploring Long Porcupine and Ironbound, but our trip heads back to Bar Harbor via Bald Porcupine. To the south of Rum Key, you will see Bald Porcupine across a mile of open ocean. Like the crossing between Sheep and Burnt Porcupine, this crossing can have heavy boat traffic as well as heavy seas, but it is also a good opportunity to paddle among seabirds and mammals.

Head for the east end of Bald Porcupine, which will be on your left. Like the rest of the Porcupine Islands, Bald Porcupine has a gently sloping northern end, with steep cliffs on its south side. This shape is a landscape feature created by glaciers known as roches moutannées, or whalebacks. The cliffs on the southern end of Bald Porcupine are impressive, rising 100 feet up out of the waters of Frenchman Bay. Stay well clear of the cliffs, especially if there are winds or swells out of the south, as rebounding surf can topple a kayak.

As you paddle around the southern end of Bald Porcupine, you eventually come to a breakwater that leads toward the shore in Bar Harbor. During most tides the breakwater is not passable, so paddle its length toward the shore. At the end of the breakwater you can continue to the shore and turn right, keeping Bar Harbor on your left as you get a good look at some of the largest houses in town. This part of town was spared during the 1947 fire, giving you a glimpse of the "cottage life" that existed before most of the large vacation homes were destroyed. As you follow the shoreline toward the harbor, you will need to maneuver around the sailboats, whale-watching boats, and lobster boats moored there. Once past the boats, you will be back at the Bar Island bar, with Bridge Street on your left.

Humpback Whales

In *Moby Dick*, Herman Melville wrote about the humpback whale, saying, "He is the most gamesome and light-hearted of all the whales, making more gay foam and whitewater than any other of them." Humpbacks are naturally curious about boats, sometimes sitting in the water within a few feet of a boat for several minutes, slapping and waving their flippers, swimming under the boat, and sticking their huge barnacle-laden heads out of the water in an apparent attempt to get a better look at the boat's occupants. Anyone who has seen one of these 25-ton behemoths breaching its entire body out of the water has definitely been impressed with its size and agility. For these reasons, humpbacks have become the darlings of the whale-watching industry, and Bar Harbor is a great place to take a whale-watching cruise. Several tour companies have two or more whale-watching trips a day during the summer, and most of them guarantee a sighting.

Humpbacks live in all of the world's oceans and tend to favor coastal waters or shallower shelf waters out at sea. They are huge animals, with adults reaching 46 to 50 feet in length and weighing as much as 30 tons. They weigh 2 tons at birth. Now, that is a big kid! Humpbacks generally migrate up to 5,000 miles between summer feeding grounds and winter breeding grounds. The animals that live in the Gulf of Maine during the summer generally swim to the Caribbean Sea in winter to breed and give birth. Like most migratory whales, humpbacks bulk up in the food-rich waters of their summer feeding grounds in order to go the rest of the year without eating. In winter, mother humpbacks will leave their yearling calves off the coast of Virginia, where they can continue to feed in relatively warm waters without making the long trip south. The young whales regroup with the mature whales during the spring migration.

Humpbacks belong to the rorqual family of whales, which also includes minke, fin, blue, sei, and Bryde's whales, all relatively large baleen whales. Minke and fin, or finback, whales are also commonly seen during whale-watching excursions in the Gulf of Maine. Baleen whales feed by filling their mouths with tons of water and then filtering out trapped fish or krill through their baleen, a substitute for teeth, which hangs down from the upper jaws of the whale in a comblike plate that includes stiff hairs to aid in trapping the smallest of prey. These huge animals rarely eat anything larger than shrimp.

Humpbacks are unique among rorqual whales in that they have a fairly rotund appearance, as opposed to the long, sleek appearance of the other members of this family. They also have very long flippers (up to 15 feet in length) with unique black and white markings that aid in the identification of individuals. Using tail and flipper markings, scientists are meticulously identifying individual North Atlantic humpbacks in an attempt to better understand their behavior, breeding success, and longevity. Naturalists on the local whale-watching boats are familiar with most of the whales by name and contribute a great deal of information to the body of knowledge being used to determine the overall health of the humpback population.

While you will not see a humpback from shore, if you take a whale-watching excursion you are likely to see one or more of the following behaviors:

- Breaching is perhaps the most exciting behavior to witness, as humpbacks propel their huge bulk out of the water. Humpbacks use their tails to shoot themselves out of the water sideways with their flippers outstretched. They then arch their backs, do a half-turn, and land on their backs in what looks like a huge explosion. Why they breach is not known for sure. It could be to stun prey or knock barnacles off their skin. It might also just be fun.

- Lobtailing is when a whale repeatedly slaps the water with its tail. The rest of the whale's body remains underwater in a "head-down" position.

- Fluking is when a whale lifts its tail high above its body as a prelude to making a deep dive. If you see humpbacks, you will most likely witness this behavior. After fluking, a whale may stay under water for as long as 45 minutes.

- Flipper slapping gives many whale watchers the impression that a whale is waving at them. Sometimes a humpback will lie at the surface of the water on its side and simply slap the water repeatedly with its huge flipper. Occasionally an individual will lie on its back and slap both flippers simultaneously.

- Spyhopping is what whales do when they just want to take a look around. While spyhopping, they slowly lift their heads straight out of the water until their eyes are above the water's surface. Spyhopping is a common behavior for whales that voluntarily approach a whale-watching boat.

TRIP 47
SUTTON AND BEAR ISLANDS

Rating: Difficulty depends on weather conditions
Distance: 6.0 miles round-trip
Estimated Time: 3.0 hours
Map: AMC's Acadia National Park Discovery Map: F7

This moderate paddle goes past a remote lighthouse and passes a sea arch providing a nice view of the mountains on Mount Desert Island.

Directions
From downtown Bar Harbor, follow Route 3 south for 8.1 miles. Seal Harbor will be on your left. A public parking area is on the right. *GPS coordinates*: 44° 17.775′ N, 68° 14.417′ W.

Trip Description
Weather and tide considerations: Tide is not an issue on this trip. With heavy boat traffic in the area, it is advisable not to paddle here in foggy weather. Strong winds (above 10 to 15 knots) from the east or west can cause problems, and winds out of the north can funnel through the mountains, making the return part of the trip difficult. Winds from the southwest are the most favorable.

This 6.0 -mile loop explores the shoreline of Mount Desert Island near Seal Harbor, as well as Sutton and Bear Islands, which are part of the group of islands known as the Cranberry Isles. A lighthouse is perched atop a cliff on the western side of Bear Island, while Sutton Island boasts a fascinating sea arch and sweeping views of the mountains on the eastern side of Mount Desert Island. Like most of the waters surrounding Acadia, this area is rich in wildlife, giving any paddler a good chance to see guillemots, loons, seals, ospreys, and bald eagles.

The put-in for this trip is at the sand beach in Seal Harbor. While you may have a long walk across the beach at low tide, the sand is firm and you do not have to worry about sinking up to your knees in muck. Seal Harbor is a picturesque spot, with sailboats filling the harbor enclosed by a gently curving shoreline populated by spruce and summer homes. The Cranberry Isles are

Paddling is a good way to explore the islands that are off Mount Desert Island.

directly across from the mouth of the harbor, inviting boaters of all types to escape the summer crowds of Mount Desert Island. Begin your trip by paddling toward the point of land on the southwest end of the harbor known as Crowninshield Point. The very large house near this point should make it apparent that the shoreline here is privately owned and landing your boat is discouraged. Stay well clear of red bell 6 in this area. In the right conditions, a large rock underwater here can cause a rogue wave to topple a kayak. After rounding Crowninshield Point, keep Mount Desert Island on your right and follow the shoreline for about 0.75 mile, at which point you will be in a protected cove known as Bracy Cove. Other than Seal Harbor, Bracy Cove is the only allowable landing spot on this trip. Directly across the road from Bracy Cove is Little Long Pond, a picturesque body of water described in Trip 37.

Continue along the shoreline, which alternates between cobble beaches and rocky coast. Some of the larger summer homes on the island are in Seal and Northeast Harbors, and this stretch of coastline boasts a few. To the southwest of Bracy Cove is Bear Island, the smallest of the Cranberry Isles. When opposite Bear Island, turn away from the coast and make the 1,200-foot crossing to the north end of the island. Like many of the islands in the area, Bear Island was used as sheep pasture for many years. Islands were popular for this purpose because the sheep were easy to keep track of without building fences. As you paddle around the western end of the island, you will see a white lighthouse sitting among tall spruce 100 feet above cliffs, caves, and rocky rubble. Bear Island Light was built in 1839 and rebuilt in 1889, and was attended until 1982, when its flashing beacon was deactivated and replaced with lighted buoys.

From the lighthouse and the west end of Bear Island, paddle due south for a little more than 0.5 mile to reach the west end of Sutton Island. While making this crossing, watch for black guillemots and double-crested cormorants. Also keep an eye out for both harbor seals and their rare cousins, gray seals. While harbor seals are much more common on the Maine coast, gray seals do frequent this area. Much bigger than harbor seals, gray seals can grow to be 10 feet long and 650 pounds, while harbor seals reach 5 feet and 250 pounds. A gray seal's uniform black or gray color contrasts with the spotted fur of a harbor seal. Gray seals can dive to almost 500 feet while feeding on fish and cuttlefish.

On the northwestern corner of Sutton Island is an amazing osprey nest built on a rock outcropping separated from the island by a thin stretch of water. The nest may be as old as 100 years, and the sticks it is made of are piled several feet high. Keep at least 0.25 mile from the nest, as the birds experience a lot of disturbance from boats in this area. If the adults are forced to leave the nest too often, the chicks may not survive. Nonetheless, it is a wonderful experience to sit in your kayak with binoculars and watch an adult osprey bring fish to its young and eager chicks. Instead of paddling around the western end of Sutton Island, turn left before reaching the osprey nest and follow the northern shore, keeping the island on your right. There is a cobble beach at the western end of the northern shore, but steep granite cliffs wall much of this side of the island. A sea arch can also be found here. The arch, created by eroding waves, is about 40 feet tall.

As you reach the eastern end of Sutton Island, Little Cranberry Island comes into view to the southeast. Great Cranberry Island is farther away to the southwest. Excellent views of Acadia's mountains can be found by looking north. Turn your boat to the north in order to return to Seal Harbor. Crowninshield Point at the entrance to Seal Harbor is about a mile due north of the eastern end of Sutton Island. This is a long crossing in an area with heavy boat traffic. If you are traveling in a group, stay close together so that you are easier for boats to spot and avoid, and try not to make this crossing in foggy conditions. As you reenter Seal Harbor, keep an eye out for bald eagles, which sometimes soar above the harbor's shoreline.

TRIP 48
SOMES SOUND

Rating: Difficulty depends on weather conditions
Distance: 7.5 miles round-trip
Estimated Time: 4.0 hours
Map: AMC's Acadia National Park Discovery Map: E5, F5, G5

This unique paddle goes to the only fjord in the eastern United States, with views of tall ocean-side cliffs and good wildlife-watching opportunities.

Directions
Just south of downtown Southwest Harbor, turn left off Route 102 onto Route 102A. After 1.0 mile, turn left onto Mansell Lane. At the end of the road, turn left onto Shore Road. The boat ramp is a short distance on the right. *GPS coordinates*: 44° 16.109′ N, 68° 18.509′ W.

Trip Description
Weather and tide considerations: When the wind and tide are moving in opposite directions, ominous standing waves can develop in the shallow and narrow mouth of the sound, known as the Narrows. Otherwise, the tides are not much of an issue in Somes Sound. The wind is another story. Running north to south, with mountains rising up on both its eastern and western shores, Somes Sound experiences a strong wind-tunnel effect when winds are out of the north or south. These winds can make it very difficult to paddle, and you are better off trying an alternate trip like Mount Desert Narrows (Trip 45). Winds out of the east or west are usually not a problem.

Somes Sound is a narrow finger of water that almost cuts Mount Desert Island in two. A glacier created Somes Sound, scouring a deep U-shaped valley between Acadia and Norumbega Mountains. The glacier carved through Mount Desert Island all the way to the ocean, and now the valley is filled with seawater. This paddling trip starts near the mouth of the sound in the working harbor of Manset, where you can explore the shoreline of Greening Island before making your way up the sound to Valley Cove, Eagle Cliff, and a waterfall at Man o' War Brook. Like all of the kayaking trips around Mount Desert Island, Somes Sound provides good opportunities for seeing wildlife such as seabirds, bald eagles, and seals.

From the boat ramp in Manset, Southwest Harbor is to your left and Greening Island is across the water to the northeast. Straight ahead is a passage between Southwest Harbor and Greening Island that is the most direct route to Somes Sound. The water is shallow in this passage, which sometimes makes for a bumpy crossing. For this trip, head to the eastern tip of Greening Island and paddle around the northeastern side of the island before heading north into the sound. With Southwest Harbor to the west and Northeast Harbor to the east, the waters around Greening Island get a fair amount of boat traffic, so keep your group together and be aware of your surroundings. Abraham Somes purchased the island in 1775 from the Wabanaki for a gallon of rum. Somes was one of the first permanent settlers on Mount Desert Island, having built a log cabin at Somes Point after sailing to Somes Sound from Gloucester, Massachusetts, in 1761. Still privately owned, Greening Island has stunning views of Somes Sound and the mountains of Mount Desert Island.

As you paddle north from Greening Island, you will make your way through the mouth of Somes Sound, known as the Narrows. Here the sound is only about 1,000 feet across and the water is very shallow—less than 10 feet deep in spots. If the wind is blowing against the tide here, there can be some fairly choppy water. Farther north in Somes Sound, the water attains depths of up to 150 feet. The gently sloping field on the western shore of the Narrows is known as Jesuit Spring. This is the site of a French colony, settled in 1613, which was quickly attacked and destroyed by the English in one of many skirmishes between the two naval powers in eastern Maine and Maritime Canada during the seventeenth and eighteenth centuries.

Just beyond Jesuit Spring, Flying Mountain rises 271 feet from the waters of Somes Sound. Follow the shoreline on your left around Flying Mountain and into Valley Cove, a sheltered inlet bordered by Flying Mountain on the south and the spectacular 400-foot cliffs of Eagle Cliff on the west. This is one of the most sheltered coves on the island, and it is still used as a place to anchor boats in extremely rough weather. The shoreline here is part of Acadia National Park and makes an excellent spot to stop and take a break. The Flying Mountain Trail is only a few yards from shore and can quickly take you to the summit of Flying Mountain or the top of Eagle Cliff, both of which have excellent views of Somes Sound. We have never seen bald eagles on Eagle Cliff, but they are common visitors to Somes Sound and can be seen at any point during this trip. To the north of Valley Cove is Acadia Mountain, and across the water to the northeast is Norumbega Mountain, which at 850 feet is the highest point above the sound.

From Valley Cove, continue north along the western shore of Somes Sound. Eagle Cliff and the northeastern shoulder of Saint Sauveur Mountain dominate the shoreline for much of the way to Man o' War Brook, which marks the low point between Saint Sauveur and Acadia Mountains. At Man o' War Brook, water rushes over steep rocks into the sound at a point where the water is deep enough for large boats. The deep water made it easy for schooners to sail into the sound, quickly collect freshwater, and head back out to sea. The easy access to freshwater in a hidden cove probably is responsible for the stories of pirate ships using this area. Today, Man o' War Brook is a scenic stop for boats, with its cool, cedar-lined shoreline flanked by the dramatic slopes of Acadia and Saint Sauveur Mountains providing beautiful visual relief.

From here you can return to Manset by either following the western shore or paddling across the sound to the rugged shoreline under Norumbega Mountain. South of Norumbega, the shoreline becomes gentler as you pass some of the biggest summer homes on Mount Desert Island in the woods on the outskirts of the town of Northeast Harbor. On your return paddle to Manset, keep your eyes open for guillemots, cormorants, and loons, as well as both harbor and gray seals. Looking south and east past Greening Island, you can see Sutton Island and the Cranberries and out to the open Atlantic.

What Is a Fjord?

Somes Sound is the only fjord on the East Coast of the United States. *Fjord* is a Norwegian word used to describe the deep bays and inlets that line the coast of Norway on the Norwegian Sea. In addition to Norway, fjords are also common in British Columbia, Alaska, and New Zealand. Most fjords were carved by glaciers during the last ice age, between 15,000 and 25,000 years ago. They are typically deep fingers of seawater surrounded by tall cliffs or mountains. In the case of Somes Sound, the mountains rise 850 feet above the water, which attains depths of 150 feet. If you drained Somes Sound, it would look much like the U-shaped valleys between Dorr Mountain and Huguenot Head, and Cadillac and Pemetic mountains. While a fjord is usually very deep for most of its length, it is often much more shallow at its mouth. In the case of Somes Sound, when the Wisconsin Glacier retreated about 13,000 years ago, it left a pile of debris, called a terminal moraine, at the mouth of the sound. The water here is only about 10 feet deep. The narrow and shallow mouth of Somes Sound makes it harder for water to leave and enter the sound during changes in tides, creating a unique mix of water and nutrients that supports a wide variety of wildlife including lobsters, loons, seals, great blue herons, and bald eagles.

Somes Sound as seen from the ledges on Acadia Mountain.

TRIP 49
SEAL COVE TO PRETTY MARSH

Rating: Difficulty depends on weather conditions
Distance: 10.0 miles
Estimated Time: 7.0 hours
Map: AMC's Acadia National Park Discovery Map:
   E3, E2, F2, F3

This paddle on the "quiet" side of Mount Desert Island is filled with wooded shoreline, beautiful islands, and bountiful wildlife.

Directions
From the intersection of Seal Cove Road and Route 102 in Seal Cove, follow Route 102 north for 0.3 mile. Turn left onto Cape Road. Drive past the boat ramp in Seal Cove to a small turnout, which is about 0.5 mile on the left. There is parking on the right. *GPS coordinates*: 44° 17.144′ N, 68° 24.889′ W.

Trip Description
Weather and tide considerations: Low tide will make it necessary to paddle on the west side of Moose Island, but this will not add additional time to your trip. A strong wind out of the southwest can cause a fair amount of choppiness at the southern ends of Moose and Hardwood Islands. Otherwise, the wind and tides should not cause too many problems. There is a small amount of boat traffic in this area, but much less than most other areas around Mount Desert Island.

Mount Desert Island is bordered on the west by a body of water known as Blue Hill Bay. From Seal Cove north to Pretty Marsh, views to the west of Blue Hill give way to the gentle shoreline of Bartlett Island as the bay funnels though the Bartlett Narrows. Here seals and porpoises regularly come to feed on the fish that become concentrated between the islands. There is much to explore here: the rocky intertidal zones of Mount Desert Island, the beautiful shoreline of Moose Island, and the pastoral views of the historically preserved farms of Bartlett Island. Trips of almost any length are possible in this area, but this trip highlights the 5.0 miles between Seal Cove and

Pretty Marsh Harbor. While there is a boat ramp in Pretty Marsh, parking is restricted to residents of the town of Mount Desert, so you must begin your trip in Seal Cove.

This trip can take most of the day, so be sure to carry plenty of food, water, and extra clothing. Also note that all of the islands in Blue Hill Bay are privately owned and landing on them for any reason is discouraged. The one exception to this is on Bartlett Island, which is owned by the Rockefeller family. If you land on Bartlett Island, try to remain below the high-tide line in order to minimize impact on the island. There is also a small picnic area in the national park on the eastern side of Pretty Marsh Harbor where it is allowable to land. The rest of Mount Desert Island in this area is private property. In addition to respecting private property, be sure to give a wide berth to seals hauled out on the ledges of Bartlett Island and north of Pretty Marsh. Seals "haul out," or come out of the water onto land, in order to rest. They are very skittish of kayaks and lose a lot of valuable energy going in and out of the water. Stay at least 0.5 mile away from any seals hauled out on land.

With those logistical concerns out of the way, be prepared to enjoy a wonderful paddle. From the put-in at Seal Cove, paddle west to leave the cove and then turn right around Reed Point. From here you can see Moose, Hardwood, and Bartlett Islands to the north and west. Moose Island is particularly beautiful, with its gravel beaches giving way to heath and blueberry bushes before a forest of tall spruce takes over. Like many of the islands in Maine, Moose Island was used to graze livestock for much of the nineteenth century. Moose Island was particularly useful for this because a gravel bar connects it with Mount Desert Island at low tide. As a kayaker, you will need to pay attention to the tide in order to avoid having to carry your boat over the bar. The bar is usually above water during the 2 hours on either side of low tide. Of course, you can paddle around the western side of the island during any tide.

From Moose Island, paddle to the northwest toward Hardwood Island. Hardwood Island is indeed named for its forest of hardwoods, in this case birch, maple, and beech. Hardwood Island has a shoreline of gravel beaches with good views to the east of Mount Desert Island's western mountains. Paddle along the eastern shore of this island until you reach its northern tip. From here it is a 0.75-mile paddle to the southern end of Bartlett Island. Feel free to take a break on Bartlett Island, but please stay below the high-tide mark, pack out all of your trash, and refrain from building fires. Bartlett Island was first settled in the 1760s and its fertile soil made it an excellent

Seal Cove is the starting point for a long, scenic paddle.

place to farm. However, by the early 1900s most families had moved to the mainland or Mount Desert Island, where access to services was much more convenient. The Rockefeller family bought the island in the early 1970s in order to prevent it from being developed into a resort community. Rockefeller family members now run the farm on the eastern side of the island that can be seen from the town landing in Pretty Marsh.

Follow the eastern shore of Bartlett Island by keeping the island on your left. You will see Folly Island to the east and the diminutive John Island to the northeast as you enter Bartlett Narrows. The waters and fish of Blue Hill Bay are funneled through this narrow passage between islands, creating an excellent feeding opportunity for harbor seals and harbor porpoises. This is one of the best areas around Acadia for spotting these marine mammals. Keep your eyes open for the periscoping, doglike heads of seals, and listen for the sounds of exhaling porpoises, which will sometimes approach quite close to a kayak. Ospreys nest in the area and can often be seen soaring above the water in search of fish. Double-crested cormorants and black guillemots are also frequent visitors to Bartlett Narrows.

Once you are past John Island, paddle east across Bartlett Narrows to the western shore of Mount Desert Island. Due east of John Island is the Pretty

Marsh picnic area in Acadia National Park. While it is a steep climb to the picnic tables from the shore, you can stop here in all but the highest tides and take a break before heading back to Seal Cove. However, the shoreline on Bartlett Island is more amenable to stopping and has good views of Acadia's mountains. No matter where you stop, to return to Seal Cove keep the shoreline of Mount Desert Island on your left. This stretch of shoreline has small cobble beaches, interesting rocky outcrops with veins of quartz, and good opportunities to observe the different layers of the intertidal zones. After returning to Seal Cove, you may want to drive to the town landing at Pretty Marsh to take in the sunset over Bartlett Island.

Intertidal Zones

The tides around Mount Desert Island rise and fall between 8 and 10 feet. This twice-daily gradual change in water levels creates unique habitats on the rocky ledges that surround the island. These habitats vary drastically in the amount of sunlight they receive and in the amount of exposure they have to the air. In 10 feet of rock at the water's edge, there are several different zones of life. Each zone supports a different group of organisms that have evolved to exploit these varying amounts of sunlight, surf, air, and water. The intertidal zones can be studied all around Mount Desert Island and the surrounding islands, most easily from a kayak. If you prefer to visit them on foot, however, look along the shore below Ocean Drive, at the end of the Ship Harbor Nature Trail, or below Bass Harbor Head Light.

Intertidal zones generally are broken down into five distinct sections, each of which supports a variety of life from blue-green algae and periwinkles to kelp and sea urchins.

The spray zone: Just above the high-tide line, this zone is never submerged in seawater but receives a constant spray of salt water from crashing surf. Sometimes called the black zone, this zone is characterized by the presence of primitive blue-green algae (*Calothrix*) and black lichen (*Verrucaria*). The algae or lichen create a thin, black, very slippery covering over the rocks. A rough-shelled variety of periwinkle feeds on the algae in this zone and seeks shelter in crevices of rocks in both this zone and the barnacle zone.

The barnacle zone: Contrasting with the black spray zone is the barnacle zone, made up of masses of white acorn barnacles (*Balanus balanoides*). The barnacle zone is below the water only at high tide, so the barnacles must be able to withstand long periods of exposure to the air as well as Maine's pounding surf. Barnacles are crustaceans, and they attach themselves to rocks with a cement-like substance they also use to build a conical shell around themselves. At the top of these shells is a small valve they can close during low tide to protect themselves from the drying effects of the air. At high tide, they open this valve to feed, extending feathery comb-shaped arms to catch microscopic organisms.

The rockweed zone: This zone is out of the water about the same amount of time it is under the water. It is characterized by a covering of stringy, rubbery, brown algae known as rockweed. There are two dominant species of rockweed around Acadia: Bladder wrack is common in the upper level of the rockweed zone, while knotted wrack proliferates in the lower level of the zone. Both types of seaweed use gas bladders filled with air to keep them suspended near the light during high tide so they can continue to photosynthesize. During low tide they form a thick, protective covering that is inhabited by a wide variety of wildlife such as common periwinkles, blue mussels, and dog whelks, which prey on both mussels and barnacles.

The Irish moss zone: Exposed to the air only during low tide, the Irish moss zone is characterized by red algae such as Irish moss and dulse. Irish moss is a maroon-colored seaweed that has an iridescent sheen in bright sunlight. Dulse is a 6-inch-long red seaweed with broad, flat fronds. Irish moss is harvested around the world to make carrageenan, a thickener used in food and cosmetic products. The Irish moss zone also provides habitat for a number of shellfish and crustaceans.

The kelp zone: This zone is above water only during extreme low tides in the spring and fall. This is a diverse underwater community that centers around kelp, a brown seaweed usually characterized by long, leathery blades. The kelp provides the ideal environment for aquatic animals such as starfish and sea urchins. Starfish feed on mussels, clams, and other shellfish by wrapping their arms around their prey, prying open the shell, inserting their stomachs and digesting the animal. Sea urchins are vegetarian, feeding mainly on kelp. Brittle stars, sea cucumbers, sea anemones, and crabs also inhabit the kelp zone.

TRIP 50
CRANBERRY ISLES

Rating: Advanced
Distance: 12.0 miles round-trip
Estimated Time: 7.0 hours
Map: AMC's Acadia National Park Discovery Map: F7

This all-day paddle goes to historic islands and offers excellent views of the mountains on Mount Desert Island.

Directions
From downtown Bar Harbor, follow Route 3 south for 8.1 miles. Seal Harbor will be on your left. A public parking area is on the right. *GPS coordinates*: 44° 17.775′ N, 68° 14.417′ W.

Trip Description
Weather and tide considerations: Tide is not a major issue on this trip. At low tide, you will have to carry you boat farther at the put-in and beware of submerged rocks in the Pool (a tidal salt marsh) at Great Cranberry Island. With heavy boat traffic in the area, it is advisable not to paddle here in foggy weather, and fog is very common in these waters. Prevailing summer winds from the southwest often blow fog into this southern part of the Mount Desert Island area before any other waters near the island. Strong winds (above 10 to 15 knots) from the east or west can cause problems, and winds out of the north can funnel through the mountains, making the return part of the trip difficult. Winds from the southwest are the most favorable, but only the most experienced paddlers should avoid this trip in winds stronger than 10 knots. In any case, the length and the exposed nature of some sections make this trip appropriate for experienced paddlers only.

The Cranberry Isles are five islands located off the southern coast of Mount Desert Island near the entrance to Somes Sound. They have a rich history of settlement that goes back 150 years, when the islands were a tight-knit community of families who made their living from the sea. There is still a small population of fishing people living year-round on Great and Little Cranberry, but most of the houses on these islands are now used as summer homes and vacation rentals. However, both islands have excellent

The Cranberry Isles provide a lovely sunset paddle.

museums worth visiting that chronicle the history of these communities. This trip visits four of the five islands: Bear, Sutton, Great Cranberry, and Little Cranberry (a.k.a. Isleford.) (The fifth island in the group, Baker Island, is also accessible by kayak, but requires advanced paddling skills and ideal conditions, and is not described in this trip.) Also, be aware that most of the shoreline on all of the Cranberry Isles is privately owned, so please respect private property and restrict your access to the islands to landing near the town docks on Great and Little Cranberry.

Like Trip 47, this paddling trip begins in Seal Harbor and proceeds to visit Bear and Sutton Islands. From the beach at Seal Harbor, paddle out of the harbor and then follow the shoreline to the right to the cobblestones of Bracy Cove. About half a mile past Bracy Cove, turn your boat to the left and aim for Bear Island, about 0.2 mile to the south. Paddle around the western shore of Bear Island, where you will pass the Bear Island Light House, and then make the 0.5-mile crossing of Eastern Way to the western end of Sutton Island. Instead of following the northern shore of Sutton, as in Trip 47, stay to the west of Sutton Island to make the crossing to Great Cranberry Island.

By paddling due south from the western end of Sutton Island, you should reach the town dock on Great Cranberry Island in about 1.0 mile. Please remember that there can be heavy boat traffic in this area. Once at Great

Cranberry, if you want to stretch your legs and explore, you can beach your boat on the cobblestone beach just to the right of the town dock and walk up into town. At the end of the dock, you will find a general store, and a quarter mile walk up the street takes you to the Preble-Marr Historical Museum, where there are public restrooms and excellent exhibits. There is also a great mile-long walking trail through beautiful mature spruce woods behind the museum that leads to a secluded sandy beach on the western side of the island. Be warned, however, that a walk on the streets of Great Cranberry will most likely cause you to dream of spending a week, a month, or a lifetime on the porch of a cedar-shingled home overlooking fields with sweeping views of the Maine Coast.

To continue paddling, follow the shoreline east past the town dock for about 1.0 mile to Long Point. Following the shoreline to the right around Long Point, brings you into he Pool, a tidal salt marsh that is a good place to watch for shorebirds and seabirds. (As mentioned at the beginning of this trip's description, be on the lookout for exposed rocks at the entrance to the Pool at low tide.) You will find this a unique landscape in a paddle that is full of cobblestone beaches that alternate with inaccessible rocky shorelines.

Once you have returned to the entrance of the Pool, aim northeast across Cranberry Harbor for the docks at Isleford in Hadlock Cove on Little Cranberry.

Caution: Do *not* paddle south and east through the "Gut" and into the waters between the Cranberry Isles and Baker Island, as there are strong tidal currents and exposed ledges that are treacherous in certain conditions without local knowledge and advanced paddling skills.

At Isleford, you can also land your boat at the beaches near the town dock and make your way into town on foot. Isleford has a few more amenities for visitors, including a few restaurants, galleries, and a bed-and-breakfast. Of real interest is the Isleford Historical Museum, which is run by the National Park Service and is home to excellent exhibits that describe life on the islands in the nineteenth century.

To make the return trip to Seal Harbor, you should paddle north from the dock at Isleford to Hadlock Point, and then head north-northeast to the eastern end of Sutton Island (about 0.6 mile), then make the 1.0 mile crossing to Seal Harbor to the north. This is a lot of open water, so be aware of other boat traffic and keep your eyes open for gray and harbor seals, and black guillemots in the open water, and bald eagles and ospreys as you get closer to shore.

5

The Other Acadia: The Schoodic Peninsula and Isle au Haut

WHILE MOUNT DESERT ISLAND MAY BE THE PHYSICAL AND SOCIAL HEART of Acadia National Park, the Schoodic Peninsula and Isle au Haut sections of the park are just as compelling. The Schoodic Peninsula is the only part of Acadia on the mainland, its 2,100 acres of headland jutting out into the open Atlantic. Isle au Haut, perhaps the wildest part of Acadia, lies 10 miles off the Maine coast and features spruce-covered highlands and dramatic seashore cliffs. Both sections of the park receive considerably less visitation than Mount Desert Island due to their distance from the main section of Acadia.

Schoodic Peninsula

The Schoodic Peninsula is a secluded section of the Maine coast an hour's drive east from Bar Harbor. It is the point of land that sits across Frenchman Bay from Mount Desert Island. Schoodic is a thickly forested headland, with a coastline that receives no protection from the relentless pounding of the Atlantic Ocean. Pink-granite ledges scoured of vegetation line the peninsula. These ledges are good places to soak in ocean views and get away from the crowds of Mount Desert Island. A visit to the Schoodic Peninsula should start with a drive on the Park Road.

The Park Road follows the coast, providing ocean views at every turn. Across Frenchman Bay, you can see the full expanse of Cadillac Mountain. About 3.0 miles from the park boundary, a rough gravel road on the left leads to the summit of Schoodic Head. This road makes a good hiking or mountain-biking trail for those without a four-wheel-drive vehicle. The views from the 440-foot summit are excellent.

Farther down the Park Road is Schoodic Point. Its massive granite ledges are a must visit. The rocks here show intense wear from glaciers in the past as well as from pounding surf in the present. Look for grooves in the rock caused by the grinding action of rocks stuck in glacier ice as it moved over the peninsula thousands of years ago. Today Schoodic Point is at the mercy of the Atlantic Ocean, as there are no islands or reefs offshore to break up the waves, which can reach heights of 30 feet during storms. While Thunder Hole on Mount Desert Island is a popular spot for watching geyser-like wave crashes, Schoodic Point may be the most reliable place in the park to see large waves making huge splashes. Like Thunder Hole, standing at Schoodic Point can present some dangers. Be very careful to avoid falling into the water.

The remainder of the peninsula continues to provide breathtaking scenery. Although there is not much hiking in the area, short trails leave from the Blueberry Hill parking area and ascend Schoodic Head as well as a small rocky hill called the Anvil. Biking options are limited to the dirt road up Schoodic Head and the 12.0-mile loop around the Park Road and Route 186. Sea-kayaking in this area can be dangerous due to the exposure to the open Atlantic.

Getting There
To get to the peninsula from Mount Desert Island, you need to drive back to Ellsworth, where you should turn right and head east on Route 1. Follow Route 186 south in West Gouldsboro until you reach the Park Road, just beyond Winter Harbor. Overnight camping is not permitted in the Schoodic section of the park, although there are several private campgrounds near the park.

Isle au Haut
Isle au Haut has a unique wilderness character that cannot be found anywhere else in Acadia National Park. Dramatic 100-foot cliffs drop down to the Atlantic Ocean on the southern end of the island. Beautiful cobblestone beaches fill the spaces between the cliffs. Seals, eagles, loons, and guillemots are common along the shore, while deer, coyote, and numerous songbirds fill the interior boreal forest. Ten miles out to sea, Isle au Haut sees fewer than

Isle au Haut is an escape from the crowds at Mount Desert Island.

10,000 visitors a year, a considerably smaller number than the 3 million who visit Mount Desert Island. The one road that circles the island does not intrude on the coastline in the national park. All these factors contribute to make this an ideal place to find quiet solitude.

Evidence of American Indians can be found all around the island in the form of shell middens and stone tools. Shell middens were basically garbage dumps where the Indians threw their used clamshells and other refuse. (If you happen to find a stone arrowhead or cutting blade, please leave it as you found it. It is illegal to disturb archaeological artifacts in a national park.) The first European to "discover" Isle au Haut was Samuel de Champlain, who first made note of the island during a voyage in 1603. He named the island Isle Haut, or High Island.

Like many of New England's outer islands, Isle au Haut was settled by fishing people who liked its proximity to fertile fishing grounds. At one point, the island had a community of around 300 permanent residents, but over the past century that number has dwindled to around 70. The introduction of the gas-powered engine made it less of an advantage for professional fishers to live on the island. However, fishing is still alive and well on Isle au Haut, accounting for the major percentage of the island's economy.

In the 1880s, residents of the big East Coast cities discovered Isle au Haut as a summer getaway. Unlike Mount Desert Island, with its proliferation of hotels, restaurants, and hectic social life, Isle au Haut was a quiet home away from home, with private summer cottages blending into the community. In 1945, descendants of one of these early summer visitors, Ernest Bowditch of Boston, donated almost half of the island to Acadia National Park. Today, 2,728 acres of Isle au Haut are part of the park.

Getting There

Getting to Isle au Haut involves taking the mail boat from Stonington, which is at the southern tip of Deer Isle. It is a long day trip from Bar Harbor, as the drive takes about 1.5 hours and the boat ride is another 35 minutes. The mail boat makes two trips a day, three in the summer. For more information, contact the Isle au Haut Company at 207-367-5193. While day trips make a good introduction to the island, the best way to experience Isle au Haut is to spend two or three nights in the Duck Harbor Campground, open from May 15 through October 15. Run by the national park, the campground has only five lean-tos and no tent sites. This limited space is highly coveted, so you will want to make reservations early. Call the Park Service (207-288-3338) for the rules regarding reservations. Currently, reservations are taken beginning April 1 for the following summer.

From the campground, you have access to 18 miles of hiking trails that explore both the dramatic seaside cliffs and the island's forested highlands. While the island's high point, Mount Champlain, reaches the lofty height of 556 feet, it is completely forested and has no views. The best views on the island are from Duck Harbor Mountain, which is a short hike from the campground. From the ledges of this modest 314-foot peak, there are spectacular views of Penobscot Bay, with its deep blue waters surrounding scores of islands. The Western Head, Cliff, and Goat Trails all provide excellent coastal hiking. Each of the three trails alternates between ascending rocky cliffs and traversing secluded cobble beaches. Harbor seals and gray seals can be seen feeding offshore, as well as black guillemots, loons, cormorants, common eiders, and harlequin ducks. (A complete list of hiking trails can be found in Appendix A.)

Experienced paddlers will find that Isle au Haut is also a great place to sea-kayak. The Isle au Haut Company can transport your kayak to the island, or you can paddle the 6.0 miles from Stonington. Contact the Maine Island

Trail Association (see Appendix E) to learn about paddling opportunities around the other islands in Penobscot Bay.

Biking on Isle au Haut is discouraged by the Park Service due to the rough nature of the roads and the fact that bikes are not allowed on hiking trails. Experienced mountain bikers will find that the dirt roads are not a difficult ride, but those who prefer pavement or the carriage roads will find biking Isle au Haut unpleasant. In any event, there are only a few miles of road on the island, so it is not really worth the extra effort of transporting a bike on the mail boat.

Like the rest of Acadia, Isle au Haut is busiest during July and August. During these months, the mail boat drops park visitors off at the campground in Duck Harbor. During the rest of the year, visitors are taken to the town of Isle au Haut, which is a 5.0-mile hike from the campground. Therefore, park visits in May and early June, as well as in the fall, take a little extra effort, but the rewards are empty trails, fewer bugs, and peaceful solitude. Whenever you visit, you are sure to be charmed by the island's slow pace, relatively empty trails, and dramatic shoreline.

Appendix A: Complete List of Hiking Trails in Acadia National Park

THE FOLLOWING BRIEF TRAIL DESCRIPTIONS list all the well-marked, officially recognized, maintained paths that give access to all of the preferred summits on Mount Desert Island and Isle au Haut. Many of these have been covered in the trip descriptions in Chapter 5, but are included here for those who would like to create their own routes. (The Schoodic Peninsula, with five short, forested trails, is excluded.) For the most part, you can reach the individual summits in comfortable half-day walks. To simplify reference and to conform with Acadia National Park nomenclature, we have divided the hikes into an eastern district and a western district. The National Park Service maintains all of the trails described here; trail markings include signs, cairns, and blue painted blazes. In addition to the map in this guide, refer to the AMC Acadia National Park Discovery Map included with this book.

The National Park Service (NPS) has rated each trail based on the following criteria:

Easy: Fairly level ground.

Moderate: Uneven ground with some steep grades and/or gradual climbing. Footing may be difficult in places.

Strenuous: Steep and/or long grades; steady climbing or descending. Sometimes difficult footing, difficult maneuvering.

Ladder: Iron-rung ladders and handrails placed on steep grades or difficult terrain. These trails are very difficult.

Please note: The NPS is in the midst of a major trails initiative that includes creating new trails, retiring some, and restoring historic trails. The

NPS is also restoring historic names to many existing trails. The trail names used in this book are considered up-to-date, but you may encounter trail signs that still use the old trail names. For this reason, we have noted the former trail names when applicable.

Eastern District   *(East of Somes Sound)*

CHAMPLAIN MOUNTAIN AREA

The Champlain Mountain area consists of Champlain and Gorham mountains, Huguenot Head, the Beehive, and Great Head, all of which provide excellent views. Champlain and the Beehive are the most popular because of their exciting ladder trails that climb steep cliff faces overlooking the open ocean, but both peaks are also accessible by easier trails, that are better options for children or those with a fear of heights.

Precipice Trail (AMC's Acadia National Park Discovery Map: D8)
NPS Rating: Ladder
This trail starts from the Precipice Trail parking area, located 1.75 mi. beyond the Sieur de Monts Spring entrance on Park Loop Road at the foot of Champlain Mountain (1,058 ft.). The trailhead is located just before the entrance-fee station on Park Loop Rd.

Following a rugged talus slope full of big boulders, the trail ascends northwest about 0.4 mi. where the Orange and Black Path (not completed as of this writing) leads right to the Champlain North Ridge Trail 0.5 mi. from the summit on the north ridge. From this intersection, the Precipice climbs southwest, rising steeply to a point directly west of the parking area. The direction is now west-northwest. Along this section of the trail, ladders and iron rungs help hikers negotiate precipitous vertical drop-offs. The final 500-ft. climb to the summit follows gentle slopes and ledges. People afraid of heights should not climb the Precipice Trail. In addition, hikers under 5 ft. tall may have difficulty reaching some handholds.

Caution: It is most important that Precipice Trail hikers remain on the designated trail. Wandering off the trail can quickly lead hikers onto cliffs that require technical mountain-climbing skills and equipment.

Note: The Precipice Trail can be closed for an undetermined amount of time each spring and summer because of the reintroduction of peregrine falcons to the park. Violators of the closure are subject to a $10,000 fine.

Those wishing the experience of a ladder trail should consider the nearby Beehive Trail, the Dorr Mountain Ladder Trail, the Jordan Cliffs Trail, the Giant Slide Trail, or the Beech Cliffs Trail.

Distances from Park Loop Rd.

to Orange and Black Path: 0.4 mi., 15 min.

to Champlain summit: 0.8 mi., 1 hr.

Champlain North Ridge Trail (formerly Bear Brook Trail)

(AMC's Acadia National Park Discovery Map: D8)

NPS Rating: Moderate

This trail begins on the Park Loop Rd., 0.2 mi. east of the entrance to the Bear Brook picnic area. The trail ends at the summit of Champlain Mountain where the Champlain South Ridge Trail continues to the Bowl Trail, located at the south end of the Bowl.

This trail climbs gradually from the parking area through a mixed forest of birch, pine, and spruce to a junction on the north slope of Champlain with the Orange and Black Path (not completed as of this writing) entering left at 0.5 mi. Continuing left, the Bear Brook Trail steadily emerges from the forest canopy giving outstanding views of Frenchman Bay and Schoodic Peninsula on the mainland to the east. At 1 mi. the trail reaches the open, rocky summit of Champlain.

Distances from Park Loop Rd.

to junction with the Champlain East Face Trail: 0.5 mi., 30 min.

to Champlain summit: 1.0 mi., 55 min.

Champlain South Ridge Trail (formerly Bear Brook Trail)

(AMC's Acadia National Park Discovery Map: E8)

NPS Rating: Moderate

This trail provides a route from the Bowl (at the base of the Beehive) to the summit of Champlain Mountain. It begins at an intersection with the Bowl Trail, 0.6 mi. from the Park Loop Road and the Sand Beach parking area. The trail skirts the southern edge of the Bowl, a small glacial tarn, before ascending to the ridgeline of Champlain Mountain's South Ridge. The trail climbs moderately and soon enters an open-air forest of pitch pines. Climbing over pink Cadillac granite, the trail reaches open views and the Precipice Trail, 1.5 mi. above the Bowl, and the summit of Champlain Mountain at 1.6 mi.

Distances from Park Loop Rd.
> to junction with the Precipice Trail: 1.5 mi., 1 hr.
> to Champlain summit and junction with Champlain North Ridge Trail:
>   1.6 mi., 1 hr. 5 min.

Beachcroft Path (AMC's Acadia National Park Discovery Map: D8)
NPS Rating: Moderate
A convenient route between Champlain Mountain and the area to the west. For the most part, the trail is entirely open. While the ascent to Hugenot Head from Route 3 is gradual and easily traveled, the character of the trail becomes more difficult on the actual ascent of Champlain.

The trail leaves Route 3 across the street from the north end of the Tarn and begins with a flight of granite steps on the east side of the highway. (There is parking above the north end of the Tarn off the west side of the highway.) It then runs southeast, often on carefully placed stone stairs. Following switchbacks and stone steps, it rises up and across the west face of Huguenot Head. The trail passes to the south of (not over) the summit of Huguenot Head at about 0.4 mi. A brief, gradual descent into the gully between Huguenot Head and Champlain Mountain is followed by a sharp, difficult ascent over rocks up the northwest slope of Champlain Mountain to the summit at 1.2 mi.

Distances from Route 3
> to shoulder of Huguenot Head: 0.4 mi., 25 min.
> to Champlain summit: 1.2 mi., 1 hr. 5 min.

Bowl Trail (AMC's Acadia National Park Discovery Map: E8)
NPS Rating: Moderate
This trail leaves from opposite the Sand Beach parking area, located 3.25 mi. beyond Sieur de Monts Spring on the Park Loop Rd. Using this trailhead means paying an entrance fee on the Park Loop Rd.

The Bowl Trail is a gently sloping path that offers access to the Beehive Trail and the Gorham Mountain Trail. It connects Sand Beach to the Bowl, a lovely lake at the base of Halfway Mountain. At the Bowl, a connector trail to the Beehive bears right.

Distances from Sand Beach parking area
> to junction with the Beehive Trail: 0.2 mi., 5 min.
> to junction with the Gorham Mountain Trail: 0.5 mi., 15 min.

to the Bowl and junction with the Beehive and Champlain South Ridge
trails: 0.7 mi., 25 min.

Beehive Trail (AMC's Acadia National Park Discovery Map: E8)
NPS Rating: Ladder
This trail begins 0.2 mi. up the Bowl Trail from the Sand Beach parking area.
Take a sharp right at the sign marked Beehive. For 0.3 mi., the trail rises
abruptly via switchbacks and iron ladders over steep ledges to the summit of
the Beehive. This trail is challenging and not for those who are uneasy on
precipitous heights. The views of Frenchman Bay, Sand Beach, and Otter
Cliff area are magnificent.

The trail continues down the northwest slope of the Beehive and dips
steeply to the south for 0.2 mi. to a junction with the Bowl and Champlain
South Ridge trails. Take the left fork for 0.7 mi. to return to Park Loop Rd.
Distances from Park Loop Rd.

to the Beehive: 0.5 mi., 25 min.
to complete loop back to the Sand Beach area (via Bowl Trail): est. 1.4
mi., 50 min.

Gorham Mountain Trail
(AMC's Acadia National Park Discovery Map: E8)
NPS Rating: Moderate
The trail starts at the Gorham Mountain Trail parking area (also known as
the Monument Cove parking area) on Park Loop Rd., 1 mi. past Sand Beach.
It rises gently over open ledges 0.3 mi. to a junction with a side trail to Cadillac Cliffs (NPS rating: Strenuous). The side trail is a loop that leads right and
rejoins the Gorham Mountain Trail 0.5 mi. later, after passing under ancient
sea cliffs and by an ancient sea cave. The Gorham Mountain Trail continues
0.3 mi. over easy open granite ledges to where the Cadillac Cliffs loop rejoins
the main trail.

The main trail continues north over the Gorham Mountain summit,
which is open and bare, with some of the finest panoramas on Mount Desert
Island. Descending, the trail reaches a junction with the Bowl Trail in another 0.7 mi. For the Bowl, go left 0.2 mi. To reach the Beehive, turn right,
then left at the next junction, about 0.1 mi. farther. (Continuing straight
ahead at this junction will bring you to Park Loop Rd. at Sand Beach.)

Distances from trailhead parking area
> to summit of Gorham Mt.: 1.1 mi., 45 min.
>
> to the Bowl Trail: 1.7 mi., 1 hr. 5 min.

Schooner Head Path

(AMC's Acadia National Park Discovery Map: D8, E8)

NPS Rating: Easy

This recently completed path provides a walking path from Bar Harbor to the Schooner Head Overlook and nearby Sand Beach. It is very flat and the trail is covered with small crushed gravel for much of its length, making it an easy walk. It is also very close to Schooner Head Rd. for most of its length.

The trail begins on the east side of Schooner Head Rd just a couple hundred yards from Route 3. It soon crosses back over the road and parallels the road, while keeping to the woods. It passes the Orange and Black Path at 0.7 mi., and Murphy Lane at 1.2 mi. (both lead right to the Park Loop Rd at the base of Champlain Mountain.) At 1.8 mi., the trail crosses the road again and reaches the Schooner Head Overlook parking area at 1.9 mi.

Distances from beginning of trail on Schooner Head Rd.
> to Orange and Black Path: 0.7 mi., 15 min.
>
> to Murphy Lane: 1.2 mi., 25 min.
>
> to Schooner Head Overlook: 1.9 mi., 40 min.

Great Head Trail (AMC's Acadia National Park Discovery Map: E8)

NPS Rating: Moderate

A scenic, short walk that passes largely along cliffs directly above the sea. From the Sand Beach parking area on Park Loop Rd., cross Sand Beach to the east end. Near the seaward end of the interior lagoon, look for a trailhead post and a series of granite steps with a handrail ascending a high bank. The trail quickly reaches a huge millstone, where the trail turns sharply right (south), switchbacking up the cliff. The path continues to the extremity of the peninsula, then turns northeast along the cliff to the high point, Great Head (145 ft.), where there are ruins of a stone teahouse. The trail descends northwest to a junction at which the right path returns more quickly to the east end of Sand Beach. The path that leads north reaches an abandoned service road in about 0.3 mi. Turn left on the road, and follow it south for about 0.3 mi. to the east side of Sand Beach.

Distances from east side of Sand Beach
   to south end of peninsula (via millstone): 0.5 mi., 15 min.
   to teahouse ruins: 0.8 mi., 20 min.
   to junction with Schooner Head Rd./Sand Beach paths: 1.3 mi., 35 min.
   to start (via service road): 1.6 mi., 55 min.

Ocean Path (also called Shore Path)
(AMC's Acadia National Park Discovery Map: E8)
NPS Rating: Easy
Park at the large, lower Sand Beach parking area on the Park Loop Rd. (fee). From the parking area, follow the asphalt trail about 50 ft. toward the beach. Where the staircase descends to the left, turn right to begin the Ocean Path. The trail leads uphill several hundred yards; crosses through a small, paved upper parking area; and continues south to Otter Point, paralleling the Park Loop Rd. for 2.2 mi. The Ocean Path offers spectacular shoreline scenery and follows a level grade. Of interest en route are Thunder Hole, Monument Cove, and Otter Cliffs.
Distance from Sand Beach
   to Otter Point: 2.2 mi., 1 hr. 5 min.

DORR MOUNTAIN
Dorr Mountain (1,265 ft.) lies immediately west of Sieur de Monts Spring. Two routes up the mountain are possible from Sieur de Monts Spring. Trails also ascend from the north and south over long ridges. The east and west slopes are steep. With properly placed cars, a party can have a good climb leaving from Sieur de Monts Spring, traversing Dorr, and continuing west to the summit of Cadillac Mountain (1,530 ft.). The route descends to about 1,000 ft. between the two summits. There is parking both at the nearby Tarn and on Cadillac's summit. (Hikers are encouraged not to park at the very congested Sieur de Monts Spring parking area. There is a connecting path between the Tarn and the spring parking areas for hikers wishing to visit or begin a hike at the spring.)

Emery Path (formerly Dorr Mountain East Face Trail, northern section) (AMC's Acadia National Park Discovery Map: D7)
NPS Rating: Strenuous
Follow the paved walkway from the Nature Center Parking Area at Sieur de Monts Spring toward the Springhouse. At the rock inscribed "Sweet Waters

of Acadia," turn right on a walkway that remains paved for a few feet. The trail continues, following a series of switchbacks up the northeast shoulder of Dorr Mountain. The first half has many stone steps. At 0.3 mi, the Homans Path enters from the right. At 0.5 mi., the Emery Path ends at its junction with Kurt Diederich's Climb, which leads left to the north end of the Tarn, and the Schiff Path, which continues to the summit.

Distances from Sieur de Monts Spring

to Homans Path junction: 0.3 mi., 20 min.

to Kurt Diederich's Climb and Schiff Path junction: 0.5 mi., 30 min.

to Dorr Mountain Summit via Schiff Path and Dorr North Ridge Trail,
    1.6 mi., 1 hr. 30 min.

Schiff Path (formerly Dorr Mountain East Face Trail, southern section) (AMC's Acadia National Park Discovery Map: D7)

NPS Rating: Strenuous

This trail begins at the intersection of the Emery Path and Kurt Diederich's Climb, 0.5 mi. above Sieur de Monts Spring and the Tarn. The trail begins by traversing the east face of the mountain, ascending moderately, and reaching an intersection with the Ladder Trail in 0.5 mi. Here the trail makes a sharp right and climbs steeply up to the Dorr North Ridge Trail, 0.1 mi. north of the summit, passing in and out of the trees on the way. Excellent views to the east can be had for most of the climb.

Distances from Emery Path and Kurt Diederich's Climb

to Ladder Trail: 0.5 mi., 20 min.

to Dorr North Ridge Trail: 1.0 mi., 1 hr.

to Dorr Mountain summit via Dorr North Ridge Trail:
    1.1 mi., 1 hr. 5 min.

Homans Path

(AMC's Acadia National Park Discovery Map: D7)

NPS Rating: Strenuous

This historic trail was restored and reopened in the summer of 2004. It allows a quick approach to Dorr Mountain for those walking from Bar Harbor via the Jesup Path by bypassing Sieur de Monts Spring. The trail begins from Hemlock Rd, a few yards west of the Jesup Path, 0.1 mi. from Sieur de Monts Spring. It rises steeply over switchbacks and stone steps to views of Great Meadow and Frenchman Bay, ending at its intersection with the Emery Path at 0.3 mi.

Distances from Hemlock Rd.
> to Emery Path: 0.3 mi.

Ladder Trail (formerly Dorr Mountain Ladder Trail)
(AMC's Acadia National Park Discovery Map: D7)
NPS Rating: Ladder
This trail climbs from a parking area on Route 3, just south of Tarn, up the eastern side of Dorr Mountain. The trail is steep, climbing many stone steps and over iron rungs. From the parking area, the trail immediately crosses the Kane Path before making its steep ascent to the Schiff Path at 0.4 mi.
Distance from Route 3
> to Schiff Path: 0.4 mi., 30 min.
> to Dorr Mountain Summit via Schiff Path and Dorr North Ridge Trail:
>> 1.0 mi., 1 hr. 10 min.

Kurt Diederich's Climb
(AMC's Acadia National Park Discovery Map: D7)
NPS Rating: Strenuous
This trail takes a direct route from the south end of the Tarn to the Schiff and Emery paths and the summit of Dorr Mountain. The trail starts at an intersection with the Kane Path (reached via the Tarn Parking lot on Route 3 or a 0.25-mi. walk from Sieur de Monts Spring). Look for an inscription in the stone stairs that says "Kurt Diederich's Climb." The trail climbs steeply via stone steps to good views and the Emery and Schiff paths at 0.5 mi.
Distances from the Tarn
> to Emery and Schiff paths: 0.5 mi., 30 min.
> to Dorr Mountain summit via Schiff Path and Dorr North Ridge Trail:
>> 1.6 mi., 1 hr. 30 min.

Kebo Mountain Trail (formerly Dorr Mountain North Ridge Trail, northern section) (AMC's Acadia National Park Discovery Map: D7)
NPS Rating: Easy
This trail begins on the south side of Park Loop Rd. about 1 mi. after the road becomes one-way. It climbs south over the summit of Kebo Mountain (407 ft.), traverses a second hump, and reaches its end at a junction with the Hemlock and Dorr North Ridge trails 0.9 mi. from the Park Loop Rd.
Distances from Park Loop Rd.
> to Hemlock and Dorr North Ridge trails: 0.9 mi., 30 min.

to Dorr Mountain Summit via Dorr North Ridge Trail: 1.8 mi.,
  1 hr. 25 min.

Dorr North Ridge Trail (formerly Dorr Mountain North Ridge Trail, southern section) (AMC's Acadia National Park Discovery Map: D7)

NPS Rating: Moderate

This trail (and the Dorr South Ridge Trail) offers a less steep alternative to the summit of Dorr Mountain than those trails that climb the east face of the mountain. It begins as an extension of the Kebo Mountain Trail, 0.9 mi. from the Park Loop Rd. It climbs the north ridge of the peak at a consistently moderate pace, reaching a junction with the Schiff Path and the Cadillac-Dorr Connector, 0.8 mi. from the Kebo Mountain Trail. It reaches the summit in another 0.1 mi.

Distance from Kebo Mountain Trail

to junction with Schiff Path and Cadillac-Dorr Connector:
  0.8 mi, 50 min.
to Dorr summit:.9 mi., 55 min.

Dorr South Ridge Trail (formerly Dorr Mountain South Ridge Trail)

(AMC's Acadia National Park Discovery Map: E7)

NPS Rating: Moderate

This trail diverges right from the Canon Brook Trail 0.9 mi. from Route 3 at the southern extremity of Dorr Mountain. It rises with moderate grade over rocky ledges and through evergreen forest. Views of Champlain, Cadillac, and the ocean are frequent during the ascent of the south ridge to the summit.

Distances from Route 3

to start (via Canon Brook Trail): 0.9 mi., 20 min.
to Dorr summit: 2.2 mi. 1 hr. 25 min.

Cadillac-Dorr Connector (formerly Cadillac-Dorr Trail)

(AMC's Acadia National Park Discovery Map: D7)

NPS Rating: Strenuous

This short trail links the summits of Dorr and Cadillac Mountains. It starts just north of the summit of Dorr Mountain, and runs east to west, connecting the Dorr North Ridge Trail with the Gorge Path at its intersection with the A. Murray Young Path. It is only 0.2 mi. in length.

The start of the trail at the summit of Cadillac may be difficult to see. Walk counterclockwise along the paved trail on the summit to the interpretive sign about Bar Harbor. Look for cairns and paint marks on the granite indicating the beginning of the trail leading to the notch. About 0.3 mi. south of the Park Loop Rd., the trail turns left to cross a brook; be careful to avoid an old wood road that goes straight ahead.

Distances from Dorr North Ridge Trail

to junction with the Gorge and A. Murray Young paths: 0.2 mi., 10 min.

A. Murray Young Path

(AMC's Acadia National Park Discovery Map: D7)

NPS Rating: Moderate

Ascending the narrow valley between Dorr and Cadillac mountains from the south, this trail leaves the Canon Brook Trail 1.1 mi. west of Route 3. It climbs gradually to the Gorge Path near its junction with the Cadillac-Dorr Connector. This point affords relatively quick (if strenuous) access to the summit of either mountain.

Distances from Route 3

to start (via Canon Brook Trail): 1.1 mi., 25 min.

to Cadillac-Dorr Connector: 2.2 mi., 1 hr.

to Dorr summit (via the Cadillac-Dorr Connector and Dorr North Ridge Trail): 2.5 mi., 1 hr. 20 min.

to Cadillac summit (via the Gorge Path): 2.6 mi., 1 hr. 25 min.

Jesup Path   (AMC's Acadia National Park Discovery Map: D7)

NPS Rating: Easy

A pleasant, level woodland walk, this path begins on Park Loop Rd. opposite the first road on the left after the beginning of the one-way section of Park Loop Rd. It follows the west margin of Great Meadow, where it may be flooded as a result of beaver activity. The path passes through a mixed forest of hemlock and hardwood to Sieur de Monts Spring at 0.8 mi. Located here are the Abbe Museum, which has displays of ancient Indian culture; the Wild Gardens of Acadia, a formal garden of native plants; and the Nature Center, with a book-sales area and natural history exhibits. The trail terminates 0.3 mi. farther at the north end of the Tarn.

Distances from Park Loop Rd.

to Sieur de Monts Spring: 0.8 mi., 20 min.

to north end of the Tarn: 1.1 mi., 30 min.

Stratheden Path (AMC's Acadia National Park Discovery Map: D7)

NPS Rating: Easy

This easy trail runs from the Hemlock Trail to the Park Loop Rd., providing an easy walk that bypasses the summit of Kebo Mountain. It begins on the Park Loop Rd., about 100 yd. east of the Kebo Mountain Trail. The trail takes a fairly level route through hemlocks on the way to the Hemlock Trail, where it ends at 0.7 mi.

Distances from Park Loop Rd.

to Hemlock Trail: 0.7 mi.

to Sieur de Monts Spring via Hemlock Trail and Hemlock Road: 1.2 mi.

Hemlock Trail (AMC's Acadia National Park Discovery Map: D7)

NPS Rating: Easy

This trail on the lower end of Dorr Mountain's north ridge connects the Gorge Path to the Dorr North Ridge Trail and Sieur de Monts Spring. It begins on the Gorge Path, 1.0 mi. below the Cadillac-Dorr notch and 0.4 mi. above the Park Loop Rd. It travels east, rising slightly to meet the Dorr North Ridge Trail in 0.2 mi. It then descends moderately to end at an intersection with the Stratheden Path and a dirt road known as the Hemlock Rd. (no cars are allowed on this road) at 0.4 mi. Sieur de Monts Spring is 0.5 mi. south via the Hemlock Rd.

Distances from Gorge Path

to Dorr North Ridge Trail: 0.2 mi., 5 min.

to Stratheden Path and Hemlock Rd.: 0.4 mi., 10 min.

to Sieur de Monts Spring via Hemlock Rd.: 0.9 mi., 20 min.

Great Meadow Loop Trail

(AMC's Acadia National Park Discovery Map: D7)

NPS Rating: Easy

This path connects the streets of Bar Harbor to the trail system within the park. It begins on Cromwell Harbor Rd., between Ledgelawn Ave. and Spring St., just to the east of a large cemetery. Paralleling roads for most of its length, it enters the woods next to the cemetery and crosses a brook and a road at 0.2 mi. At 0.6 mi., the trail crosses the road again and walks next to the Kebo Valley Golf Course. At 0.9 mi. and 1.0 mi., respectively, the Hemlock Rd. and Jesup Path lead left to Sieur de Monts Spring and the trails on

Dorr Mountain. Over the next 0.6 mi., the trail crosses two roads and a driveway and then comes out on Cromwell Harbor Rd. at 1.8 mi., completing the loop in another 0.1 mi.

Distances from Cromwell Harbor Rd.
> to Hemlock Road: 0.9 mi., 20 min.
> to Jesup Path: 1.0 mi., 20 min.
> to beginning of loop: 1.9 mi., 35 min.

Kane Path (formerly Tarn Trail)
(AMC's Acadia National Park Discovery Map: D7)
NPS Rating: Moderate
This path leads from the north end of the Tarn south to the Canon Brook Trail, and links the Sieur de Monts Spring area to the southern trails of Dorr and Cadillac mountains, while avoiding Route 3. At its start the path runs south, over a rocky talus slope directly along the west side of the Tarn. After reaching the south end of the Tarn, the trail continues past the Ladder Trail at 0.5 mi., then ends at the Canon Brook Trail at 0.8 mi.

Distance from north end of the Tarn
> to Ladder Trail: 0.5 mi., 20 min.
> to Canon Brook Trail: 0.8 mi., 25 min.

Canon Brook Trail (AMC's Acadia National Park Discovery Map: E7)
NPS Rating: Strenuous
From a pullout on Route 3 about 0.5 mi. south of the south end of the Tarn and about 2 mi. north of Otter Creek Village, the Canon Brook Trail runs west to join the Bubble and Jordan Ponds Path in the valley south of Bubble Pond. It gives access (via the Bubble and Jordan Ponds Path) to the Jordan Pond area, as well as to the trails running north to Dorr and Cadillac Mountains.

From the highway, the trail descends west to Otter Creek and intersects the Kane Path at 0.2 mi. Turn left (south) at the intersection and follow the trail in the valley of Otter Creek. After a brief, sharp rise from the valley, the trail reaches a junction with the Dorr South Ridge Trail, which diverges right at 0.9 mi. The trail descends to a junction with the A. Murray Young Path, which goes right at 1.1 mi. Then the trail runs steeply westward up the south bank of Canon Brook for about 0.5 mi. At this point, the trail swings away from the brook, passes a beaver pond, and ascends to a small pond known as the Featherbed, where it crosses the Cadillac South Ridge Trail at 2.0.

Descending the west face of Cadillac Mountain, the Canon Brook Trail ends in the valley between Cadillac and Pemetic Mountains at its junction with the Bubble and Jordan Ponds Path at 2.7 mi.

Distances from Route 3

to the Kane Path junction: 0.2 mi., 10 min.

to Dorr South Ridge Trail junction: 0.9 mi., 25 min.

to A. Murray Young Path junction: 1.1 mi., 30 min.

to junction with the Cadillac South Ridge Trail: 2.0 mi., 1 hr. 5 min.

to junction with the Bubble and Jordan Ponds Path: 2.7 mi., 1 hr. 40 min.

CADILLAC MOUNTAIN

Cadillac Mountain (1,530 ft.) is the highest point on the island. There is an automobile road to the summit, which has parking, a small gift shop, and bathrooms. Accessibility by car makes this summit the busiest in the park. Its height offers commanding views.

The North Ridge Trail, beginning on Park Loop Rd., can be connected with the Gorge Path, which ends on Park Loop Rd. about 0.5 mi. east of the North Ridge trailhead, creating a pleasant loop up and down Cadillac.

Cadillac South Ridge Trail

(AMC's Acadia National Park Discovery Map: D7, F8)

NPS Rating: Moderate

A relatively long hike for Mount Desert Island, this trail starts on the north side of Route 3, about 50 yd. west of the entrance to the NPS Blackwoods Campground. (A flat, 0.7-mi. connector links the campground to the trailhead.) It climbs generally north. At 1.0 mi. a short loop trail on the right leads to Eagle Crag, which has good views to the east and southeast. The loop trail rejoins the main trail in 0.2 mi. After leaving the woods, the South Ridge Trail rises gently over open ledges. It crosses the Canon Brook Trail about 2.3 mi. from Route 3, in a slight col at the Featherbed. Continuing in the open, it passes close to a switchback in the Summit Rd. and ends at the summit parking area.

Distances from Route 3

to junction with the Eagle Crag Spur: 1.0 mi., 40 min.

to Cadillac summit: 3.5 mi., 2 hrs. 30 min. (descending Cadillac summit to Route 3, subtract 45 min.)

Cadillac West Face Trail

(AMC's Acadia National Park Discovery Map: E6, E7)

NPS Rating: Strenuous

This steep trail, which starts at the north end of Bubble Pond, is the shortest route to the summit. Begin where Park Loop Rd. passes north of Bubble Pond, using the short spur road off Park Loop Rd. to reach the pond and trailhead. The trail rises steeply through woods and over open ledges to a junction with the Cadillac South Ridge Trail 0.5 mi. from the summit. For the summit, turn left (north).

Distances from north end of Bubble Pond

to Cadillac South Ridge Trail junction: 0.9 mi., 1 hr. 5 min.

to Cadillac summit: 1.4 mi, 1 hr. 25 min.

Cadillac North Ridge Trail

(AMC's Acadia National Park Discovery Map: D7)

NPS Rating: Moderate

This trail follows the north ridge of Cadillac, quickly rising through the stunted evergreens onto open ledges. In winter, the North Ridge Trail is often clear of snow when Summit Rd. and trails on the other parts of the mountain are blocked. To reach the trailhead, follow Park Loop Rd. south from the visitor center. Take the third left turn (about 3 mi.), following the sign for Sand Beach and Park Loop Rd. Park at a paved pulloff on the north side of the road 0.6 mi. beyond the intersection. The trail starts on the south side of the road. It climbs steadily, always keeping to the east of the automobile road, although it closely approaches road switchbacks on two occasions. For much of the distance both sides of the ridge are visible. The views of Bar Harbor, Eagle Lake, Egg Rock, and Dorr Mt. are excellent.

Distance from Park Loop Rd.

to Cadillac summit: 2.2 mi., 1 hr. 30 min.

Gorge Path (AMC's Acadia National Park Discovery Map: D7)

NPS Rating: Moderate

Follow Park Loop Rd. south from the visitor center. Take the third left turn (about 3 mi.), following the sign for Sand Beach and Park Loop Rd. The Gorge Path starts from a gravel pullout on the south side of Park Loop Rd. 0.8 mi. beyond the intersection. The trail rises south up the gorge between Cadillac and Dorr mountains, passing the Hemlock Trail at 0.4 mi. and reaching a junction with the Cadillac-Dorr Connector and the A. Murray Young Path at

1.4 mi. At this point, the trail turns right, climbing steeply to the summit of Cadillac at 1.8 mi.

Distances from Park Loop Rd.

> to Dorr-Cadillac notch: 1.4 mi., 1 hr. 5 min.
> to Cadillac summit: 1.8 mi., 1 hr. 35 min. (in reverse direction, Cadillac summit to Park Loop Rd., subtract about 40 min.)

Bar Island Trail (AMC's Acadia National Park Discovery Map: C8)

NPS Rating: Easy

A short trail that leads from the Bar Island Bar to the summit of Bar Island. The trail must be hiked during low tide, as the Bar Island Bar connecting Bar Island to Bar Harbor is completely underwater at high tide. Return to Bar Harbor no later than two hours after low tide. Trail begins at the end of Bridge Street in Bar Harbor. Walk 0.25 mi. across the bar to the island, then follow a dirt road through the forest. After about 300 yd., the Bar Island Trail leads to the left. At 0.2 mi. from the road it reaches the summit, offering good views of the harbor and the mountains of Acadia.

Distance from Bridge St., via Bar Island Bar and Bar Island dirt road

> to Bar Island Summit: 0.6 mi., 20 min.

JORDAN POND AND SOUTHERN TRAILS AREA

Jordan Pond (274 ft.) is a central trailhead to the eastern side of Mount Desert Island. The view from the Jordan Pond House across the pond to the Bubbles is justifiably famous.

Jordan Pond Path (formerly Jordan Pond Loop Trail)

(AMC's Acadia National Park Discovery Map: E6)

NPS Rating: Moderate

This circuit around Jordan Pond is level most of the way, but crosses a rocky slope with occasional loose boulders at the pond's northeastern shore. It is 3.4 mi. long; directions here are for traveling the east shore first. Park at the Jordan Pond parking area, located off the west side of Park Loop Rd., about 0.1 mi. north of the Jordan Pond House. Follow the boat-launch road to the south shore of the pond.

When you reach the pond, turn right to start the circuit. The trails listed below all diverge to the right, because the route described is counterclockwise around the lake.

Along the west side of the pond, the trail runs under the sharp Jordan Cliffs and loses the sun early in the day. The trail along the west shore also has many wet spots and exposed tree trunks. An alternative route is a carriage road that runs along the pond uphill from the trail. Use the Deer Brook Trail to reach the carriage road. The circuit is completed at the south end of Jordan Pond.

Distances from Jordan Pond parking area
   to Bubble and Jordan Ponds Path (to Canon Brook Trail):
      0.2 mi., 5 min.
   to Jordan Pond Carry (to Eagle Lake): 1.1 mi., 30 min.
   to Bubbles Trail (to South Bubble summit): 1.1 mi., 30 min.
   to Bubbles Divide Trail (leads to Bubble Gap): 1.5 mi., 45 min.
   to Deer Brook Trail (to Penobscot Mountain): 1.6 mi., 50 min.
   to Jordan Pond parking area: 3.2 mi., 1 hr. 40 min.

Jordan Pond Carry (AMC's Acadia National Park Discovery Map: E6)
NPS Rating: Moderate
This trail connects the northeastern shore of Jordan Pond with the Southern Shore Eagle Lake. From Jordan Pond, the Jordan Pond Carry leaves the Jordan Pond Path and climbs moderately to its junction with the Bubbles Divide Trail at 0.4 mi. It then gently descends through forests to Eagle Lake and the Eagle Lake Hiking Trail at 1.1 mi.

Distances from Jordan Pond Loop Trail
   to Bubbles-Divide Trail (at Bubble Rock Parking area):
      0.4 mi., 10 min.
   to Eagle Lake Trail: 1.0 mi., 20 min.

Jordan Stream Path (AMC's Acadia National Park Discovery Map: F6)
NPS Rating: Moderate
This walk along the outlet of Jordan Pond passes through pleasant cedar, maple, and spruce woods. The trailhead is reached by a short connecting path from the Jordan Pond House. The path essentially parallels a carriage road, which can be hiked for a return trip.

At 0.6 mi., the trail passes under a cobblestone bridge and continues descending along the stream. The trail takes a sharp left from the stream at 1.2 mi. and rises to end at a carriage road at the base of Lookout Ledge, close to Little Long Pond.

Distances from the Jordan Pond House
   to trailhead: 0.1 mi., 5 min.
   to cobblestone bridge: 0.6 mi., 20 min.
   to carriage road: 1.3 mi., 45 min.

Jordan Pond Seaside Trail

(AMC's Acadia National Park Discovery Map: F6)

NPS Rating: Easy

The Jordan Pond Seaside Trail offers an easy, level walk between the Jordan Pond House and Seal Harbor. Starting from the south side of the Jordan Pond House, the trail passes through an evergreen forest. After crossing a carriage road at 0.2 mi., the trail continues on a level course to a private driveway just west of Seal Harbor. Follow the driveway south to Route 3 and Seal Harbor. Parking on the southern terminus of the trail is best found at the entrance to the Park Loop Rd. at Seal Harbor.

Distance from the Jordan Pond House
   to Seal Harbor: est. 2.0 mi., 1 hr.

Asticou and Jordan Pond Path (formerly Asticou Trail)

(AMC's Acadia National Park Discovery Map: F5, F6)

NPS Rating: Easy

The Asticou and Jordan Pond Path is reached by the short connecting path from the west side of the Jordan Pond House. This trail follows a level course for most of its distance, yet gains some elevation to reach the Asticou Ridge Trail. It provides an important link to Eliot Mountain as well as a potential leg of a loop over Sargent and Penobscot Mountains.

Leaving from the trailhead, the trail goes through a mixed forest of birch, maple, white pine, and spruce. At 0.9 mi., the trail crosses a carriage road. At 1.0 mi., it crosses another carriage road, and at 1.1 mi., the Penobscot Mountain Trail leaves right, with the Harbor Brook Trail entering from the left shortly after that. The trail then begins to climb up the Asticou Ridge. At 1.5 mi., the Asticou Ridge Trail leaves left, and the trail levels once again. The Asticou Trail follows straight ahead to a junction with the Sargent South Ridge Trail at 1.8 mi. At 2.0 mi., the trail ends at a private drive. Note: the private drive is not open to the public. It is recommended that hikers turn back or take other trails leading from the Asticou and Jordan Pond Path to reach public areas.

Distances from the Jordan Pond House
    to start of the Asticou Trail: 0.1 mi., 5 min.
    to junction with the Penobscot Mountain Trail: 1.1 mi., 30 min.
    to junction with the Asticou Ridge Trail: 1.5 mi., 50 min.
    to junction with the Sargent South Ridge Trail: 1.8 mi., 1 hr.

Asticou Ridge Trail (AMC's Acadia National Park Discovery Map: F6)
NPS Rating: Moderate
This trail is reached by following the Asticou and Jordan Pond Path for 1.5 mi. from Jordan Pond. Traversing a rocky ridge, this trail climbs over Eliot Mtn., offering views to the south and east of the ocean, Day Mtn., and the Triad. Gradually descending from the summit, the trail reaches a monument to Charles William Eliot, one of the founders of the park, at 0.9 mi. Descending into the woods, the trail reaches a junction with a side trail to Route 3 (0.4 mi. in length). Keeping right, the trail descends into the beautiful Thuya Gardens.
Distances from junction with the Asticou and Jordan Pond Path
    to summit of Eliot Mt.: 0.8 mi., 25 min.
    to monument: 0.9 mi., 30 min.
    to junction with Route 3 spur trail: 1.1 mi., 35 min.
    to Thuya Gardens: 1.4 mi., 45 min.

Amphitheater Trail (AMC's Acadia National Park Discovery Map: F6)
NPS Rating: Moderate
The Amphitheater Trail connects the Hadlock Brook Trail to the Sargent South Ridge Trail and the carriage roads near Jordan Pond. It begins on a carriage road between posts 20 and 22, about 1.5 mi. from Jordan Pond via the Asticou and Jordan Pond Path and a carriage road. The trail parallels Harbor Brook, crossing it numerous times before and after passing under the Amphitheater Bridge at 0.8 mi. The Amphitheater Bridge is the largest carriage road bridge in the park. After passing under the bridge, the trail climbs more steeply to Birch Spring and an intersection with the Sargent South Ridge Trail at 1.4 mi. The Amphitheater Trail then descends for 0.3 mi. to its end at the Hadlock Brook Trail.
Distances from Beginning of Trail at Carriage Road crossing between posts 20 and 22
    to Amphitheater Bridge: 0.8 mi., 25 min.
    to Sargent South Ridge Trail: 1.6 mi., 1 hr. 15 min.

to Hadlock Brook Trail: 1.9 mi., 1 hr., 30 min.

Harbor Brook Trail (AMC's Acadia National Park Discovery Map: F5)
NPS Rating: Moderate
The Harbor Brook Trail connects the Asticou and Jordan Pond Path with a
point on Route 3 between Bracy Cove and Northeast Harbor. Following the
brook for its entire length, the trail passes through beautiful cedar groves, as
well as mixed forest. At 1.1 mi., a connector to Eliot Mountain and the Asticou Ridge Trail leaves west. The trail ends on Route 3 at 2.0 mi.
Distance from the Asticou and Jordan Pond Path
    to Route 3: 2.0 mi., 1 hr.

THE BUBBLES

The finely shaped, almost symmetrical North Bubble (872 ft.) and South
Bubble (766 ft.) rise above the north end of Jordan Pond. Formerly covered
with heavy evergreen growth, they were swept by fire in 1947, leaving many
open views. The best access is from the Bubble Rock parking area about 1.1
mi. south of Bubble Pond on the west side of Park Loop Rd.

Bubbles Trail (formerly North Bubble Trail and South Bubble Trail)
(AMC's Acadia National Park Discovery Map: E6)
NPS Rating: Strenuous
Like the Jordan Pond Carry, the 2.2-mi.-long Bubbles Trail connects the
north shore of Jordan Pond with Eagle Lake, but the Bubbles Trail takes the
high route, climbing up and over both of the Bubbles and Conner's Nubble in
the process. The trail starts on the north shore of Jordan Pond at an intersection with the Jordan Pond Path, 1.1 mi. from the Jordan Pond parking
area. It rises very steeply almost immediately, climbing over boulders and
scrambling over ledge before leveling off just before reaching the summit of
South Bubble in 0.4 mi. The views of Jordan Pond and beyond from the
ledges before the summit are spectacular. At the summit, a spur trail leaves
right for a short walk to Bubble Rock, a large glacial erratic, seemingly
perched on the edge of the mountain.

From the summit of South Bubble, the trail descends moderately for 0.2
mi., then turns right coinciding with the Bubbles Divide Trail for a short
distance before turning left, making a steep climb to the summit of North
Bubble at 0.9 mi. The trail continues north past the summit, descending at
an easy pace over open ridgeline for several hundred yards. At 1.7 mi., the

trail crosses a carriage road before making a short climb to the summit of Conner's Nubble and its excellent views of Eagle Lake and Cadillac Mountain at 1.8 mi. The trail continues north over the summit, and descends into the woods, reaching the Eagle Lake Trail near the shore of Eagle Lake at 2.2 mi.

Distances from the Jordan Pond Path
> to summit of South Bubble: 0.4 mi., 25 min.
> to summit of North Bubble Mountain: 0.9 mi., 1 hr.
> to Conner's Nubble: 1.8 mi., 1 hr. 30 min.
> to Eagle Lake Trail: 2.2 mi., 1 hr. 45 min.

Bubbles-Divide Trail (formerly North Bubble Trail and South Bubble Trail) (AMC's Acadia National Park Discovery Map: E6)
NPS Rating: Moderate
The Bubbles-Divide Trail leaves the Bubble Rock Parking area on the Park Loop Road and heads east over the small notch between the Bubbles and down to the north shore of Jordan Pond. By providing quick access to the Bubbles Trail, it is the quickest route to the summit of either mountain.

Distances from the Bubble Rock parking area
> to junction with Jordan Pond Carry: 0.1 mi., 5 min.
> to summit of North Bubble, via Bubbles Trail: 0.5 mi., 25 min.
> to summit of South Bubble, via Bubbles Trail: 0.5 mi., 25 min.
> to junction with the Jordan Pond Path: 0.6 mi., 30 min.

Eagle Lake Trail (AMC's Acadia National Park Discovery Map: D6)
NPS Rating: Moderate
This trail walks along the northern shore of Eagle Lake. It allows hikers to circumnavigate Eagle Lake via the carriage roads without making the climb up and around Conner's Nubble. It begins from a carriage road, 1.3 mi. south of the Eagle Lake parking area. After about 100 yards, the Bubbles Trail enters from the right. It follows the shoreline of the lake for 1.2 mi., ending at the carriage road near post 7, 0.4 mi. north of the Bubble Pond parking area.

Distances from Eagle Lake Parking area
> to beginning of Eagle Lake Hiking Trail: 1.3 mi., 30 min.
> to Jordan Pond Carry: 2.5 mi., 1 hr.
> to Carriage Road post 7: 3.1 mi., 1 hr. 15 min.
> to Bubble Pond parking area (via carriage road): 3.5 mi., 1 hr. 30 min.

PEMETIC MOUNTAIN AREA

Pemetic Mountain (1,247 ft.) is located roughly in the center of the eastern district of the island and offers some of Mount Desert Island's best views. Trails up the west side are short and relatively steep, while routes from the north and south are more gradual and wooded. For the trails from the south, park at the Jordan Pond parking area. From the north, there is parking at Bubble Pond. From the west, parking is located at Bubble Rock.

Pemetic North Ridge Trail (formerly called Pemetic Mountain Trail, Pemetic SE) (AMC's Acadia National Park Discovery Map: E6)

NPS Rating: Strenuous

This trail ascends the mountain from the north. The views of Jordan Pond, the Bubbles, Sargent Mountain, and Eagle Lake are outstanding.

From the north, the trail leaves from the Bubble Pond parking area at the north end of Bubble Pond. It quickly climbs through spruce-fir forest to a junction with the Pemetic Northwest Trail at 1.0 mi. The trail reaches the summit of Pemetic Mountain at 1.1 mi. There are excellent views of the Triad, Cadillac Mountain, and Jordan Pond from the summit. The trail continues down the south ridge as the Pemetic South Ridge Trail (described below).

Distances from Bubble Pond parking area

to Pemetic Northwest Trail junction: 1.0 mi., 55 min.

to Pemetic summit: 1.1 mi., 1 hr.

Pemetic South Ridge Trail (formerly called Pemetic Mountain Trail, West Cliff Trail) AMC's Acadia National Park Discovery Map: E6)

NPS Rating: Strenuous

This trail climbs to the summit of Pemetic Mountain via the mountain's south ridge. It begins at the Bubble and Jordan Ponds Path, 0.5 mi. east of the Jordan Pond parking area. It climbs steadily to a junction at 0.6 mi. with the Pemetic East Cliff Trail, which leads to the right. The Pemetic South Ridge Trail continues straight, climbing over open ledges with spectacular views to the summit and the Pemetic North Ridge Trail at 1.2 mi.

Distances from Bubble and Jordan Ponds Path

to Pemetic East Cliff Trail, 0.6 mi., 25 min.

to Pemetic Mountain summit, 1.2 mi., 1 hr.

to Bubble Pond via Pemetic North Ridge Trail, 2.3 mi., 1 hr. 45 min.

Pemetic East Cliff Trail (formerly a portion of Pemetic Mountain Trail)
(AMC's Acadia National Park Discovery Map: E6)
NPS Rating: Strenuous
This trail is short, but steep, climbing from the intersection of the Bubble and Jordan Ponds Path and the Triad Trail to the Pemetic South Ridge Trail in 0.3 mi. and approximately 10 min.

Pemetic Northwest Trail (formerly Bubbles-Pemetic Trail)
(AMC's Acadia National Park Discovery Map: E6)
NPS Rating: Strenuous
This trail begins at the Bubble Rock parking area, on the west side of Park Loop Rd. about 1.1 mi. south of Bubble Pond.

The path enters the woods east of Park Loop Rd. and climbs in almost constant cover. Sometimes following a rocky stream bed, the trail ends at a junction with the Pemetic North Ridge Trail about 0.1 mi. north of the summit.
Distances from Bubble Rock parking area
    to Pemetic North Ridge Trail junction: 0.5 mi., 35 min.
    to Pemetic summit (via Pemetic North Ridge Trail): 0.6 mi., 40 min.

Bubble and Jordan Ponds Path
(AMC's Acadia National Park Discovery Map: E6, E7)
NPS Rating: Moderate
This slightly graded path leaves from the southeast shore of Jordan Pond to the valley south of Bubble Pond, where it meets the west end of the Canon Brook Trail.

The Bubble and Jordan Ponds Path leaves the shore of Jordan Pond, traveling east, and crosses Park Loop Rd. at 0.1 mi. There is a small parking area at this crossing. Continuing through heavy woods and by easy grades, the path swings in the valley between the Triad and Pemetic Mountain. It crosses the Pemetic South Ridge Trail at 0.5 mi., then turn left at an intersection with the Triad Pass. It continues northeast to cross the Pemetic East Cliff Trail at 0.8 mi., and a carriage road at 1.1 mi. Continuing to climb for another 0.4 mi., the trail ends at the Canon Brook Trail, which climbs to the south ridge of Cadillac Mountain, 1.2 mi. south of the summit.
Distances from Jordan Pond
    to Pemetic South Ridge Trail: 0.5 mi., 20 min.
    to carriage road: 1.1 mi., 40 min.
    to Canon Brook Trail: 1.5 mi., 1 hr. 5 min.

Triad Pass (AMC's Acadia National Park Discovery Map: E6)
NPS Rating: Easy
This short trail begins on the Bubble and Jordan Ponds Path, 0.5 mi. east of Jordan Pond and heads southeast for 0.2 mi., ending at the Hunters Brook Trail. This short link provides trail access from Jordan Pond to the Triad and Day Mountain.
Distances from Jordan Pond hiker parking
    to start of trail via Bubble and Jordan Ponds Path: 0.5 mi., 20 min.
    to Hunters Brook Trail: 0.7 mi., 25 min.

Triad Trail (the northern half of this trail was formerly called the Pemetic Mountain Trail) AMC's Acadia National Park Discovery Map: E6)
NPS Rating: Moderate
The Triad Trail provides a route from Pemetic Mountain to Day Mountain via a hill known as the Triad. It heads southeast from the Bubble and Jordan Ponds Path (0.8 mi. from Jordan Pond) where the Pemetic East Cliff Trail heads northwest. The trail rises moderately for 0.4 mi., where it crosses the Hunters Brook Trail before reaching the top of the Triad. It then descends for 0.4 mi. before ending at a Carriage Road and the Day Mountain Trail.
Distances from Bubble and Jordan Ponds Path
    to Hunters Brook Trail: 0.4 mi., 15 min.
    to Day Mountain Trail: 0.8 mi., 25 min.

Day Mountain Trail (AMC's Acadia National Park Discovery Map: F7)
NPS Rating: Moderate
The Day Mountain Trail starts on the north side of Route 3 approximately 1.5 mi. south of the Blackwoods Campground. The parking area is located on the south side of the highway.
    The Day Mountain Trail climbs moderately through the forest for its entire length. Periodically crossing carriage roads, the trail offers beautiful views of Hunter's Beach and Seal Harbor from ledges 0.6 mi. from the trailhead. At 0.8 mi., the summit of Day Mountain is reached. (A carriage road also rises to the summit of Day.) Then descending into the forest quickly, the trail ends at another carriage road at 1.3 mi., where the Triad Trail continues north toward the Triad and Pemetic Mountain.

Distances from Route 3
> to summit of Day Mountain: 0.8 mi., 35 min.
>
> to carriage road: 1.3 mi., 50 min.
>
> to Pemetic Mountain summit via Triad, Pemetic East Cliff, and Pemetic South Ridge Trails: 3.0 mi., 2 hrs.

Hunter's Brook Trail (formerly Triad-Hunter's Brook Trail)

(AMC's Acadia National Park Discovery Map: E7, F7)

NPS Rating: Strenuous

This trail begins on the Park Loop Rd. near the southern overpass of Route 3. It follows along Hunter's Brook, passing through a canopy of cedar, maple, and spruce. At 1.25 mi. the trail bears west from the brook and climbs to a carriage road at 1.4 mi. Crossing the carriage path, the trail continues to climb to a junction with the Triad Trail near the Triad at 1.8 mi. (Turning right onto the Triad Trail will take you to the summit of Pemetic Mountain in an additional 1.3 mi.) Then the trail descends for 0.3 mi., passes the Triad Pass Trail on the right, takes a left, and heads south, ending at a carriage road (0.2 mi. west of post 17) at 2.6 mi.

Distances from Park Loop Rd.
> to carriage path: 1.4 mi., 45 min.
>
> to junction with the Triad Trail: 1.8 mi., 1 hr. 15 min.
>
> to Triad Pass Trail: 2.1 mi., 1 hr. 25 min.
>
> to carriage road near post 17: 2.6 mi., 1 hr. 45 min.

SARGENT MOUNTAIN AND PENOBSCOT MOUNTAIN

Sargent Mountain (1,379 ft.) and Penobscot Mountain (1,196 ft.) are open summits about 1 mi. apart. Sargent Pond, a pleasant mountain pond, lies between the two summits. From the south, the preferred starting point is Jordan Pond parking area. The outlying territory to the southwest contains an interesting maze of trails and carriage roads around Bald Peak (974 ft.) and Parkman Mountain (941 ft.). Ample parking is available at two areas: One is on the west side of Route 3/198 and about 0.3 mi. north of Upper Hadlock Pond (reservoir, no swimming); and the other, Parkman Mountain parking area, is on the east side of Route 3/198, about 0.5 mi. north of Upper Hadlock Pond. Upper Hadlock Pond is approximately 2.5 mi. south of where Route 3/198 splits from Route 233.

Penobscot Mountain Trail

(AMC's Acadia National Park Discovery Map: E6, F6)

NPS Rating: Strenuous

The lower section of this trail was recently rerouted to extend the trail to the Asticou and Jordan Pond Path, 1.1 mi. west of the Jordan Pond House. The original lower part of the trail that starts near the Jordan Pond House is now called the Spring Trail.

The trail heads north from the Asticou and Jordan Pond Path, climbing at an easy pace and making three carriage road crossings in its first 0.3 mi. It then climbs more steeply, occasionally breaking out into the open with excellent views to the south. It attains the south ridge of Penobscot Mountain and a junction with the Spring Trail at 1.2 mi. The trail then climbs gradually over open granite ledges to the summit of Penobscot Mountain at 2.2 mi., and then continues north, descending to an intersection with the Deer Brook Trail at 2.3 mi. The trail turns left here and reaches Sargent Pond in about 100 yd. From the pond, the trail makes a short climb to the Sargent South Ridge Trail at 2.5 mi.

Distances from Asticou and Jordan Pond Path

> to Spring Trail: 1.2 mi., 1 hr.
>
> to Penobscot Mountain summit : 2.2 mi., 1 hr. 30 min.
>
> to Sargent Mountain summit (via Sargent South Ridge Trail):
> est. 2.9 mi., 2 hr.

Spring Trail (formerly part of the Penobscot Mountain Trail)

(AMC's Acadia National Park Discovery Map: E6)

NPS Rating: Strenuous

This trail provides the quickest access to Penobscot Mountain from the Jordan Pond House. It is short, but very steep in places and should be avoided for descents, especially in wet conditions. The trail starts from the west side of Jordan Stream, about 100 yd. west of the Jordan Pond House at an intersection with a carriage road and the Asticou and Jordan Pond Path. The trail runs west and passes the Jordan Cliffs Trail at 0.3 mi. shortly before crossing a carriage road. It then climbs very steeply with the assistance of iron rungs and wooden handrails to the Penobscot Mountain Trail at 0.5 mi.

Distances from Jordan Pond House

> to Jordan Cliffs Trail: 0.3 mi., 15 min.

to Penobscot Mountain Trail: 0.5 mi., 30 min.

to Penobscot Mountain summit via Penobscot Mountain Trail:
    1.5 mi., 1 hr.

Jordan Cliffs Trail (AMC's Acadia National Park Discovery Map: E6)
NPS Rating: Ladder
This challenging yet scenic trail leaves the Spring Trail 0.3 mi. west of the
Jordan Pond House, just northeast of the junction of the Spring Trail and a
carriage road. Bearing right soon after crossing the carriage road, the trail to
Jordan Cliffs heads north and rises up the east shoulder of Penobscot Moun-
tain in gradual pitches to the cliffs at 0.8 mi. The trail traverses the Jordan
Cliffs, via ladders and handrails, to a junction with the Penobscot East Trail
at 1.2 mi. Turn left on the Penobscot East Trail to reach the summit of
Penobscot Mountain. While very steep, the trail is spectacular, with views of
the Bubbles, Pemetic Mountain, and Jordan Pond.

Continuing straight past the Penobscot East Trail, the Jordan Cliffs Trail
traverses the cliffs above Jordan Pond and ends at its intersection with the
Deer Brook Trail and the Sargent East Cliff Trail at 1.5 mi.
Distances from Jordan Pond House
    to Jordan Cliffs Trail (via Spring Trail): 0.3 mi., 15 min.
    to Jordan Cliffs: 1.1 mi., 55 min.
    to Penobscot summit (via Penobscot East Trail): 1.8 mi., 1 hr. 20 min.
    to junction with the Deer Brook Trail: 1.8 mi., 1 hr. 15 min.
    to summit of Sargent Mountain via Sargent East Cliff Trail:
        2.5 mi., 1 hr. 50 min.

Sargent East Cliff Trail (AMC's Acadia National Park Discovery Map: E6)
NPS Rating: Strenuous
This short but steep trail connects the Jordan Cliffs Trail to the summit of
Sargent Mountain. It is recommended more for ascending than descending,
especially in wet weather, when the steep climb down wet rocks and ledges
can be troublesome. The trail starts at Deer Brook and an intersection with
the Jordan Cliffs Trail and the Deer Brook Trail. It climbs quickly up the
south east face of Sargent Mountain, and has excellent views for much of its
0.7 mi.
Distances from Deer Brook Trail
    to Sargent Mountain Summit: 0.7 mi., 35 min.

Deer Brook Trail (AMC's Acadia National Park Discovery Map: E6)
NPS Rating: Strenuous
This is a steep, quick ascent of 0.8 mi. to Sargent Pond from the Jordan Pond Path at the north end of Jordan Pond. The route is entirely wooded and follows the course of Deer Brook, crossing a carriage road at 0.2 mi. and reaching an intersection with the Jordan Cliffs and Sargent East Cliff trails at 0.3 mi. This trail joins the Penobscot Mountain Trail in the valley between Sargent and Penobscot, 0.8 mi. from the shore of Jordan Pond.
Distance from Jordan Pond Path
    to Penobscot Mountain Trail junction: 0.8 mi., 45 min.

Sargent South Ridge Trail
(AMC's Acadia National Park Discovery Map: E6)
NPS Rating: Moderate
This trail starts from a carriage path leaving from the parking lot at the Brown Mountain gatehouse in Northeast Harbor. The trailhead is located about 1 mi. south of Upper Hadlock Pond, on the east side of Route 3/198. The trail begins at an intersection with the Asticou and Jordan Pond Path, 0.1 mi. south of a carriage road, which is the easiest way to access the trail. From the parking area, follow the carriage path east, always bearing right at junctions for about 0.7 mi. There, the trail heads north to the summit of Sargent Mountain or south to the Asticou and Jordan Pond Path.

The Sargent South Ridge Trail rises over the wooded shoulder and passes just southeast of the summit of Cedar Swamp Mountain at 1.4 mi. from the carriage road. A spur trail bears left to the summit. It drops to cross Little Harbor Brook at 1.5 mi., where it crosses the Amphitheater Trail. The trail then leaves the woods and rises sharply 0.5 mi. to a junction with the Penobscot Mountain Trail, which comes in from the right. The trail continues north over open granite ledges, past junctions to the left with the Hadlock Brook Trail at 2.2 mi. and the Maple Spring Trail at 2.4 mi. It reaches the summit at 2.7 mi.
Distances from carriage road
    to Cedar Swamp Mountain spur path: 1.4 mi., 1 hr.
    to Penobscot Mountain Trail: 2.0 mi., 1 hr. 40 min.
    to Hadlock Brook Trail: 2.2 mi., 1 hr. 55 min.
    to Maple Spring Trail: 2.4 mi., 2 hr.
    to Sargent summit: 2.7 mi., 2 hr. 15 min.

Giant Slide Trail

(AMC's Acadia National Park Discovery Map: E5)

NPS Rating: Ladder

This trail is the approach to the Sargent Mountain area from the northwest. The beginning of this trail has been relocated to a trailhead on the east side of Route 198, 1.0 mi. south of Route 233 (limited parking is available on the west side of the road). The trail climbs through mature softwoods up a gradual slope to a carriage road, at 0.7 mi. The trail turns sharply right (south) and, following Sargent Brook, rises steeply over the tumbled boulders of Giant Slide. At 1.1 mi., the Parkman Mountain Trail diverges right and the Sargent Northwest Trail leaves left. The Giant Slide Trail continues through the notch between Parkman Mountain and Gilmore Peak at an intersection with the Grandgent Trail at 1.7 mi. and descends to end at a junction with the Maple Spring Trail at 2.3 mi.

Distances from Route 198

   to carriage road crossing: 0.7 mi., 15 min.

   to Parkman Mountain Trail and Sargent Northwest Trail junction:
       1.1 mi., 45 min.

   to Maple Spring Trail junction: 2.3 mi., 1 hr. 30 min.

Sargent Northwest Trail

(AMC's Acadia National Park Discovery Map: E5)

NPS Rating: Moderate

Leaving the Giant Slide Trail 1.1 mi. from Route 198, this trail ascends east and crosses a carriage road at 0.3 mi. Continuing essentially east, it rises over slanting pitches for 0.3 mi. before making a sharp right (south) turn. The final 0.4 mi. to the summit of Sargent is over open ledges offering spectacular views.

Distance from Giant Slide Trail

   to Sargent summit: 1.0 mi., 1 hr.

Hadlock Brook Trail   (AMC's Acadia National Park Discovery Map: E6)

NPS Rating: Strenuous

The Hadlock Brook Trail provides access to Sargent Mountain from the southwest, as well as leading to several other trails without roadside access. From the east side of Route 198 just north of Upper Hadlock Pond and opposite the Norumbega Mountain parking area, the Hadlock Brook Trail heads east, passing the Bald Peak Trail, Parkman Mountain Trail, a carriage road, the Hadlock Ponds Trail, and the Maple Spring Trail, all in the first 0.4 mi. From here, the trail follows the east branch of Hadlock Brook through mature forest for 0.4 mi. before crossing a carriage road at Waterfall Bridge and its excellent view of a 40-ft. waterfall. The trail then gets steeper, continuing to parallel the brook over rough footing to a junction with the Amphitheater Trail at 1.1 mi. The trail then climbs very steeply before reaching the open terrain of Sargent Mountain's south ridge and the Sargent South Ridge Trail at 1.7 mi.

Distances from Route 198

to junction with the Maple Spring Trail: 0.4 mi., 10 min.

to junction with the Amphitheater Trail: 1.1 mi., 40 min.

to summit of Sargent Mountain via Sargent South Ridge Trail:
2.2 mi., 1 hr. 30 min.

Maple Spring Trail (AMC's Acadia National Park Discovery Map: E5)

NPS Rating: Strenuous

This trail climbs to the south ridge of Sargent Mountain from the southwest, following the west branch of Hadlock Brook for much of its length. A recent relocation on the upper part of this trail means it now also provides access to Gilmore Peak via the Grandgent Trail.

The beginning of the Maple Spring Trail is reached by following the Hadlock Brook Trail from the Norumbega Mountain parking area on Route 198 for 0.4 mi., where the Maple Spring Trail leads left. The trail closely follows Hadlock Brook, crossing it several times. In high water, there are some very nice cascades and small waterfalls before and after crossing under the Hemlock Bridge 0.3 mi. from the Hadlock Brook Trail. The trail climbs through a small gorge before reaching the Giant Slide Trail at 0.4 mi., and then the Grandgent Trail at 0.9 mi. (Gilmore Peak is 0.1 mi. to the left via the Grandgent Trail.) Here the Maple Spring Trail makes a sharp right and climbs steeply, reaching the open south ridge and the Sargent South Ridge Trail at 1.4 mi. The summit of Sargent Mountain is 0.3 mi. to the left via the Sargent South Ridge Trail.

Distances from Hadlock Brook Trail

to Giant Slide Trail, 0.4 mi., 15 min.

to Grandgent Trail, 0.9 mi., 40 min.

to Sargent Mountain summit via Sargent South Ridge Trail,
1.7 mi., 1 hr. 20 min.

Grandgent Trail

(AMC's Acadia National Park Discovery Map: E5)

NPS Rating: Strenuous

This trail runs between the summits of Sargent Mountain, Gilmore Peak, and Parkman Mountain. From the summit of Sargent, the trail leaves west and steeply descends into a saddle at the base of Gilmore Peak, where there is an intersection with the Maple Spring Trail at 0.5 mi. After a right turn and a short climb of 0.1 mi., the trail reaches Gilmore Peak. Then it gradually descends for 0.3 mi., crossing the Giant Slide Trail before climbing another 0.2 mi. to the summit of Parkman Mountain.

Distances from the summit of Sargent Mountain
> to Maple Spring Trail: 0.5 mi., 20 min.
> to Gilmore Peak: 0.6 mi., 25 min.
> to junction with the Giant Slide Trail: 0.9 mi., 35 min.
> to Parkman Mountain summit: 1.1 mi., 45 min.

Parkman Mountain Trail

(AMC's Acadia National Park Discovery Map: E5)

NPS Rating: Moderate

The Parkman Mountain Trail starts out with the Hadlock Brook Trail but soon diverges north (left) to lead 1.5 mi. through woods and over a series of knobs to the summit of Parkman Mountain. The trail crosses a carriage road three times on the way to the summit. The Bald Peak Trail joins the trail from the right at 1.4 mi. At the summit, the Grandgent Trail leaves right toward Gilmore Peak. The Parkman Mountain Trail continues north over open ledges, then through the woods, crossing a carriage road 0.5 mi. beyond the summit. The trail ends 0.3 mi. farther, at the junction of the Giant Slide Trail and the Sargent North Ridge Trail.

Distances from Route 198
> to Parkman summit: 1.4 mi., 50 min.
> to Giant Slide Trail-Sargent North Ridge Trail junction:
>   2.2 mi., 1 hr. 10 min.

Bald Peak Trail

(AMC's Acadia National Park Discovery Map: E5)

NPS Rating: Moderate

This trail is the most direct route up Bald Peak, one of several small and rocky, open summits to the west of Sargent Mountain. The trail is reached by following the Hadlock Brook Trail for 0.2 mi. from the Norumbega Mountain parking area on Route 198. At this point, the Bald Peak Trail leaves left. Gradually climbing through the forest, the trail reaches the summit of Bald Peak at 0.9 mi. The trail reaches the Parkman Mountain Trail 0.2 mi. beyond the summit of Bald Peak.

Distances from Route 198 (via the Hadlock Brook Trail)
> to beginning of Bald Peak Trail: 0.2 mi., 10 min.
> to summit of Bald Peak: 0.9 mi., 30 min.
> to Parkman Mountain Trail: 1.1 mi., 40 min.

NORUMBEGA MOUNTAIN

The summit of Norumbega Mountain (852 ft.) is wooded, but the blueberries on the north slope make it attractive and appealing in season. The trail offers very good views of Somes Sound and the mountains west of the sound. Note: This area is honeycombed with abandoned and unofficial paths, and the names of existing trails have recently changed. Pay careful attention to trail markers and maps.

Goat Trail (formerly a portion of the Norumbega Mountain Trail)
(AMC's Acadia National Park Discovery Map: E5)
NPS Rating: Strenuous
This trail leaves the Norumbega Mountain parking lot on the west side of Route 198 about 0.3 mi. north of Upper Hadlock Pond. It ascends quickly and very steeply for the first 0.3 mi. through woods to granite ledges, then swings south to the summit, 0.6 mi. from the parking area. There are occasional views from the ledges prior to reaching the wooded summit and excellent views from the Norumbega Mountain trail about 150 yd. beyond the summit.

Distance from Route 198
> to summit of Norumbega Mountain: 0.6 mi., 45 min.

Norumbega Mountain Trail
(AMC's Acadia National Park Discovery Map: E5 F5)
NPS Rating: Moderate
This trail connects the Hadlock Ponds Trail on the north shore of Lower Hadlock Pond to the summit of Norumbega Mountain. Beginning at the Goat Trail and the summit of Norumbega, the Norumbega Mountain Trail follows south ridge over semi-open ledges with occasional views, descending

moderately before entering the forest and reaching junction with the Golf Course Trail, 0.8 mi. below the summit. Veering left at this junction, the trail continues its moderate descent, reaching Lower Hadlock Pond and the Hadlock Ponds Trail at 1.4 mi.

Distances from Norumbega Mountain Summit
> to Golf Course Trail, 0.8 mi., 15 min. (25 min. in reverse)
> to Hadlock Ponds Trail, 1.4 mi., 30 min. (45 min. in reverse)

Hadlock Ponds Trail (formerly Hadlock Trail)

(AMC's Acadia National Park Discovery Map: F5)

NPS Rating: Moderate

This relatively flat trail starts on the Hadlock Brook Trail, 0.3 mi. from the Norumbega Mountain parking area on Route 198; follows the eastern shoreline of Upper Hadlock Pond; crosses Route 198; and continues to Lower Hadlock Pond and the Lower Norumbega Trail and Norumbega Mountain Trail. The views of the ponds from the trail are excellent. As of this writing, the section from Route 198 south to the Lower Norumbega Trail is not passable but is under construction.

Distances from Hadlock Brook Trail
> to Route 198 at south end of Upper Hadlock Pond: 0.7 mi., 15 min.
> to Lower Norumbega Trail (not passable as of this writing):
>> 1.0 mi., 20 min.
> to Norumbega Mountain Trail: 1.6 mi., 35 min.

Lower Norumbega Trail (formerly part of Norumbega Mountain Trail)   (AMC's Acadia National Park Discovery Map: F5

NPS Rating: Moderate

This trail connects the Goat Trail, just west of the Norumbega Mountain parking area to the Hadlock Ponds Trail near the northern shore of Lower Hadlock Pond. It is 0.9 mi. long, following uneven terrain in a spruce forest while paralleling Route 198.

Distances from Goat Trail
> to Hadlock Ponds Trail: 0.9 mi., 30 min.

Lower Hadlock Trail   (AMC's Acadia National Park Discovery Map: F5)

NPS Rating: Easy

This short trail follows the eastern shoreline of Lower Hadlock Pond. It starts at the inlet to Lower Hadlock Pond where it leaves the Hadlock Ponds

Trail, crosses the stream and follows the shoreline through a nice evergreen forest, reaching Hadlock Pond Road in 0.7 mi.

Distances from Hadlock Ponds Trail
> to Hadlock Pond Road, 0.7 mi., 15 min.
> to southern terminus of Hadlock Ponds Trail via Hadlock Pond Road, 1.2 mi., 25 min.

Western District *(West of Somes Sound)*

ACADIA MOUNTAIN

The high point on the western side of Somes Sound, Acadia Mountain provides dramatic views of the sound and the Cranberry Isles from open ledges interspersed with pitch pines and scrub oaks. A loop over the summit can be made using the Acadia Mountain Trail and the Man 'o War Brook fire road.

Acadia Mountain Trail (AMC's Acadia National Park Discovery Map: E4)
NPS Rating: Strenuous
Parking is located at the Acadia Mountain parking area on the west side of Route 102, 3 mi. south of Somesville and 3 mi. north of Southwest Harbor. (Please do not block the fire road gates on the east side of Route 102.) The Acadia Mountain Trail begins on the east side of Route 102, across the road from the parking area. Go left at the fork 0.1 mi. down the trail.

The trail ascends the west slope, soon leaving woods for open rocks and frequent views. It passes over the highest summit (681 ft.) and reaches the east summit, with views of the sound, at about 1 mi. The trail then descends southeast and south very steeply to cross Man o' War Brook. A junction about 50 yd. beyond the stream marks the end of the Acadia Mountain Trail. To return to Route 102 via the fire road, go west (right) at the junction and proceed past trails to St. Sauveur and Valley Cove, which diverge left about 100 yd. east of the stream. The east end of the Man o' War Brook fire road is in another 200 yd. Follow the fire road west over gradual grades for 0.9 mi. back to Route 102, 50 yd. north of the parking area. You will cross the Acadia Mountain Trail shortly before Route 102; turn left onto the trail to reach the parking lot directly.

Distances from Route 102
> to Acadia Mountain, east summit: 1 mi., 45 min.
> to Man o' War Brook: 1.4 mi., 1 hr.

to Route 102 via Man o' War Brook fire road: 2.3 mi., 1 hr. 30 min.

ST. SAUVEUR MOUNTAIN

St. Sauveur Mountain (690 ft.) can be climbed from the north via the Man o' War Brook fire road (NPS fire service road from Route 102), from Route 102 on the west, and from Fernald Cove Rd. on the south. There are good views of Somes Sound from Eagle Cliff, just east of the summit.

St. Sauveur Trail (AMC's Acadia National Park Discovery Map: F4)
NPS Rating: Moderate
This trail is an easy route to the summit of St. Sauveur Mountain from the north. Follow the Acadia Mountain Trail description to reach the parking lot and trailhead. Start 0.1 mi. down the Acadia Mountain Trail, and go right at the fork.

The path runs south through evergreens and over open slopes, rising constantly for 0.8 mi. to a junction with the Ledge Trail entering on the right. From there it is 0.2 mi. to the summit, where the St. Sauveur Trail continues past the summit while a spur of the Valley Peak Trail leaves left. The St. Sauveur Trail descends the south ridge of the mountain for 0.4 mi., where it ends at the Valley Peak Trail, 0.5 mi. from Fernald Point Rd.
Distances from Route 102
  to Ledge Trail junction: 0.9 mi., 40 min.
  to St. Sauveur summit: 1.2 mi., 55 min.
  to Fernald Point Road via Valley Peak Trail: 2.1 mi., 1 hr. 20 min.

Ledge Trail (AMC's Acadia National Park Discovery Map: F4)
NPS Rating: Moderate
This trail begins at St. Sauveur parking area on the east side of Route 102 about 0.2 mi. north of the entrance road to the NPS swimming facilities at the south end of Echo Lake. The parking area is also about 0.2 mi. south of the access road to the Appalachian Mountain Club's Echo Lake Camp. (For more information visit the camp's website at www.amcecholakecamp.org.)

The path enters the woods and rises over ledges to its end. It meets the St. Sauveur Trail 0.6 mi. from the highway and 0.2 mi. northwest of the summit.
Distances from Route 102
  to St. Sauveur Trail junction: 0.6 mi., 25 min.
  to St. Sauveur summit: 0.8 mi., 40 min.

Valley Peak Trail (AMC's Acadia National Park Discovery Map: F4)
NPS Rating: Strenuous
This trail leaves the west side of the Valley Cove truck road a few yards north of the parking area at Fernald Cove. It rises steeply northwest through shady woods over Valley Peak (the south shoulder of St. Sauveur Mountain), where the St. Sauveur Trail leads left. The trail then skirts the top of Eagle Cliff, with outstanding views of Valley Cove below and the mountains to the east of Somes Sound. At 0.7 mi., a spur path leads to the summit of St. Sauveur Mountain, while the Valley Peak Trail continues straight, steeply descending the northeast shoulder of St. Sauveur to end at a junction with the Acadia Mountain Trail near Man o' War Brook and the east terminus of the Man o' War Brook fire road at 1.5 mi.
Distances from the Valley Cove truck road
 to St. Sauveur Trail: 0.4 mi., 20 min.
 to St. Sauveur summit via spur path: 0.8 mi., 45 min.
 to Acadia Mountain Trail junction: 1.5 mi., 1 hr. 10 min.

FLYING MOUNTAIN

A few minutes' climb to the open top of Flying Mountain (284 ft.) gives a fine panorama of the sound, Southwest Harbor, Northeast Harbor, and the islands to the south: the Cranberries, Greening, Sutton, Baker, and Bear.

Flying Mountain Trail
(AMC's Acadia National Park Discovery Map: F4)
NPS Rating: Moderate
This scenic trail over tiny Flying Mountain leaves the east side of the parking area at the Fernald Cove end of the Valley Cove truck road and rises quickly and steeply through spruce woods, reaching the summit of Flying Mountain in 0.6 mi. The trail then descends to the shoreline of Valley Cove and follows the cove to the left, reaching the Valley Cove Trail and Valley Cove fire road at 0.9 mi. For an easy return to the Fernald Cove parking area, follow the fire road south for about 0.5 mi.
Distances from Fernald Cove parking area
 to Flying Mountain summit: 0.6 mi., 15 min.
 to Valley Cove Trail and fire road: 0.9 mi., 25 min.
 to Fernald Cove parking area (via fire road from Valley Cove):
  1.4 mi., 45 min.
 to Acadia Mountain Trail junction via Valley Cove Trail: 2.0 mi., 1 hr.

Valley Cove Trail (formerly part of the Flying Mountain Trail)
(AMC's Acadia National Park Discovery Map: F4)
NPS Rating: Easy
This trail connects the Fernald Cove parking area to the Acadia Mountain Trail. It starts on the shoreline of Valley Cove at the end of the Valley Cove fire road, 0.5 mi. from the parking area. From the fire road, the Valley Cove Trail goes left, while the Flying Mountain Trail goes right. The Valley Cove Trail follows the shoreline under the ledges of Eagle Cliff high above. It ends at the Acadia Mountain Trail in 1.1 mi.
Distances from Fernald Cove parking area
   to beginning of Valley Cove Trail via Valley Cove fire road: 0.5 mi., 10 min.
   to Acadia Mountain Trail: 1.6 mi., 45 min.

BEECH MOUNTAIN
Beech Mountain (841 ft.) lies between Echo Lake and Long Pond (Great Pond on some maps). Its summit is easy to reach from either the Beech Cliff parking area (located at the end of Beech Hill Rd., in the notch between Beech Cliff and Beech Mountain) or the pumping station area at the foot of Long Pond. To reach the pumping station, follow Seal Cove Road west from Southwest Harbor. Take the first right (toward the landfill) and follow this road until it ends at the pumping station. Beech Mountain can also be climbed on its southwest flank, beginning at the south end of Long Pond. An added attraction near Beech Mountain is the Beech Cliff–Canada Cliff area just to the east of the Beech Cliff parking area. These rugged cliffs offer spectacular views of Echo Lake.

Beech Cliff Trail (AMC's Acadia National Park Discovery Map: F3)
NPS Rating: Ladder
This trail offers quick but extremely steep access to Beech Cliff from the beach parking area at the southern end of Echo Lake. The trail is usually closed from early spring through early August to protect peregrine falcons nesting on the cliffs, so check with park personnel to confirm that the trail is open. After about 0.1 mi. of moderate hiking through the woods, the trail climbs very steeply for the rest of the way, climbing the cliff via a series of stone staircases and iron ladders. This trail reaches the level top of Beech Cliff 0.5 mi. from the parking area, where the Canada Cliff Trail leads left. The Beech Cliff trail

continues right for about 100 yards, where it ends at the Beech Cliff Loop Trail. Views of Echo Lake and the mountains to the east are excellent.

Distance from parking area

   to Canada Cliff Trail and Beech Cliff Loop Trail: 0.5 mi., 40 min.

Canada Cliff Trail (AMC's Acadia National Park Discovery Map: F3)

NPS Rating: Moderate

This trail starts from the Valley Trail, 0.2 mi. south of the Beech Cliff parking area located at the end of Beech Hill Rd. To reach this trailhead, follow Route 102 south through Somesville and take Pretty Marsh Rd., the first right after the fire station. Follow Pretty Marsh Rd. west for about 0.5 mi., where the Beech Hill Rd. intersects from the left. Follow Beech Hill Rd. south until it ends at the trailhead, 3.2 mi. from Pretty Marsh Road.

   The trail heads east from the Valley Trail, going over a small knoll and then crossing a cedar swamp on bog bridges, before reaching a fork, 0.2 mi. from the Valley Trail. Either fork will take you to the Beech Cliff and Beech Cliff Loop Trails. The left fork is shorter (0.4 mi. vs. 0.6 mi.), but the right fork provides views from Canada Cliff on the way.

Distances from Beech Cliff parking area

   to beginning of trail via Valley Trail: 0.2 mi., 5 min.

   to fork in trail: 0.4 mi., 10 min.

   to Beech Cliff and Beech Cliff Loop Trails (via right fork): 1.0 mi., 35 min.

   to Beech Cliff and Beech Cliff Loop Trails (via left fork): 0.8 mi., 30 min.

Beech Cliff Loop Trail (AMC's Acadia National Park Discovery Map: E3)

NPS Rating: Moderate

This trail climbs Beech Cliff from the Beech Cliff parking area at the end of Beech Hill Rd. (See Canada Cliff Trail description for directions.) The trail starts with the Valley Trail and soon leaves left, climbing moderately and sometimes steeply up the western, wooded slope of Beech Cliff. In 0.2 mi., it reaches an intersection, where the Beech Cliff Trail leads right toward Echo Lake and the Beech Cliff Loop Trail leads straight or left, depending on which direction the loop is walked. The loop is 0.4 mi. long and follows the edge of the cliff for about half of its length. The views are spectacular to the east.

Distances from Beech Cliff parking area

   to loop junction and Beech Cliff Trail: 0.2 mi., 15 min.

   to return to parking area via loop: 0.8 mi., 35 min.

Beech Mountain Loop Trail

(AMC's Acadia National Park Discovery Map: F3)

NPS Rating: Moderate

The trail leaves the northwest side of the Beech Cliff parking area and forks in 0.1 mi. The trail to the right (northwest) is 0.7 mi. long and provides a beautiful vista of Long Pond before climbing to the summit. The trail to the left (south) is 0.4 mi. long and climbs more steeply to the summit of Beech Mountain, with its fire tower. The two trails can be combined to form a scenic loop hike.

From the summit, the Beech West Ridge and Beech South Ridge Trails depart to the southwest and south, respectively, providing access to the parking area the south end of Long Pond.

Distances from Beech Cliff parking area

to Beech Mountain summit (via north fork): 0.4 mi., 30 min.

to Beech Cliff Parking area (via north fork, then south fork):
1.1 mi., 1 hr. 15 min.

Valley Trail

(AMC's Acadia National Park Discovery Map: F3)

NPS Rating: Moderate

This graded path is a convenient link between the Long Pond area and the Beech Cliff parking area, which is located in the notch between Beech Cliff and Beech Mountain. It also permits a circuit or one-way trip over Beech Mountain, since it provides direct access to the Beech South Ridge Trail.

The trail starts at the parking area next to the pumping station at the south end of Long Pond and crosses a service road in 0.3 mi. By easy grades over wooded slopes, the trail runs north briefly and then swings east (right) before entering a series of switchbacks on the south slopes of Beech Mountain. At 0.7 mi., the Beech South Ridge Trail to Beech Mountain leaves left. Continuing east the Valley Trail soon swings north to maintain altitude as it runs up the valley separating Beech Mountain and Canada Cliff. At 1.3 mi. the Canada Cliff Trail comes in from the right. Continue directly ahead to reach the Beech Cliff parking area at 1.5 mi.

Distances from parking area at Long Pond

to Beech South Ridge Trail junction: 0.7 mi., 15 min.

to Canada Ridge Trail junction: 1.3 mi., 40 min.

to Beech Cliff parking area: 1.5 mi., 50 min.

Beech South Ridge Trail (AMC's Acadia National Park Discovery Map: F3)
NPS Rating: Moderate
This well-marked trail diverges left from the Valley Trail about 0.7 mi. east of the parking area at the south end of Long Pond and steadily ascends the south ridge to the summit along open ledges, offering views to the south.
Distances from Long Pond parking area
    to start (via Valley Trail): 0.7 mi., 15 min.
    to summit of Beech Mountain: 1.5 mi., 45 min.

Beech West Ridge Trail (AMC's Acadia National Park Discovery Map: F3)
NPS Rating: Moderate
Leaving from the east side of the Long Pond pumping station, this trail skirts the edge of Long Pond for 0.3 mi. At this point the trail begins to climb from the shore, rising steeply at times. Ledges offer good views of the pond and Mansell Mountain. The trail reaches the Beech Mountain Loop Trail at 0.9 mi.
Distances from Long Pond parking area at pumping station
    to junction with the Beech Mountain Loop Trail: 0.9 mi., 40 min.
    to summit of Beech Mountain (via the Beech Mountain Loop Trail):
        1.0 mi., 45 min.

Western Mountains

BERNARD MOUNTAIN AND MANSELL MOUNTAIN

This area has two main summits: Bernard Mountain (1,071 ft.) to the west and Mansell Mountain (938 ft.) to the east. Both summits are wooded, and extensive views are rare. You can reach all of the southern approaches from the parking area at the foot of Long Pond near the pumping station. To reach the pumping station, follow Seal Cove Road west from Southwest Harbor. Take the first right (toward the landfill) and follow this road until it ends at the pumping station.

Great Notch Trail (formerly Great Notch and Western Mountain Trails) (AMC's Acadia National Park Discovery Map: F2, F3)
NPS Rating: Moderate
This is the only trail providing access to the western mountains from the north. There are no open vistas. To reach the trailhead, go about 1 mi. east

from the western loop of Route 102 on the Long Pond (Great Pond) fire road. Parking is available here. The fire road crosses Route 102 just north of Seal Cove Pond. The Western Trail starts on the southeast side of the road about 0.1 mi. beyond the Pine Hill turnaround and parking area.

The trail trends southeast and rises by easy grades to a junction with the Great Pond Trail (entering left) 1.1 mi. from the fire road. It reaches the Great Notch at 1.5 mi., where the Bernard Mountain Trail leads right toward Bernard Mountain and the Razorback Trail leads left toward Mansell Mountain. The Great Notch trail continues through the notch and down to the Gilley Field parking area at the Gilley Trail at 2.0 mi., 0.7 mi. from the Gilley Field parking area.

Distances from Great Pond fire road
> to Great Pond Trail junction: 1.1 mi., 1 hr. 5 min.
> to Great Notch: 1.5 mi., 1 hr. 25 min.
> to Gilley Field parking area via Gilley Trail, 2.7 mi., 2 hr. 5 min.

Gilley Trail (formerly part of the Great Notch Trail)   (AMC's Acadia National Park Discovery Map: F3)
NPS Rating: Easy
This trail starts at the Gilley Field Parking area at the eastern end of the Western Mountain Fire Road. It provides access to Mansell and Bernard Mountains via the Razorback, Great Notch, and Sluiceway Trails. The trail starts next to the Mansell Mountain Trail, but instead of climbing the peak, it follows easy grades to the west, passing the Razorback Trail in 0.1 mi., crossing a fire road at 0.3 mi., then turning north and climbing moderately to its end at the Great Notch and Sluiceway Trails at 0.6 mi.
Distances from Gilley Field parking area
> to Razorback Trail: 0.1 mi., 5 min.
> to Great Notch and Sluiceway Trails: 0.6 mi., 15 min.

Long Pond Trail (Formerly Great Pond Trail)
(AMC's Acadia National Park Discovery Map: F3)
NPS Rating: Easy
This excellent footpath starts at the parking area at the south end of Long Pond. It follows the west shore of the pond for 1.5 mi., then bears west away from it. Turning south, the trail passes through a beautiful birch forest and follows Great Brook to a junction with the Great Notch Trail. This route to

the Great Notch Trail leads to the complex of trails on Bernard and Mansell and completes a circuit back to the parking area.

Distances from pumping station

to junction with Perpendicular Trail: 0.2 mi., 5 min.

to Western Trail junction: 2.9 mi., 1 hr. 40 min.

Perpendicular Trail (AMC's Acadia National Park Discovery Map: F3)

NPS Rating: Strenuous

This trail, ascending the Mansell peak, leaves left from the Long Pond Trail on the west shore of Long Pond, 0.2 mi. north of the parking area at the south end of Long Pond. It follows a steep course up the east slope of Mansell, crossing a rock slide. The trail is very steep, much of it passing over stone steps. There are a few iron rungs and one iron ladder along the course of the trail. The upper portion has an excellent view southeast. At an open ledge near the top, watch for a sign marked "Path," where an abrupt turn left leads down sharply into woods and marsh before the trail goes up to the actual summit. The summit is wooded. A loop hike is possible by taking the Mansell Mountain Trail south from the summit to the Cold Brook Trail (at Gilley Field), which can then be followed back to the parking area.

Distances from parking area

to start (via Long Pond Trail): 0.2 mi., 5 min.

to Mansell summit: 1.2 mi., 1 hr. 10 min.

Sluiceway Trail (AMC's Acadia National Park Discovery Map: F3)

NPS Rating: Strenuous

This trail starts at Mill Field on the Western Mountain fire road. To reach Mill Field, follow Seal Cove Rd. west from Route 102 in Southwest Harbor. The pavement ends at the Acadia Park border. Take the first right off the dirt road, bear right at the first fork, and left at the second fork. The road ends at Mill Field. The trail runs north 0.4 mi. to a junction with the Great Notch and Gilley Trails. At this junction, the Sluiceway Trail swings northwest and climbs rather steeply, to a junction with the Bernard Mountain Trail 0.5 mi. farther. To reach Bernard Peak, follow the Bernard Mountain Trail left (south) for 0.2 mi.

Distances from Mill Field parking area

to Great Notch Trail junction: 0.4 mi., 25 min.

to Bernard Mountain Trail junction: 0.9 mi., 50 min.

to Bernard summit (via Bernard Mountain Trail): 1.1 mi., 1 hr.

Bernard Mountain Trail (formerly South Face Trail)
(AMC's Acadia National Park Discovery Map: F3)

NPS Rating: Strenuous

This trail also starts at Mill Field on the Western Mountain fire road. (For directions to Mill Field, see the Sluiceway Trail description.) As do many of the trails on the western mountains, it runs through a magnificent spruce-fir forest and affords fine views of western Mount Desert Island and Blue Hill Bay. It leads west for 1.0 mi., where the West Ledge Trail enters from the left and the Bernard Mountain Trail turns right. From here it rises north to Bernard peak at 1.5 mi. and reaches a junction with the Sluiceway Trail at 1.7 mi. The trail continues straight, passing over Knight Nubble before descending to the Great Notch at 2.2 mi.

Distances from Mill Field parking area
> to West Ledge Trail: 1.0 mi., 1 hr.
> to Bernard summit: 1.5 mi., 1 hr. 20 min.
> to Great Notch: 2.2 mi., 1 hr. 50 min.

Razorback Trail   (AMC's Acadia National Park Discovery Map: F3)
NPS Rating: Strenuous

The Razorback Trail leaves from the Gilley Trail, which in turn begins at the Gilley Field parking area at the east end of the Western Mountain Fire Road. To reach Gilley Field, follow Seal Cove Rd. west from Route 102 in Southwest Harbor. The pavement ends at the Acadia Park border. Take the first right off the dirt road, bear right at the first fork, and right at the second fork. The road ends at Gilley Field. Follow the Gilley Trail for 0.2 mi., where the Razorback Trail bears right.

This hike moderately climbs the western side of Mansell, offering views of the Great Notch and Bernard. The trail climbs over ledges and through softwood forest, to reach a fork between the summit of Mansell and Great Notch at 0.7 mi. The left fork leads to the Great Notch in 0.2 mi. The right fork leads 0.2 mi. to the Mansell Mountain Trail, 0.2 mi. below Mansell Mountain.

Distances from Gilley Field
> to start of Razorback Trail (via Gilley Trail): 0.2 mi., 5 min.
> to Mansell Mountain via right fork and Mansell Mountain Trail:
> > 1.3 mi., 50 min.
> to the Great Notch via right fork: 1.1 mi., 40 min.

Cold Brook Trail (AMC's Acadia National Park Discovery Map: F3)

NPS Rating: Easy

This trail is an important link between the parking area at the south end of Long Pond and the western mountains. Running between the Long Pond Trail and Gilley Field, this trail is an easy hike, following the lowlands around Mt. Mansell. It provides access to the Mansell Mountain and Gilley Trails. More important, it is a natural beginning or finish to a circuit hike over both Mansell and Bernard, and it is a lovely woodlands walk.

Distances from parking area

to Gilley Field: 0.4 mi., 15 min.

Mansell Mountain Trail

(AMC's Acadia National Park Discovery Map: F3)

NPS Rating: Moderate

This trail leaves from Gilley Field and offers a beautiful hike up Mount Mansell. Gradually climbing from the trailhead, this trail passes through softwood forest. It continues to climb onto ledges, giving views to the east and south of Southwest Harbor, Beech Mountain, Long Pond, and Northeast Harbor. At 0.8 mi., the Razorback Trail enters from the left. It is then a short walk the summit of Mansell.

Distances from Gilley Field

to Razorback Trail: 0.8 mi., 30 min.

to Mansell summit: 1.0 mi., 35 min.

West Ledge Trail (AMC's Acadia National Park Discovery Map: F2)

NPS Rating: Strenuous

The West Ledge Trail connects the west end of Western Mountain Road to the system of trails on Bernard and Mansell mountains. The views to the west of Blue Hill Bay, the Atlantic Ocean, and the islands south and west of Mount Desert Island are spectacular. The trail begins from Western Mountain Rd., approximately 0.3 mi. east of Seal Cove Pond. This road is closed to cars during the winter and early spring. The trail begins climbing moderately up the west face of Bernard Mountain, reaching open ledges very quickly. It briefly reenters the woods twice before beginning a very steep climb over open granite ledges. From here, the views stretch from Bass Harbor to the Camden Hills, 30 mi. to the west. After entering the woods, at 1.1 mi., the trail ends at its intersection with the Bernard Mountain Trail.

Distances from Western Mountain Road
    to junction with Bernard Mountain Trail 1.1 mi., 45 min.
    to summit of Bernard Mountain via Bernard Mountain Trail,
        1.6 mi., 1 hr. 5 min.

Western Mountain Connector

(AMC's Acadia National Park Discovery Map: F3)
NPS Rating: Easy
This wide gravel path connects Long Pond Rd., across from Lurvey Spring Rd. (0.8 mi. from Seal Cove Road in Southwest Harbor), to the trails at Gilley Field. During the course of its 0.4-mi. length, the trail passes a municipal building and a view of the town dump before entering a grove of beautiful spruce trees. The trail ends at a dirt road that leads right 0.4 mi. to Gilley Field.
Distances from Long Pond Road
    to Gilley Field: 0.8 mi., 20 min.

Isle au Haut

A range of mountains extends for 6 mi., the length of the island. Mount Champlain (543 ft.), near the north end, is its highest summit. Farther south along the ridge are Rocky Mountain (500 ft.), Sawyer Mountain (480 ft.), and Jerusalem Mountain (440 ft.). Near the southwest tip is Duck Harbor Mountain (314 ft.).

The island is reached by mail boat from Stonington (45 min.). The schedule should be checked locally (see Chapter 5).

About half of the island is within Acadia National Park. The NPS maintains a camping area at Duck Harbor, on the southwest side of the island and about 4 mi. from Isle au Haut Village. There are five lean-tos (no tent sites), which are available by reservation only. The NPS has established daily limits on the number of people allowed to visit Isle au Haut. For the latest information and reservations (available no earlier than April 1 for the following calendar year), call the park headquarters on Mount Desert Island (207-288-3338), or write to Acadia National Park, PO Box 177, Bar Harbor, ME 04609.

The 12-mi. road around the island is partly paved. Some sections of the road, however, are very rough and not recommended for bike riding. The road passes the foot of Long Pond, where there is a place to swim.

Numerous trails offer opportunities to explore wild and rocky shoreline, heavily wooded uplands, marshes, and mountain summits. For current hiking information, write to Acadia National Park, stop at the park visitor center in Hulls Cove, or pick up a map from the mail-boat operators. From mid-May to mid-October, park rangers will meet the mail boat and provide you with detailed hiking information. Isle Au Haut and the Schoodic Peninsula can be found at the bottom of the Eastern Mount Desert Island side of the map found in the pocket of this book.

Goat Trail

NPS Rating: Moderate

This trail runs from the southern portion of the main road to the Western Head Rd. It parallels the shoreline and offers spectacular views of Head Harbor, Merchant Cove, Barred Harbor, Squeaker Cove, and Deep Cove.

The trail begins in a marshy lowland and gradually rises to the coastal ridge. Passing through an evergreen forest, at 0.6 mi. the trail emerges onto a rocky beach. Shortly thereafter, the trail climbs again and passes the southern terminus of the Median Ridge Trail (0.9 mi.). Once again, the trail passes intermittently through both beaches and highlands offering a variety of perspectives on the southern coast of Isle au Haut.

Distances from main road

to junction with Median Ridge Trail: 0.9 mi., 30 min.

to junction with Duck Harbor Mountain Trail: 1.8 mi., 1 hr.

to junction with Western Head Rd.: 2.2 mi., 1 hr. 15 min.

Cliff Trail

NPS Rating: Moderate

This trail leaves from Western Head Rd. It offers the shortest possible route to the Western Ear, which is a small island accessible only during low tide. It begins by climbing steeply (50 ft.) to reach the coastal ridge. Then it follows the ridge, passing through an evergreen forest. At 0.6 mi., the trail passes through a rocky beach, offering views of Deep Cove and the coast.

Distances from Western Head Rd.

to junction with Western Head Trail: 0.7 mi., 40 min.

to Western Ear: 0.8 mi., 45 min.

Western Head Trail

NPS Rating: Moderate

This trail follows the western shore of Western Head. It offers spectacular views of the ocean from oceanside cliffs. Included in these views are rock outcroppings in the Western Bay. Combined with the Cliff Trail, the Western Head Trail offers a very nice loop around Western Head. The trailheads are a short walk apart on the Western Head Road.

The trail begins in lowlands. At 0.2 mi., it begins to gradually climb to a shoreline ridge. Shortly thereafter, it crosses an active stream. As it continues to ascend through an evergreen forest on a ledge, views of the coast are evident to the west. At 0.4 mi., the trail descends onto a rocky beach. The terrain continues to follow along the coast, ascending and descending between ridge and beach.

Distances from Western Head Rd.

to view of rock outcroppings in the Western Bay: 0.7 mi., 45 min.

to cliffs: 1.2 mi., 1 hr.

to junction with Cliff Trail: 1.6 mi., 1 hr. 15 min.

Duck Harbor Trail

NPS Rating: Moderate

This trail begins at the park ranger station on the north end of the island. As a major connector, this trail offers hiking access to Duck Harbor, Moore's Harbor, Eli Creek, the Bowditch Trail, the Nat Merchant Trail, and the park campground.

Following the marshy lowlands, this trail passes through mature stands of softwoods. At 0.9 mi., a small pond will appear to the left. At 1.5 mi., the Bowditch Trail bears to the left. Shortly thereafter, another junction with the town road cuts off to the right. The trail crosses a sandy beach at 1.9 mi., offering views of the western coast. At 2.2 mi., a Park Service cabin will be visible. A small side trail that offers views of Deep Cove bears off to the right at 2.7 mi. After crossing the road, the trail offers outstanding views of the ocean and harbor.

Distances from park ranger station

to junction with Bowditch Trail: 1.5 mi., 45 min.

to junction with town road: 1.5 mi., 45 min.

to Park Service cabin: 2.3 mi., 1 hr. 10 min.

to junction with side trail to Deep Cove: 2.7 mi., 1 hr. 20 min.

to second junction with road: 3.0 mi., 1 hr. 30 min.

to views of harbor and ocean: 3.7 mi., 1 hr. 50 min.

to Duck Harbor and road: 3.9 mi., 2 hrs.

Duck Harbor Mountain Trail

NPS Rating: Strenuous

This trail begins on the Western Head Rd. and is one of the most physically challenging trails on Isle au Haut. It climbs over Duck Harbor Mountain, offering terrific views of the harbor as well as the southern end of the island. The trail begins on rapidly ascending ledges. At 0.2 mi., the trail briefly crests. Then, at 0.3 mi., after a short descent, the trail again ascends steeply. It passes through a mixture of softwood forest and open ledge to the summit of Duck Harbor Mountain.

After the summit, this trail continues along the ridge. It goes over the Puddings, offering more views, and descends rapidly through softwood forest and ledges down to a junction with the Goat Trail.

Distances from Western Head Rd.

to summit of Duck Harbor Mountain: 0.4 mi., 35 min.

to junction with Goat Trail: 1.2 mi., 1 hr. 30 min.

Median Ridge Trail

NPS Rating: Moderate

The trailhead is located on the main road in the southern part of the island. This trail has two spurs, north and south, from this point. The south spur connects quickly (0.3 mi.) with the Goat Trail by following low marshlands. The north spur quickly ascends to the ridge. At 0.3 mi., a blue blaze marks the park boundary. The trail follows the ridge into a Japanese garden, offering views to the east. At 0.7 mi., excellent views can be seen from a ledge area surrounded by small conifers. The trail then descends into a bog. At 1.0 mi., it crosses the Nat Merchant Trail. The trail continues through marsh, evergreens, and a cedar bog to a junction with the Long Pond Trail.

Distances from main road

to junction of south spur with the Goat Trail: 0.3 mi., 25 min.

to junction of north spur with the Nat Merchant Trail: 1 mi., 45 min.

to junction of north spur with the Long Pond Trail: 1.6 mi, 1 hr. 30 min.

Nat Merchant Trail

NPS Rating: Moderate

The Nat Merchant Trail is located on the main road on the western shore of the island. This trail begins by entering low marshlands covered in cedar and pine. It crosses several intermittent streams until it meets with the Median Ridge Trail (0.8 mi.). After this junction, the trail begins to climb gradually. It passes over a boulder field and crests at the top of this field offering fine views. Once this ridge is crested, the trail passes through a softwood forest. The trail ends at the main road on the island's eastern side.

Distances from main road

> to junction with Median Ridge Trail: 0.8 mi., 25 min.
>
> to junction with road: 1.2 mi., 45 min.

Long Pond Trail

NPS Rating: Strenuous

This trailhead is located on the main road on the western portion of the island. While this trail is relatively flat to begin, once on the loop the change of elevation is quite severe. Despite the difficult climb, this trail offers wonderful views of the largest pond on Isle au Haut, not to mention access to the summit of Bowditch Mountain, the Bowditch Trail, and the Median Ridge Trail. The trail forms a nice loop for a day hike.

Beginning at the road, the trail follows a low, wet area for 0.4 mi., where the trail meets the Median Ridge Trail (entering right) and splits into its two legs of the loop. The southern loop follows along an old streambed for quite some time. At 1.1 mi., the trail passes over the old foundation of a building, follows along a stone wall, and then gradually climbs onto a ridge. At 1.7 mi., you will see Long Pond. The trail follows Long Pond north for a short time, bears west, and climbs gradually through evergreens to the summit of Bowditch Mountain. At the summit, the Bowditch Trail enters from the right. The Long Pond Trail continues straight ahead and returns to the junction with the southern leg and the Median Ridge Trail.

Distances from main road

> to junction with the Median Ridge Trail: 0.4 mi., 15 min.
>
> to foundation of old building: 1.1 mi., 35 min.
>
> to Long Pond (via south leg): 1.7 mi., 55 min.
>
> to summit and junction with Bowditch Trail (via south leg):
>   2.4 mi., 1 hr. 30 min.
>
> to complete the Long Pond Loop: 3.2 mi., 2 hr.

Bowditch Trail

NPS Rating: Moderate

This trail runs between the Duck Harbor Trail and the Median Ridge Trail. It offers spectacular views from Bowditch Mountain.

Beginning from the Duck Harbor Trail, this trail follows low marshlands for its first 0.8 mi., where it crosses an active stream and turns onto an old firebreak. After following the firebreak, the trail begins to climb gradually, offering wonderful views of the ocean to the west. It continues to climb through a softwood forest over wet ledge for 1.1 mi., where it reaches the summit of Bowditch Mountain. At this point, it connects with the Median Ridge Trail.

Distances from junction with Duck Harbor Trail

to sign marking trail:1.1 mi., 40 min.

to ledges with views to the west: 1.6 mi., 1 hr.

to summit and junction with Median Ridge Trail: 2.0 mi., 1 hr. 30 min.

Appendix B:
Other Sunny- and
Rainy-Day Activities

ACADIA OFFERS SO MUCH TO DO, you could spend years there and never run out of ideas. This chapter lists things you can do to fill in the spaces between your hiking, bicycling, and paddling trips.

Airplane/Glider Rides
Nothing helps you get the big picture of Acadia better than seeing it from above. There are two options for getting airborne:
- Acadia Air Tours—Bar Harbor Airport, Trenton, ME; 207-667-SOAR; www.acadiaairtours.com. Scenic Biplane and Glider Rides.
- Scenic Flights of Acadia—Bar Harbor Airport, Trenton, ME; 207-667-6527; www.mainecoastalflight.com. Scenic Cessna 172.

Boats and Ferries
Seeing the beauty of Acadia from the water provides you with a unique perspective of the park. Boat rides are a great way to see seabirds and marine mammals up close. Ferries can take you to some of the outer islands in the area, each of which has its own culture and scenery separate from Mount Desert Island. See Appendix C for a list of ferries and tour companies.

Guided Tours
Let someone else do the driving—sit back and enjoy the scenery while you listen to the story of the land. If you have never visited the park before, taking a guided tour is a good introduction to Acadia and Mount Desert Island.

- Oli's Trolley—56 Cottage Street, Bar Harbor, ME; 207-288-9899; www .acadiaislandtours.com. Go on a historical tour and hear tales of a lost era, the cottage days of Bar Harbor. Also find out about the park's flora and fauna.
- Acadia National Park Tours—Testa's Restaurant, 53 Main Street, Bar Harbor, ME; 207-288-0300; www.acadiatours.com. Learn about the island's history, flora and fauna, geology, and mansions, and see the major sights. Handicapped accessible.

Gardens
Enjoy a peaceful stroll through a lovely garden.
- Asticou Azalea Garden—Asticou Way, Maine Highway 3 and 198, Northeast Harbor, ME; no phone; www.gardenpreserve.org. This garden has an Oriental style. Enjoy some peace and quiet away from the summer crowds. June is the best time to find the azaleas in bloom.
- Thuya Garden—Route 3, Northeast Harbor, ME; 207-276-5130; www .gardenpreserve.org. This garden is open 7 days a week, late June through September. It is an English-style garden, featuring 80 percent perennials and 20 percent annuals. The best time to catch everything in bloom is August. It also has hiking trails on its 260 acres of land.
- Wild Gardens of Acadia—Sieur de Monts, Acadia National Park, ME; 207-288-3338; no website. These gardens are perfect for those of you who want to study the local flora of Acadia. They have a wide variety of the flowers and foliage typically found in the park, and everything is labeled with common and scientific names.

Horse-Drawn-Carriage Rides
Experience the carriage roads as they were originally intended.
- Wildwood Stables—Park Loop Road, Acadia National Park, ME; 207-276-3622; no website. A handicapped-accessible carriage is available.

Internet Café
- The Opera House Internet Café, 27 Cottage Street, Bar Harbor, ME; 207-288-3509; www.barharborinternetcafe.com. Check your e-mail or check the weather online. Download your digital pictures and send them to Mom.

Jordan Pond House Restaurant

• On the Park Loop Road, Acadia National Park, ME; 207-276-3316; www. jordanpond.com. One of our favorite things to do is stop in at the Jordan Pond House Restaurant for afternoon tea and popovers. The food is delicious, and the scenery is spectacular. Take the bus!

Museums

A great way to learn about the island (especially on a rainy day). Most museums are seasonal, so be sure to call ahead for hours.

• Abbe Museum—26 Mt. Desert Street, Bar Harbor and Sieur de Monts Spring, Acadia National Park, ME; 207-288-3519; www.abbemuseum .org. This museum celebrates Maine's American Indian heritage through exhibits, craft workshops with native people, and ongoing archaeological research.

• Bar Harbor Historical Society—33 Ledgelawn Avenue, Bar Harbor, ME; 207-288-0000; www.barharborhistorical.org. Experience the "lost" Bar Harbor and its famous summer colony through this fine collection of early drawings, hotel memorabilia, photographs, sketches, and pictures of the devastating fire of 1947.

• Bar Harbor Whale Museum, 55 West Street, Bar Harbor, ME; 207-288-0288; www.barharborwhalemuseum.org. Explore and learn about many different species of whales. Great gift shop. Free admission.

• Islesford Museum—Little Cranberry Island, ME; 207-244-9224; no website. This historic maritime museum is part of Acadia National Park. The exhibits portray the lives of the hardy seafaring people of the Cranberry Isles. You need to take a ferry to get there (see Appendix C); call Acadia National Park for information: 207-288-3338.

• Mount Desert Island Historical Society—Somesville Museum, 1119 Main Street, Somesville, ME; 207-244-5043; www.mdihistory.org. Explore Mount Desert Island's history with the historical society's settlement artifacts (furniture, household items). Learn about the hotels, shipbuilding, and mills in the islands history. Be sure to visit the first town office by walking over the scenic (and highly photographed) decorative bridge.

• Mount Desert Island Historical Society—Somes Sound School House, 373 Sound Drive, 207-276-9323; www.mdihistory.org. Originally built in 1892, this building survived as a school until 1926. When you visit, check out the genealogy collection, photo archives, and business records.

- Mount Desert Oceanarium—Two locations: Route 3, Bar Harbor, ME; 207-288-5005; and Clark Point Road, Southwest Harbor, ME; 207-244-7330; www.theoceanarium.com. These museums offer a great way for kids to explore the ocean life of Acadia. The Southwest Harbor location has 26 tanks filled with local sea life, as well as informal staff talks and hands-on and interactive exhibits. The Bar Harbor location (which opens in June each year) offers a lobster museum; staff walks out on a salt marsh; a lobster hatchery; and programs about lobsters, lobster fishing, and harbor seals.
- Wendell Gilley Museum—Corner of Main and Herrick, Southeast Harbor, ME; 207-244-7555; www.wendellgilleymuseum.org. This museum features wood bird carvings made by Wendell Gilley, a famous native Maine carver. It also has wildlife art exhibits and natural-history video programs.

Nature Tours
- Down East Nature Tours—150 Knox Road, Bar Harbor, ME; 207-288-8128; www.downeastnaturetours.com. Explore the natural beauty of the park with qualified naturalists and biologists. Get a personalized tour, one-on-one with a guide. Down East's specialty is native birds. Please call in advance to make reservations.

Photography
Of course you can aim your camera practically anywhere and get a nice photo, but for some special tips and free advice, contact the Park Service and hook up with their photography tours, 207-288-8832.

Picnics
The places to picnic are limited only by your imagination. If you like official picnic sites complete with tables and restrooms, try these:
- Bear Brook—Park Loop Road between the visitor center and Champlain Mountain (handicapped accessible).
- Fabbri—Park Loop Road just after Otter Cliffs (handicapped accessible).
- Frazer Point—Schoodic Peninsula.
- Pretty Marsh—on Route 102 between Pretty Marsh and Seal Cove.
- Seawall—across Route 102A from the Seawall Campground (handicapped accessible).

- Thompson Island—Route 3 just before Mount Desert Island (handicapped accessible).

Ranger Programs

The Park Service has programs on just about everything. There are ranger programs for hikers as well as programs on sea cruises, on bus tours, and in the campground amphitheaters and other special areas like the base of Champlain Mountain for peregrine watching. Ask at the visitor center for a complete list of programs available during your stay; read up on the different programs in the Beaver Log or Acadia Weekly (provided free and found in many restaurants, shops, and at the visitor centers); call 207-288-3338; or search at www.nps.gov/acad.

Rock Climbing

While Acadia is not one of the premier climbing areas in the East, the glaciers did leave behind some wonderful rock-climbing in places such as Otter Cliffs, Champlain Mountain, and South Bubble. For information about climbing routes or to explore these climbs safely by hiring a guide, contact:

- Acadia Mountain Guides Climbing School—198 Main Street, Bar Harbor, ME; 207-288-8186; www.acadiamountainguides.com.
- Atlantic Climbing School—24 Cottage Street, Bar Harbor, ME; 207-288-2521; www.climbacadia.com.

Snowshoeing or Cross-Country Skiing/Winter Hiking

On those rare occasions when the coast gets hit with a big snow, the carriage roads are a fantastic place to get into the backcountry. Use this book's biking chapter as a guide for snowshoeing or cross-country skiing.

Only experienced winter hikers should try to use the hiking trails in winter, since the steep trails often require crampon use. When planning a hike, you should realize that the Park Loop Road is closed in winter, except for the Ocean Drive portion of the road and the access to Jordan Pond from Seal Harbor.

Swimming

On a hot summer day, nothing will cool you off faster than jumping into re-freshing Maine waters. There are only two places to swim in Acadia: Echo Lake Beach and Sand Beach. By July, the water at Echo Lake Beach, at the south end of Echo Lake, is considerably warmer than the cold waters of the Atlantic, which rarely get warmer than 55 degrees. Most of the lakes and ponds on Mount Desert Island are used as public water supplies, so please respect the no-swimming rules.

Theaters

- Acadia Repertory Theatre—Route 102, Mount Desert, ME; 207-244-7260; www.acadiarep.com. Enjoy live, professional theater.
- Reel Pizza—Top of Rodick Street, Bar Harbor, ME; 207-288-3811; www .reelpizza.net. Enjoy a pizza while you watch the movie.
- Criterion Theatre and Arts Center—35 Cottage Street, Bar Harbor, ME; 207-288-3441; www.criteriontheater.com. Enjoy films and live events.

Whale Watch

If you have never gone on a whale watch before, Acadia is a fantastic place to give it a try. Sighting whales is so common that all of the tour operators guarantee that you will see at least one whale (or your money back or a free ride on another trip). See Appendix C for a list of whale-watch tours.

Zoo

Acadia Zoological Park, Rt. 3, Trenton, ME; 207-667-3244; no website. See native Maine species like moose and deer as well as non-native species. Shows daily. Open May to December.

Appendix C: Boating

Company	Phone number and website	Name of boat
Bar Harbor Whale Watch Co.	1-888-WHALES-4 www.barharborwhales.com	Atlanticat
		Miss Samantha
		The Bay King III
		Acadian
Bay Ferries	1-877-359-3760 www.catferry.com	The Cat
Beal & Bunker Mailboat Ferry	207-244-3575	Sea Queen
Cranberry Cove Boating Co.	207-244-5882	Southwest Harbor Ferry
The Delight Water Taxi	207-244-5724 www.islesford.com	The Delight
Diver Ed Dive in Theater	207-288-DIVE www.divered.com	The Starfish Enterprise
Down East Friendship Sloop Charters	207-266-5210 www.sailacadia.com	Alice E
		Helen Brooks
Down East Sailing Adventures	207-288-2216 www.downeastsail.com	Rachel B. Jackson
		Hurricane
		Friendship Sloop Surprise

Destination/Trip	Leaves From	Notes
Whale watching and other wildlife, including seabirds, seals, and porpoises	1 West Street, Harbor Place, Bar Harbor	High-speed catamaran; Cash-back guarantee
Watch lobster trapping and observe seals. Also offers a Baker Island tour narrated by a park ranger.	1 West Street, Harbor Place, Bar Harbor	
A historic lighthouse and National Park Tour	1 West Street, Harbor Place, Bar Harbor	
Granite cliffs of Schooner Head and the rock beaches behind Ironbound Island	1 West Street, Harbor Place, Bar Harbor	
Yarmouth, Nova Scotia	121 Eden Street, Bay Ferries Terminal	Fastest car ferry in North America: Go to Canada in three hours; casino on board
Ferry to Cranberry Isles	Northeast Harbor	Runs all year
Ferry to Isleford/Cranberry Isles	Southwest Harbor	
Custom cruises serving Northeast Harbor, Southwest Harbor, Manset, Seal Harbor and Private Docks	105 Eden Street, Bar Harbor	Maximum six passengers
Frenchman Bay and Porcupines	Harborside Hotel	Live underwater video marine education trip: Watch Diver Ed on a 6-ft. screen as he explores the ocean, then get to touch whatever he brings up into his catchbag
Private Charters	Southwest Harbor	Built in 1899, the oldest Friendship Sloop sailing today
Private Charters	Northeast Harbor	
Sails around Cranberry Isles and Somes Sound	Beals Lobster Pier, Southwest Harbor	Working replica of an 1890's coastal schooner; Help raise the sails or steer
Real lobster boat, 2-hour tour	Southwest Harbor	Help haul in the traps
2.5-hour sailing adventure. Available for private parties of six	Southwest Harbor	

Company	Phone number and website	Name of boat
Down East Windjammer	207-288-4585 (winter 207-546-2927) www.downeastwindjammer.com	Margaret Todd Ada C. Lore Bar Harbor Ferry Cranberry Cove Ferry Tiger Shark
Greensleeves Charters	207-460-8999 www.greensleevescharters.com	Greensleeves
Isle Au Haut Co.	207-367-5193 www.isleauhaut.com	Miss Lizzy & Mink
Island Cruises	207-244-5785 www.bassharborcruises.com	RL Gott
Lulu Lobster Boat Ride	207-963-2341 www.lululobsterboat.com	Lulu
Quietside Cruises	207-244-7312 www.sailacadia.com	The Elizabeth T
Sea Princess Cruises	207-276-5352 www.barharborcruises.com	Sea Princess
Sea Venture Custom Boat Tours	207-288-3355 www.svboattours.com	Reflection
Swans Island Ferry	207-244-3254; www.state.me.us/ mdot/opt/ferry/215-swan.php	Captain Henry Lee

Destination/Trip	Leaves From	Notes
1.5-2.0-hour windjammer cruise	Bar Harbor Inn Pier	150-ft four-masted schooner
1.5-hour Oyster Schooner Cruise	Harborside Hotel	Fully restored 1923 Oyster Schooner
Ferry from Bar Harbor to Winter Harbor	Bar Harbor Inn Pier	
Ferry from Southwest Harbor to Manset, Great Cranberry and Little Cranberry	SW Harbor	
Deep-sea fishing and wildlife watching in Frenchman Bay	Bar Harbor Inn Pier	
Private half-day sailboat charters	Northeast Harbor	Maximum six passengers
Ferry to Isle Au Haut—either Town Landing or Duck Harbor	Stonington	Runs Monday to Saturday all year to village, only goes to Duck Harbor mid-June to early September
Lobster Cruise (Monday–Friday)	Stonington	
Scenic Cruise (Monday–Saturday)	Stonington	
Lunch cruise to Frenchboro	Bass Harbor	Stops on Long Island for lunch and a walk around Frenchboro
Afternoon nature cruise	Bass Harbor	
Lobster fishing, seal watching and sightseeing	55 West Street, The Harborside Hotel	2.0-hour tour with twelve passengers on traditional Down East-style lobster boat
Island Lunch Cruise, Lobster and Lighthouse Cruise, Sunset Dinner Cruise to the Isleford Dock Restaurant.	Southwest Harbor	Real Maine lobster boat, built on Mt. Desert Island
Little Cranberry, Somes Sound, lighthouse narrated by a park service naturalist	Northeast Harbor	2.75-hour trip
Somes Sound with a naturalist	Northeast Harbor	1.5-hour trip
Litte Cranberry Island, dinner trip	Northeast Harbor	Dinner at a restaurant on Little Cranberry Island
Customized boat tours; will show you whatever you want to see	Atlantic Oaks pier, Bar Harbor	Bald Eagle researcher will let you design your own trip; specializes in birds and wildlife, nature and lighthouses
Swans Island	Bass Harbor	Runs all year

Appendix D: Outfitters

Name	Address	Phone/Website	When Open	Bike Rentals
Acadia Bike	48 Cottage Street, Bar Harbor	800-526-8615 www.acadiabike.com	Year-round	Yes
Acadia Outfitters	106 Cottage Street, Bar Harbor	207-288-8118	May–Oct.	Yes
Acadia 1 Water Sports (formerly Loon Bay Kayak)	Lamoine	888-786-0676 www.kayak1.com	June–Sept.	
Aquaterra Adventures	1 West Street, Bar Harbor	207-288-0007; www .aquaterra-adventures .com	May–Sept.	
Bar Harbor Bicycle	193 Main Street, Ellsworth	207-667-6886 www.barharborbike.com	April–Oct.	Yes
Bar Harbor Bicycle	141 Cottage Street, Bar Harbor	207-288-3886 www.barharborbike.com	March–Dec.	Yes
Coastal Kayaking Tours	48 Cottage Street, Bar Harbor	207-288-9605 www.acadiafun.com	Year-round	
Cadillac Mountain Sports	32 High Street, Ellsworth	207-667-7819 www.cadillacsports.com	Year-round	
Maine State Kayak	254 Main Street, Southwest Harbor	877-481-9500; www .mainestateseakayak.com	May–Sept.	
National Park Canoe & Kayak	Pretty Marsh Road, Rt. 102 Mount Desert	207-244-5854 www .nationalparkcanoerental .com	May–Oct.	
National Park Sea Kayak Tours	39 Cottage Street, Bar Harbor	207-288-0342 or 800-347-0940 www.acadiakayak.com	May–Sept.	
Southwest Cycle	370 Main Street, Southwest Harbor	207-244-5856 www.southwestcycle .com	April–Jan.	Yes

Bike Repairs	Bike Sales	Kayak Rentals (not on tours)	Kayak Sales	Kayak Tours	Canoe Rentals	Other
Yes	Yes					Bike accessories, group rentals and tours.
Yes	Yes	Yes	Yes	Yes	Yes	Scooter Rentals too.
		Yes		Yes	Yes	Guided tours include fresh cooked mussels on shore for lunch, or they deliver and pick up rentals.
				Yes		Variety of kayaking tours. Paddling accessories.
Yes	Yes					Skateboards, jogging strollers, cycling clothing.
Yes	Yes					Biking accessories, clothing, and shoes. Baby joggers.
			Yes	Yes		Wide variety of tours.
	Yes					Bike accessories, outdoor clothing
				Yes		Tours of western (quiet) side of the island.
		Yes			Yes	Boat right there on Long Pond, or get a car top rack and go anywhere.
				Yes		Tours of western (quiet) side of the island.
Yes	Yes					A variety of bike accessories and child carriers.

Appendix E: Conservation and Recreation Organizations

American Oceans Campaign: 202-833-3900; www.oceana.org

Appalachian Mountain Club: 617-523-0655; www.outdoors.org

Frenchman Bay Conservancy: 207-422-2328; www.frenchmanbay.org

Friends of Acadia: 207-288-3340; www.foacadia.org

Island Institute: 207-594-9209; www.islandinstitute.org

Leave No Trace: 303-442-8222; www.lnt.org

Maine Audubon Society: 207-781-2330; www.maineaudubon.org

Maine Coast Heritage Trust: 207-244-5100; www.mcht.org

Maine Island Trail Association: 207-596-6456; www.mita.org

National Park Conservation Association: 800-628-7275, www.npca.org

Natural Resources Council of Maine: 800-287-2345; www.nrcm.org

The Nature Conservancy: 207-729-5182; www.nature.org

Sierra Club, Maine Chapter: 207-761-5616; maine.sierraclub.org

The Trust for Public Land: 207-772-7424; www.tpl.org

Appendix F: Recommended Reading

Appalachian Mountain Club. *Maine Mountain Guide*, 9th edition. Boston: AMC Books, 2005.

Blagden, Thomas. *First Light*. Boulder, Colo.: Westcliffe Publishing, 2003.

Grierson, Ruth Gortner. *Wildlife Watcher's Guide: Acadia National Park*. Boulder, Colo.: NorthWord Press, 1995.

Hill, Ruth Ann. *Discovering Old Bar Harbor and Acadia National Park*. Camden, Maine: Down East Books, 1996.

Monkman, Jerry, and Marcy Monkman. *A Photographer's Guide to Acadia National Park*. Woodstock, Vt.: The Countryman Press, 2010.

Monkman, Jerry, and Marcy Monkman. *Wild Acadia*. Lebanon, N.H.: University Press of New England, 2007.

Paigen, Jennifer Alisa. *The Sea Kayaker's Guide to Mount Desert Island*. Camden, Maine: Down East Books, 1997.

Roberts, Ann Rockefeller. *Mr. Rockefeller's Roads: The Untold Story of Acadia's Carriage Roads & Their Creator*. Camden, Maine: Down East Books, 1990.

St. Germain, Tom, and Jay Saunders. *Trails of History: The Story of Mount Desert Island's Paths from Norumbega to Acadia*. Bar Harbor, Maine: Parkman Publications, 1993.

Thayer, Robert A. *The Park Loop Road: A Guide to Acadia National Park's Scenic Byway*. Bar Harbor, Maine: Down East Books, 1999.

Wilson, Alex and John Hayes. *Quiet Water: Maine*. Boston: AMC Books, 2005.

Wivell, Ty. *Discover Maine: AMC Outdoor Traveler's Guide to the Pine Tree State*. Boston: AMC Books, 2006.

Index

Bracketed information indicates the location of a trail on the pull-out map, by section letter and number.

About the Authors

KNOWN FOR THEIR CONSERVATION WORK IN NEW ENGLAND'S wild places, Jerry and Marcy Monkman have spent the last fifteen years artfully documenting the mountains, forests, and coastlines that define the region. In 2002, they were awarded a communications award by the Northern Forest Alliance in recognition for their "vision and excellence in chronicling the story of the Northern Forest through photography." Authors of six books, including three AMC Discover guides, their work has appeared in publications worldwide and their client list includes *National Geographic Adventure*, Audubon, *Men's Journal*, *The Washington Post*, *Outdoor Photographer*, L.L. Bean, Princess Cruises, and The Nature Conservancy. Jerry and Marcy live in Portsmouth, N.H., with their daughter Acadia and their son Quinn.

Appalachian Mountain Club

Founded in 1876, the AMC is the nation's oldest outdoor recreation and conservation organization. The AMC promotes the protection, enjoyment, and understanding of the mountains, forests, waters, and trails of the Appalachian region.

People

We are more than 100,000 members, advocates, and supporters; 16,000 volunteers; and more than 450 full-time and seasonal staff. Our 12 chapters reach from Maine to Washington, D.C.

Outdoor Adventure and Fun

We offer more than 8,000 trips each year, from local chapter activities to major excursions worldwide, for every ability level and outdoor interest— from hiking and climbing to paddling, snowshoeing, and skiing.

Great Places to Stay

We host more than 140,000 guests each year at our lodges, huts, camps, shelters, and campgrounds. Each AMC destination is a model for environmental education and stewardship.

Opportunities for Learning

We teach people the skills to be safe outdoors and to care for the natural world around us through programs for children, teens, and adults, as well as outdoor leadership training.

Caring for Trails

We maintain more than 1,500 miles of trails throughout the Northeast, including nearly 350 miles of the Appalachian Trail in five states.

Protecting Wild Places

We advocate for land and riverway conservation, monitor air quality and climate change, and work to protect alpine and forest ecosystems throughout the Northern Forest and Mid-Atlantic Highlands regions.

Engaging the Public

We seek to educate and inform our own members and an additional 2 million people annually through AMC Books, our website, our White Mountain visitor centers, and AMC destinations.

Join Us!

Members support our mission while enjoying great AMC programs, our award-winning *AMC Outdoors* magazine, and special discounts. Visit www.outdoors.org or call 800-372-1758 for more information.

APPALACHIAN MOUNTAIN CLUB
Recreation • Education • Conservation
www.outdoors.org

The AMC in Maine

The AMC Maine Chapter offers a wide variety of hiking, backpacking, climbing, paddling, and skiing trips each year, as well as social and young member programs and instructional workshops. The chapter also offers trail volunteer opportunities.

To view a list AMC activities in Maine and other parts of the Northeast, visit: trips.outdoors.org

APPALACHIAN MOUNTAIN CLUB

MAINE WOODS INITIATIVE

The AMC is engaged in the Maine Woods Initiative, a conservation effort that has a goal of protecting 100,000 acres of forest land in the 100-Mile Wilderness region. The initiative is an innovative approach to conservation that combines outdoor recreation, resource protection, sustainable forestry, and community partnerships. The strategy represents the most significant investment in conservation and recreation in the AMC's history. The public is welcome to hike paddle, snowshoe, and ski on AMC's 66,000 acres of conservation and recreation land, which includes a growing trail netwok and AMC's Maine Wilderness Lodges. For more information about this effort and how to support it, visit www.outdoors.org/mwi.

AMC Books Updates

AMC Books strives to keep our guidebooks as up-to-date as possible to help you plan safe and enjoyable adventures. If we learn after publishing a book that trails are relocated or that route or contact information has changed, we will post the updated information online. Before you hit the trail, check for updates at www.outdoors.org/publications/books/updates.

If you notice discrepancies in the descriptions or maps while hiking or paddling, or if you find other errors in the book, please let us know by submitting them to amcbookupdates@outdoors.org or in writing to Books Editor, c/o AMC, 5 Joy Street, Boston, MA 02108. We will verify all submissions and post key updates each month.

AMC Books is dedicated to being a recognized leader in outdoor publishing. Thank you for your participation.